Welcome to Basis for Business B1

Mit dem neuen **Basis for Business B1** lernen Sie die zentralen Fertigkeiten, um sich im englischsprachigen Arbeitsalltag sicher zu fühlen. Denn **Basis for Business B1** wurde speziell für deutschsprachige Lernende entwickelt.

Die *Welcome-Unit* ermöglicht Ihnen einen sanften Einstieg in das Lehrwerk. Sie lernen verschiedene Personen aus dem Buch kennen, können sich den anderen Kursteilnehmer/innen vorstellen und sich mit ihnen über Ihre Kursziele austauschen.

Alle *Units* bieten Ihnen ein klar strukturiertes Thema mit aktuellem Praxisbezug aus dem Geschäftsleben. Am Anfang bieten die Lernziele einen kurzen Überblick über den Inhalt der *Unit*. Eine kommunikative *warm-up*-Übung (**1**) stimmt Sie auf das Thema der *Unit* ein. Die zehn *Units* sind in fünf Abschnitte untergliedert (*Part A*, *Part B*, *Business file*, *Grammar summary*, *Extra practice*). Darin finden Sie unter anderem:

→ Die regulären Parts *(A & B)*, in denen die Grundlagen für die neuen Strukturen und Sprachmittel gelegt werden. *Did you know?*-Kästen (**2**) vermitteln interessante Hintergrundinformationen; Redemittel werden in blauen *Phrase boxes* (**3**) zusammengefasst.

→ Die Grammatik an der jeweils passenden Stelle in der *Unit* (**4**). Eine ausführliche Erläuterung folgt dann in der *Grammar summary* jeder *Unit*.

→ Die *Business files*, in denen der Fokus auf einem bestimmten Aspekt der geschäftlichen Kommunikation (z.B. Small talk, Telefonieren, Verhandeln) liegt.

→ Die Bereiche *Extra practice*, in denen Sie das Gelernte anwenden und vertiefen können. Die Kategorie *Typical mistakes* (**5**) weist Sie hier auf mögliche (Transfer)fehler vom Deutschen ins Englische hin. Im *Culture spot* (**6**) erhalten Sie Informationen zu interkulturellen Themen.

→ Den *Business Correspondence*-Anhang, in dem Sie Ihre Schreibfertigkeit verbessern können. Hier lernen Sie, dem (beruflichen) Anlass angemessene E-Mails, Briefe oder Faxe zu formulieren und erfolgreich kommunizieren.

Das handliche *Phrasebook* ist ein nützlicher Begleiter: Hier können Sie unbekannte Wörter nachschlagen und finden in den *Useful phrases*-Kästen Beispiele für idiomatische Wendungen.

Das separat erhältliche *Pocket Workbook* im praktischen A5 Format bietet Ihnen viele zusätzliche Übungen, um das Erlernte zu vertiefen.

Viel Spaß und Erfolg mit **Basis for Business B1** wünschen Ihnen Autorenteam und Redaktion!

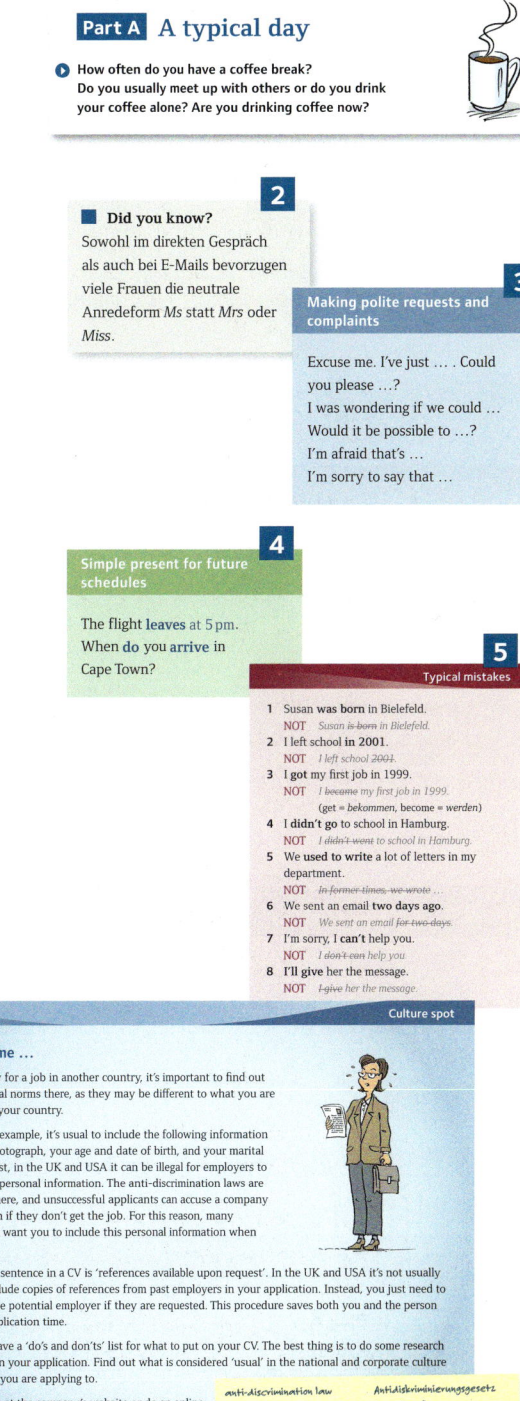

Table of contents

	Welcome!			6
		· Greeting colleagues and new acquaintances · Talking about learning objectives · Meeting the characters		

Unit 1	First impressions			10
Part A	A typical day	· Talking about your job, responsibilities and current projects	Simple present Present continuous	
Part B	Working together	· Describing companies and products	Passive: simple present	
Business file	Here's my card	· Giving your contact details · Introducing yourself and your company	Extra practice Culture spot: The first 30 seconds	19

Unit 2	Then & now			22
Part A	Working here	· Talking about your job experience and your past	Simple past *Used to*	
Part B	Old job, new job	· Talking about your skills and abilities	*Can, could, be able to* Passive: simple past and modals	
Business file	I'm calling about …	· Making telephone calls and leaving messages · Exchanging information	Extra practice Culture spot: When in Rome …	31

Unit 3	A company tour			34
Part A	Meeting people	· Welcoming visitors and socializing	Adjectives and adverbs Past continuous	
Part B	How things work	· Talking about rules and regulations · Describing a process · Writing emails	*Must(n't), need(n't), (not) have to*	
Business file	Tell me more …	· Developing small talk tactics	Extra practice Culture spot: What is the point of small talk?	43

Unit 4	Big plans			46
Part A	Looking ahead	· Talking about plans and projects · Looking at graphs and sales figures	*Will* future *Going to* future	
Part B	Projects & planning	· Taking part in meetings	Passive: *will* future Word order with adverbs of manner	
Business file	Have I got that right?	· Checking and comparing information · Placing orders	Extra practice Culture spot: Being polite	55

Unit 5	It's a deal			58
Part A	Terms & conditions	· Discussing terms · Negotiating a deal	First conditional *if* vs *when*	
Part B	Work-life balance	· Talking about differences · Persuading others	Making comparisons *Fewer/fewest, less/least, more/most*	
Business file	What are your terms?	· Talking about prices and terms	Extra practice Culture spot: 'What does that stand for?'	67

Unit 6	Changing times			70
Part A	A new job	· Talking about your experiences	Present perfect (with *ever*, *never*, *so far*)	
Part B	Making arrangements	· Discussing and making arrangements · Checking and reporting progress	Present continuous for future arrangements Simple present for fixed future schedules Present perfect with *already*, *not … yet*, *just*	
Business file	Can we find a time?	· Updating a diary · Writing emails to make and change appointments	Extra practice Culture spot: Time matters	79
Unit 7	Out of the office			82
Part A	Presenting ideas	· Talking about recent activities and new developments · Making small talk and saying goodbye	Present perfect with *for* and *since* Passive: present perfect Present perfect vs simple past	
Part B	Travelling on business	· Communicating at the hotel · Making polite requests and complaints	*Some* and *any*	
Business file	I'd like to begin with …	· Structuring and giving presentations	Extra practice Culture spot: Doing business in other countries	91
Unit 8	At a trade fair			94
Part A	The eco trade fair	· Describing features and benefits of products · Linking words	Adjective + infinitive Adverb + past participle Past perfect	
Part B	Back in the office	· Writing formal and informal emails		
Business file	A product review	· Analysing data and writing reports	Extra practice Culture spot: Email etiquette	103
Unit 9	A company tour			106
Part A	New management	· Talking about a company's history	Present perfect continuous	
Part B	At a restaurant	· Discussing international management styles · Explaining a menu	Verb + object + infinitive	
Business file	I'm very sorry about this	· Making and dealing with complaints	Extra practice Culture spot: Wining, dining … and paying!	115
Unit 10	Smooth operations			118
Part A	Supply chains	· Talking about supply chains · Discussing hypothetical situations and consequences	Second conditional First conditional vs second conditional	
Part B	Budget talk	· Asking for and giving approval · Exploring the next steps for learning	*Unless* and *in case*	
Business file	Here's my idea	· Pitching a proposal	Extra practice Culture spot: Time to say goodbye	127

Partner files page 130
Numbers, dates, years and times page 144
Telephone numbers and addresses page 146
Business correspondence page 147
Extra practice – Answer key page 167
Transcripts page 174
Irregular verb list page 194
Copyright page 199
Audio CDs – Track list page 200

Welcome!

1 Which responses go with the situations below? Discuss with a partner.

1. ☐ Nice to see you too. How are you?
2. ☐ One moment, sir. I'll put you through.
3. ☐ My name's Anne Singer. I have an appointment at nine o'clock.
4. ☐ How do you do?
5. ☐ Not too bad. And how are you, Alison?
6. ☐ Ah, it's nice to finally meet you in person.

A: Good morning. Welcome to Clarkes Ltd. How can I help you?

B: Hi, Janet! How are you doing?

C: How do you do?

D: Lisa? I'm Sven, from Sales. We always talk on the phone.

E: This is Ken Bennett from LSI. Can I speak to Marion Braun, please?

F: Nice to see you here, Mr Becker. I wasn't sure you were coming.

2 Introduce yourself to your partner and try to find something you have in common.

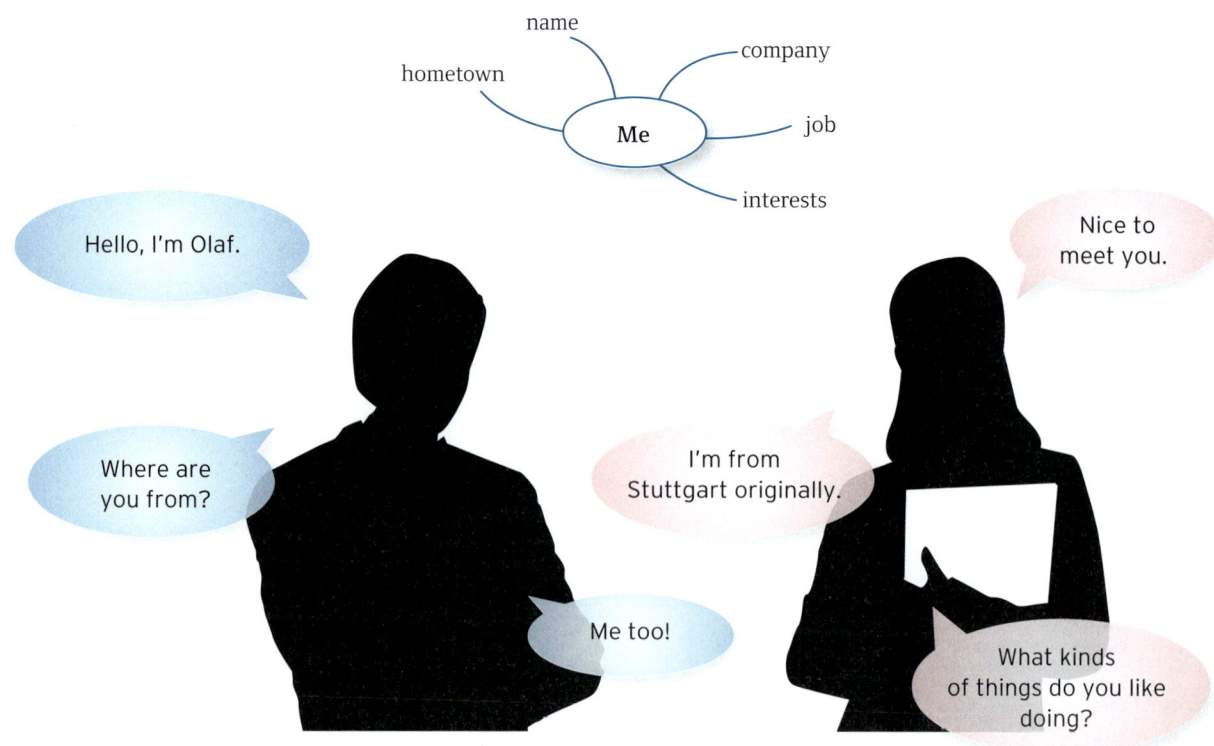

3 Do you ever use English to do the things below? What do you want to use English for in the future? Tick ✔ the boxes. (You can also add your own items to the list.)

		Now	In the future
1	talk to people face-to-face	☐	☐
2	talk on the phone	☐	☐
3	show people around the company	☐	☐
4	make small talk	☐	☐
5	talk in meetings	☐	☐
6	take part in teleconferences or video conferences	☐	☐
7	present information	☐	☐
8	read and write emails	☐	☐
9	read reports	☐	☐
10	write reports	☐	☐
11	read trade journals	☐	☐
12	sell products at a trade fair	☐	☐
13	....	☐	☐
14	....	☐	☐
15	....	☐	☐

👥 Tell your partner about what you do in English now, and what you need to or would like to do in English in the future.

> In my current job I only talk on the phone in English. But soon I want to talk in meetings and write emails in English. How about you?

> Well, I talk to business partners in Russia and Poland in English. In the future I want to travel more and visit customers in the UK and Ireland.

4 Write about your own goals. What do you do? Why do you need English? What do you want to be able to do (better) at the end of your course?

My English Goals

7

Welcome!

5 The people you will meet in this book have different jobs and are of different nationalities, but they all have one thing in common: they use English to do business.

Look at the map and the pictures of some of the characters from the book. Use the clues in a–j to write the correct name next to each picture.

.... 1
I often travel to Germany to talk to local marketing people about selling our electronic products.
Unit 10

.... 2
We're based in Cleveland, Ohio, but we have offices in London and Munich. We help international teams work together.
Unit 9

.... 3
We have a new yogurt coming on the market here next month.
Unit 4

.... 5
I work for an English company in Germany.
Unit 1

.... 4
I work for a medium-sized German company. I sometimes visit Cape Town on business.
Unit 6

a The headquarters of Karin Schröder's company are in London, but she works in Cologne.
b Aysun Greenfield's assistant in the Dortmund office booked her a flight to Africa a few days ago.
c Uli Rietz works in sales. His company is called HRT and is based in Bremen.
d Martin Kehler works for a dairy product company in Regensburg. The UK is a big market for his company's products.
e Stefan Altmann works for the Credmasse Group in Munich. The group's headquarters are in Milan.
f Most of Margaret Hughes' customers are in Northern Europe and the USA, and she often goes there on business.
g Declan O'Connor's company in Ireland exports tablet PCs all over Europe. Germany is one of their main markets.
h Petra Schöder's company does business with a factory in Asia.
i Tony Alda is head of Sutton Associates. They offer training programmes to companies around the world.
j Andrea Duff runs a company in Frankfurt that supplies and stocks vending machines.

6 I visit trade fairs all over Europe and sell different sorts of cleaning products.
Unit 8

7 A supplier of vending machines from the UK is visiting me today.
Unit 5

8 I normally work in Munich, but I'm in Milan on a business trip today.
Unit 7

9 I'm here for a few days to visit the factory that makes our shoes.
Unit 3

10 I have a winery near Melbourne. We export most of our wine to Europe and America.
Unit 1

6 Work with a partner and take turns asking and answering questions.

- Do you do business with more native or non-native English speakers? Where are they based?
- Where are your company headquarters?
- Does your company have any branches or subsidiaries? Where are they located?
- Do you ever go to Spain / the UK / …? What do you do there?
- What country would you like to go to next?

1 First impressions

In this unit you will ...

- talk about your job, your responsibilities and your current projects
- describe companies and products

Business file

- practise giving your contact details
- learn how to introduce yourself and your company

Part A A typical day

▶ How often do you have a coffee break? Do you usually meet up with others or do you drink your coffee alone? Are you drinking coffee now?

1 Read the article from a business magazine. Which jobs do you think the people do?

bank employee · lab technician · warehouse supervisor · personal assistant · call centre agent · safety engineer · production line manager

Our readers tell us how they work.
This month's question: When do you have your coffee break?

Frank

In our East European headquarters we usually meet up at around eleven o'clock in the kitchen at the end of the corridor. I usually drink decaf because, in my job, I need a steady hand. My colleagues and I have a quick chat, but the break is only a quarter of an hour long and, before you know it, it's time to go back to the microscopes.

Karin

On a typical day I meet up with a few of my colleagues first thing in the morning. Personally I never drink coffee, I prefer green tea. One of us is always responsible for light refreshments like pastries or sandwiches. It's usually me! Then it's time to get started. I make a second cup of tea, go to my desk, and have a look at my boss's diary.

Denise

I rarely have a break in the mornings. Most of the deliveries arrive then, and it's hard to get away. I have a lot of responsibility, so I have my phone on all day. My deputy and I always take our breaks on a rotating basis. In fact, my first coffee break isn't usually until the early afternoon. Things are a bit quieter then and I can really enjoy a nice cup of coffee.

Answer these questions about the people in the article.

1 Who always needs to be available even in the breaks?
2 Who usually has quite an early break?
3 Who often talks to colleagues during the break?
4 Who doesn't spend much time on coffee breaks?

2 Interview your partner. What is his/her typical workday like? When does he/she get up, get to work, have lunch, go home for the day, etc.?

3 Match the company departments with the descriptions below.

1 Our buyers contact suppliers and order goods.
2 We deal with matters related to staff, such as payroll and training.
3 Our main focus is on getting and keeping customers.
4 We develop and test new products here.
5 We are responsible for moving goods around.
6 We draw up contracts and other important documents.

HR · R&D · Sales · Legal · Purchasing · Logistics and Distribution

How many other departments can you think of? What do people do there?

Did you know?
HR = Human Resources
IT = Information Technology
R&D = Research and Development

Part A

1

4 🔊 1.2 **Karin and Roger work for Logan Germany, a mail-order and e-tail company. Listen. What department does Karin work in?**

Starting a conversation

It's Karin, isn't it?
Are you Karin Schröder, by any chance?
Excuse me. Do you mind if I ask you a question?
Uhm, do you have a moment?
I hope I'm not disturbing you.

Now answer the questions.

1. How does Roger start the conversation?
2. Why is he asking Karin about her job?
3. What are some of Karin's regular duties?
4. What is Karin doing this week?
5. What is Jürgen Löwe doing this week? Why?
6. What does Karin like about her job? Why?

5 **What did Karin say? Tick the phrases you heard, then listen again to check.**

1. I make a lot of ☐ phone calls ☑ appointments for my boss.
2. I sometimes update ☐ HR documentation ☐ the diary.
3. A colleague is off sick, so I'm doing ☐ some work for her too ☐ some research into the company for her.
4. We're doing ☐ training schedules this week ☐ more and more business with Asia at the moment.
5. I am currently coordinating ☐ his travel arrangements ☐ several business trips.
6. We all have ☐ a chat before work ☐ a great time here.

Which things happen on a regular basis? Which things are going on at the moment?

Merken Sie sich, welche Verben und Nomen zusammen gehören, sogenannte „collocations".

6 **Complete these sentences so that they are true for you and/or a colleague.**

1. I sometimes ....
2. At the moment I am ....
3. At work I am currently ....
4. A colleague of mine is ....
5. He/She never ....
6. We usually ....

👥 Tell a partner.

Simple present vs present continuous

What **do** you **do** (for a living)?
I often **make** appointments for my boss.
She **works** in the purchasing department.

What projects **are** you **working** on at the moment?
We **are** currently **doing** more and more business with Asia.

1 First impressions — Part A

7 🔊 1.3 Listen to Karin describing her relationships to different people in the company. Who does she probably meet up with after work?

Listen again and complete the diagram with the missing names and departments.

Did you know?
- CEO = Chief Executive Officer
- CFO = Chief Financial Officer
- CIO = Chief Information Officer
- COO = Chief Operating Officer
- CRO = Chief Risk Officer
- CTO = Chief Technology Officer

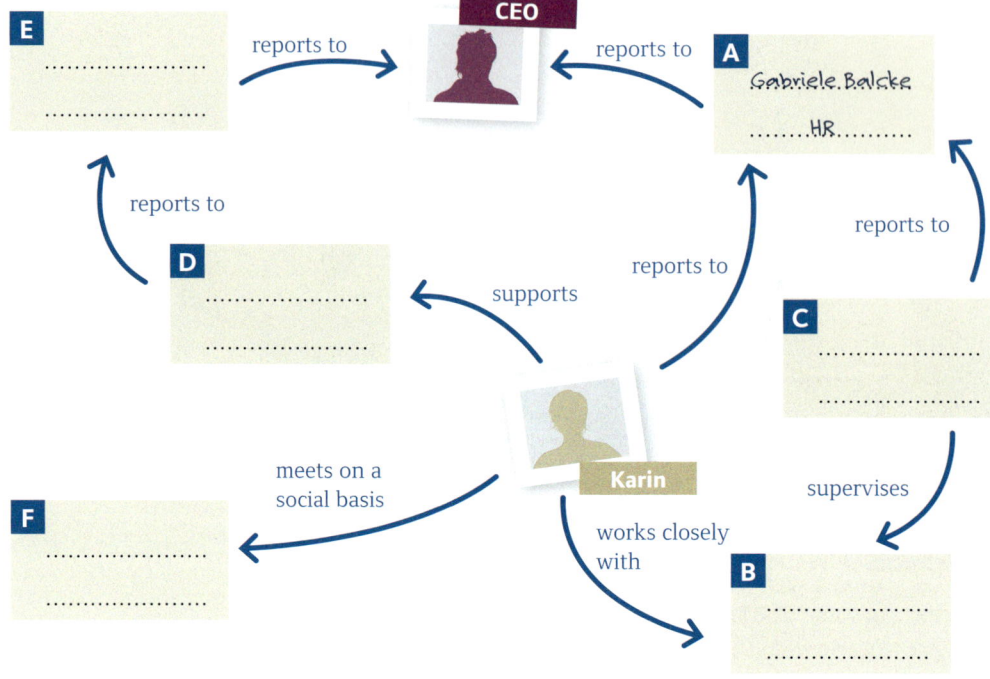

Use the diagram to talk about the different people in the company and the relationships between them.

Karin reports directly to Gabriele Balcke. She's head of the HR department.

8 👥 Work with a partner. Either make your own diagram and describe it to a partner, or talk about the diagrams in the partner files.

→ Partner A: file 1, page 130; → Partner B: file 16, page 136

9 👥 Start a conversation with a new partner. Find out something about his/her role at work, regular activities and current projects.

👥 Introduce your partner to the class and include one statement that isn't true. Can the class spot the lie?

Talking about responsibilities and roles

- He works for an oil company / in the IT department.
- She's in sales / banking / the civil service / …
- I'm responsible for …
- I update / arrange / deal with / handle / coordinate …
- My boss is the team leader. She has five direct reports.
- I report directly to …
- He works closely with …
- I'm between jobs / looking for a new opening …

This is Marius. He works as a sales rep. He sells medical equipment to doctors, dentists and hospitals. He makes a lot of phone calls, arranges appointments with customers and does some general administration every day. He always takes a three-hour lunch break on Fridays. At the moment he is preparing to move to a new sales area.

Part B Working together

▶ Which aspects of a company are most important to you?

- location
- corporate culture
- training programmes
- company structure
- the products and services it offers

1 Read this description of a company. Would you like to work for it? Why (not)?

FELIX ADHESIVES

» Search | Sitemap | Contact | Home | E-Business

About us | Product & Industries | Innovations | Sustainability | Jobs & Careers

About us
- Business Units
- Management
- Strategy
- Vision
- Employees

About us

Felix Adhesives plc is a global company with a vibrant corporate culture. We manufacture industrial glues and adhesives that are used in diverse consumer and industrial products from aeroplanes to nappies. Our products are sold in more than 40 countries on four continents.
We operate in three regions: Europe, Asia and America. Overall 4,140 people are employed throughout our organization. Our headquarters are located in London, and we have production facilities and sales operations in 29 countries. Our strategic team is based in London. It sets the objectives, and coordinates and supports the business activities.
Our business is divided into four global business units: Automotive, Aeronautics, Hygiene and Furniture. We have six divisions: Research & Development, HR & Communications, Manufacturing, Supply, Business Development and Finance.

From aeroplanes to nappies ... just a few examples of where our products are used

Are the following statements true or false?

1. More than four thousand staff are employed in London.
2. The strategic staff are based at company headquarters.
3. The company's products are only sold in Europe and America.
4. The company is organized into six global business units.
5. The adhesives are used in industrial and consumer products.
6. The production facilities are located in different countries.

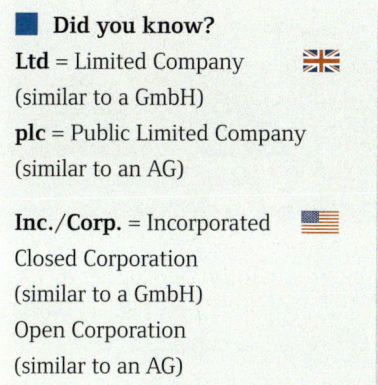

■ **Did you know?**
Ltd = Limited Company
(similar to a GmbH)
plc = Public Limited Company
(similar to an AG)

Inc./Corp. = Incorporated
Closed Corporation
(similar to a GmbH)
Open Corporation
(similar to an AG)

1 First impressions — Part B

2 Which diagram matches Felix Adhesives' organization best?

A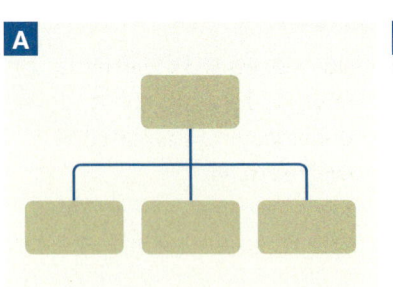
B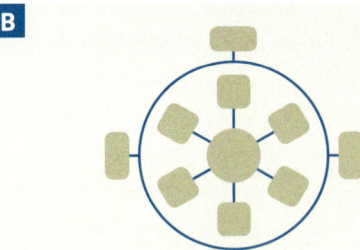
C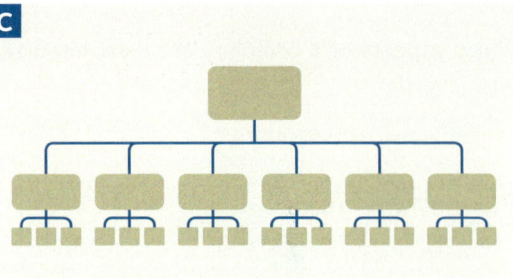

Now match these descriptions to the other two diagrams.

> **1** My company structure is quite flat. It's basically divided into three layers. There's one person at the top. That's the CEO. Then there are six people in the second layer: the senior managers of various departments. Then come the rest of us.

> **2** Our structure is very traditional. There is a parent company – that's us – and then there are three subsidiaries operating in different regions of the world: Germany, Poland and Canada.

3 Which word doesn't fit with the others in each row? Why not?

1. business unit · division · consumer · department
2. facilities · products · headquarters · sales operations
3. diverse · flat · traditional · layer
4. parent company · finance · subsidiary · branch

4 🔊 1.4-5 Listen to two people introducing themselves and presenting their companies at a careers fair. What products or services do their companies sell?

1. Petra Weber

   ....

2. Johan Svensen

   ....

What did they say? Select the right words to complete the sentences. Then listen and check.

Petra Weber

1. Our head office / subsidiary / training department is in Sheffield.
2. We're currently developing a new brand / line of products / product range .
3. The structure of our company is … divided according to region / product / country .

Johan Svensen

4. Our company structure is traditional / quite flat / straightforward .
5. Safe work habits / International safety standards / Innovative communications skills are taught to managers and workers on a regular basis.
6. Lasco is an environmentally friendly / a growing / a long-established company.

Part B 1

5 In pairs, ask each other questions about Felix Adhesives, Fresh Look and Lasco Energy.

- What products or services are offered?
- Where is it based?
- How is the company organized?
- What kind of training is done there?

Now ask your partner questions about his/her company or a company he/she is familiar with.

Passive: simple present

Our business **is divided** into four global business units.
Our products **are exported** all over the world.
Are the goods **produced** locally, or **are** they **made** abroad?

6 Complete the sentences with the simple present passive form of the verbs in the box.

generate · make · make · sell · ~~target~~ · use

1 I think these products ..are........ ..targeted.. at men.
2 Surprisingly, most of our garments .... still .... in retail outlets and not online.
3 I think this .... by hand. That's probably why the price is so high.
4 I wonder why adhesives .... in this product.
5 .... energy often .... by hydroelectric power in your country, too?
6 We guarantee that this premium product .... with fresh natural ingredients like Alpine milk and real vanilla.

Match the sentences above to these pictures.

7 Your partner has three products that are trusted brand names in Germany. Can you guess each product in 10 questions or less?

→ Partner A: file 2, page 130; → Partner B: file 17, page 136

15

1 First impressions

Business file

📁 Here's my card

1 🔊 1.6-8 Listen and fill in the missing contact information.

......................¹ **Rentals Ltd**

......................² Parker

Sales Assistant
14 Bay Avenue
Bromley, Kent BR1 1EX

+44 (0) 181 460 6682
+44 (0) 172 387 127
e.parker@globex.co.uk

Mohan Gupta

Staying at Regent Hotel

....
....⁷

Tel: ....⁸

Last name ....³
First name **Margaret**
Company ....⁴
Mobile ....⁵
Email ....⁶

Passing on and checking contact details

I'm sorry, I didn't catch that.
What's your last name again?
Excuse me, how do you spell that, please?
Could you please say that again / repeat that?
Can I read that back?
Go ahead.
OK, so that's 476 208.
So, what do you do exactly?
Sorry, is that spelled with a double 'g'?

---

2 👥 Now work with a partner to practise exchanging contact information.

→ *Partner A: file 3, page 131*
→ *Partner B: file 18, page 137*

→ *See page 146 for help with saying telephone numbers and addresses.*

3 🔊 1.9-11 Listen to Liz, Margaret and Mohan introducing themselves at a networking event. Who works for a company based outside of Europe?

Liz Parker

Margaret Hughes

Mohan Gupta

Listen again and take notes. What stands out about …

the person? · the company? · the products or services?

Business file

4 Read this article from a business magazine.

Networking. How to stand out from the crowd.

These days it is becoming more and more important to reach out and meet other professionals from similar or even completely different fields. But how do you make a memorable first impression? Just include the following three factors:

Your company
Say something memorable to introduce your business. Describe your business. Choose something concrete and not abstract. What do you do? What kind of products or services do you have? What makes you or your company unique?
- We have the biggest range of kitchen furniture in Europe.
- We're the only company that offers home deliveries free of charge.

Your products and services
Give some specific information about the kind of products you sell or the clients you serve.
Use numbers or details about location. Which are your most important or most interesting products, services or clients?
- One of our clients is the oldest estate agency in Stuttgart.
- We have over 40 different kinds of cupcakes, and they are all homemade and decorated by hand.

Yourself
Give one or two personal details about yourself.
What do you love about your job? What do you get to do in this job that you would never get to do in any other job?
- I love meeting new people and in my job I get to meet new people every day.
- I like balance sheets and statistics. My colleagues call me the number cruncher. Not many of my friends know this.

Now think of three sentences of your own.

My company: ....

My products and services: ....

Myself: ....

5 Write a short self-introduction. Try to keep it under 60 seconds. Then use it to introduce yourself to the rest of the class.

Introducing yourself and your company
Hello, I'm / my name is …   I work as / for …   I'm responsible for / I'm in …   I work for a unique sort of company.   We are actually the only … company in the world / region / industry / … that …   You simply can't find a company anywhere with a better …   What makes us / our products / services so special?   It's really the only product of its kind that …   We have some rather amazing … . For example, …   I like my job because …   That's why I love my job so much.

1 Grammar summary

Simple present

1. We **develop** and **test** new products here.
   I **report** to Bill.
   Do you **work** here full time?
2. She sometimes **updates** the HR documentation.
   They **don't** usually **take** a coffee break.
   Does Jon ever **work** from home?
3. Lisa **is** sometimes away from the office on business trips.

I	make … / 'm …
	don't make … / 'm not …
he / she / it	makes … / 's …
	doesn't make … / isn't …
you / we / they	make … / 're …
	don't make … / aren't …

Mit dem *simple present* beschreibt man
- gleichbleibende Zustände und Fakten, beispielsweise Angaben zur Person, Arbeit oder Firma (**1**).
- routinemäßig ausgeführte Handlungen und Gewohnheiten. Signalwörter dafür sind u. a.: *always*, *often*, *usually* oder *sometimes*. Diese Signalwörter stehen im Allgemeinen vor dem Verb (**2**) aber hinter Formen von *be* (**3**).

Present continuous

1. Sorry, I can't help you. I**'m writing** a very important email now.
2. He**'s** currently **doing** a lot of extra jobs.
   We**'re doing** more and more business in Asia at the moment.
   Are you **working** overtime this week?
3. Mary **isn't** in today – she **has** the day off.
   Bob**'s having** a meeting with the supplier now.

I	'm taking …
	'm not taking …
he / she / it	's taking …
	isn't taking …
you / we / they	're taking …
	aren't taking …

Mit dem *present continuous* werden
- vorübergehende Vorgänge beschrieben, die in dem Moment stattfinden, in dem man spricht (**1**).
- langfristige aber zeitlich begrenzte Vorgänge beschrieben (z. B. ein aktuell in der Firma laufendes Projekt oder ein Trend) (**2**).

Signalwörter dafür sind u. a.: *now*, *at the moment* oder *currently*.

Das *present continuous* wird normalerweise nicht mit Verben wie u. a. *be*, *believe*, *know*, *like* oder *have* verwendet. In Wendungen wie *have a chat* sowie *have a meeting* kann *have* auch in der *continuous form* verwendet werden (**3**).

Passive: simple present

1. The company **is organized** into six global business units.
   The teams **aren't based** in London.
2. The files **are updated** once a month.
3. The toys **are** all **designed** by artists.
   Are the goods **produced** locally?

I	'm	given …
	'm not	
he / she / it	's	taught …
	isn't	
you / we / they	're	based …
	aren't	

Das Passiv wird verwendet, wenn man auf unpersönliche Art und Weise über Fakten und Daten berichten möchte, z. B. bei
- statischen Zuständen (**1**).
- Handlungen, bei denen das Subjekt unbekannt oder unwichtig ist (**2**).
- Prozessen, wie z. B. der Herstellung eines Produktes (**3**).

Das *simple present passive* wird mit *am/is/are* und dem Partizip Perfekt gebildet. Für die Liste der unregelmäßigen Verben und deren dritten Formen, siehe S. 194.

> „Von" bzw. „durch" wird in Passivsätzen durch <u>by</u> ausgedrückt.

Extra practice 1

1 Fill in the correct form of the verb. Use the simple present or present continuous.

1 .Do.you.know. (you/know) Jill? She ....works......... (work) in the IT department too.
2 David .... (make) some coffee for us now. .... (you/like) yours with or without sugar?
3 I usually .... (start) work at 7.30. But this week I .... (start) half an hour earlier because my colleague .... (be) on holiday and I .... (do) some of his work too.
4 I often .... (have) lunch just after noon, but today we .... (have) a very late lunch because there is so much to do.
5 'What .... Gina .... (do)?'
'I .... (think) she .... (be) on the phone. Maybe she .... (make) an appointment with one of the suppliers.'
6 More and more customers .... (buy) environmentally friendly products these days.

2 Match the questions to the answers.

1 Where is Kazue Sato from?	a	Yes, it certainly is.
2 Where does she work?	b	She works in Bangalore, India.
3 What does she do?	c	No, she isn't. Not as far as I know.
4 What's that?	d	This type of engineer provides technical support to suppliers.
5 Is she working on any special projects?	e	She comes from Japan.
6 Is the Indian market expanding?	f	She's a purchase engineer.

3 Rearrange the words to make questions.

1 this / are / week / you / who / with / working .Who.are.you.working.with.this.week?...............................
2 people / do / why / like / iPhone / the / many / so? ....
3 she / files / often / update / how / does / the? ....
4 your / based / where / company / is? ....
5 company's / abroad / your / sold / products / are? ....
6 break / a / usually / have / you / when / do? ....

4 Fill in the gaps with the simple present passive form of the verbs in the box.

base · divide · export · make · manufacture · use

1 The company .... into three main parts.
2 Where .... your company ....? In Paris or Lyon?
3 .... this box really .... of plastic? It feels like wood!
4 These bicycles .... in Germany and .... to over thirty different countries, including a few in Asia.
5 This type of adhesive .... in consumer products.

1 Extra practice

5 Match the job descriptions to the departments or workplaces.

1. I make sure the meals are prepared on time.
2. She updates drug records and arranges business trips for her boss.
3. They interview job candidates and process wages and salaries.
4. I answer questions and try to keep everybody happy.
5. He develops and tests new products.
6. They provide support for all computer applications.

a HR department
b pharmaceutical company
c canteen
d R&D
e customer care
f IT

6 Complete the sentences with the words in the box.

boss · division · colleague · culture · range · staff

1. Mark actually works for the same company as I do, but he's in a different ....
2. A .... of mine is off sick this week, so I'm doing some of her work.
3. I report to Jürgen Eichermüller. He's my immediate ....
4. We're lucky to have Jackie as a member of ....
5. Our company has a huge product .... We sell everything from shampoo to adhesives.
6. Last year a French company bought us. Now the corporate .... here is slowly changing.

7 Choose the correct words to complete the text.

I work in the R&D department / area ¹ of a multinational food manufacturer. I'm responsible for doing / making ² research into new kinds of dairy products. I report for / to ³ Stephan Price. He's my supervisor / direct report ⁴. That's him over there – the man who's doing / making ⁵ a phone call. I hope that he's asking his chief / boss ⁶ for some extra facilities / staff ⁷ because we really need some more people here. We're all doing / making ⁸ so much work at the moment.

8 🔊 1.12 Listen and write down the contact information.

Extra practice 1

9 Translate into English.

1. Er arbeitet bei Toyota (*feste Stelle*).
2. Was macht Anna gerade? Sie telefoniert.
3. Normalerweise trinke ich Kaffee, aber heute trinke ich Tee.
4. Sie trifft sich manchmal mit ihren Kollegen nach der Arbeit.
5. Diese Produkte werden häufig von Eltern gekauft.
6. Ich kann im Moment leider nicht helfen.
7. Ich arbeite bei einer deutschen Firma. Ich bin Ingenieurin.
8. Wir verkaufen gerade sehr viele umweltfreundliche Produkte.

Typical mistakes

1. Remember the difference:
   I **work** for BMW. (*Ich habe hier eine feste Stelle.*)
   I**'m working** for BMW. (*Ich arbeite hier nur vorübergehend.*)
2. What are you doing **at the moment**?
   NOT   … *in the moment?*
3. My boss **often goes** on business trips.
   NOT   My boss *goes often* on business trips.
4. She **makes** a lot of phone calls every day.
   NOT   She *does* a lot of phone calls …
5. He's **an** engineer.
   NOT   *He's engineer.*
6. It **is sold** in supermarkets.
   NOT   It *will sold* in supermarkets.
7. I **work for** a German company.
   NOT   I *work by* a German company.
8. It is **made by** Beiersdorf.
   NOT   It is *made from* Beiersdorf.

Culture spot

The first 30 seconds

Three tricky questions and all in the first 30 seconds!
When business people from different countries meet for the first time, there are three questions that are often asked in the first 30 seconds. They sound harmless but can be tricky to answer.

00 sec.

Do you speak English?
It seems obvious to say *Yes, I do* and wait for your partner to react. But you can make a much better impression if you say something light-hearted. Say *I know enough to get by* or *It depends on the situation* or *Some days are better than others – I hope today's a good day.* English people in particular love understatement, and your quick-thinking reply will put a smile on their face and help them connect with you.

10 sec.

What's your name?
This question seems perfectly harmless but it is trickier than it sounds. Do you answer with your first name only, *Alex*, or with your surname, *Klein*, or with both, *Alex Klein*? German speakers know that in many countries like Britain and Sweden business partners prefer to be on a first-name basis. So is it too formal to use both names? Or is it impolite to just use first names? The best advice is to follow the other person's lead. If they use first names, *Hi, I'm Janet. What's your name?*, say something like *Hi Janet, I'm Alex. Nice to meet you!* If they say *Hi, I'm John Brown. But please call me John*, say *Hi, John. I'm Alex. Alex Klein.* When in doubt, use both your names and see how the situation develops.

20 sec.

Do you work with Günther?
This is another situation where a simple *Yes, I do* often isn't enough. Your partner may want to know something about your business relationship. If Günther is a colleague and you don't want to specify your relationship, say something like *Yes, we work on the same team.* If you want to specify hierarchy, but in a gentle way, say something like *Yes, he's a member of my team* or *He's our team leader.*

30 sec.

light-hearted	unbeschwert
to follow the other person's lead	sich an der anderen Person orientieren
in a gentle way	vorsichtig

2 Then & now

In this unit you will ...
- talk about your job experience and your past
- talk about your skills and abilities

Business file
- practise making telephone calls and leaving messages
- practise telephoning a business contact for information

Part A Working here

▶ How is your current job different from those you had in the past? What made some of your jobs better than others?

1 🔊 1.13 Listen. Which syllable is stressed? Put the words in the right columns.

automotive · components · innovation · bureaucracy · development · manufacturer · opportunity · importance

•.•	.•..	..•.	..•..
		automotive	

Match 1–4 to the words above with a similar meaning. Explain the remaining words.

1 producer   3 official rules
2 parts   4 chance

Oft wird im Englischen anders betont als im Deutschen. Ein Wörterbuch gibt Auskunft. Z. B.
automotive [ɔːtəˈməʊtɪv]

2 Read the article about Dieter Weigl, an employee at ZMM Mechanics. Are these statements true or false?

1 ZMM produces parts for the automobile industry.
2 Dieter started working at ZMM in 2004.
3 In his first job, his team had problems meeting deadlines.
4 He next worked for a multinational.
5 He moved to ZMM because he wanted to work for a more innovative company.

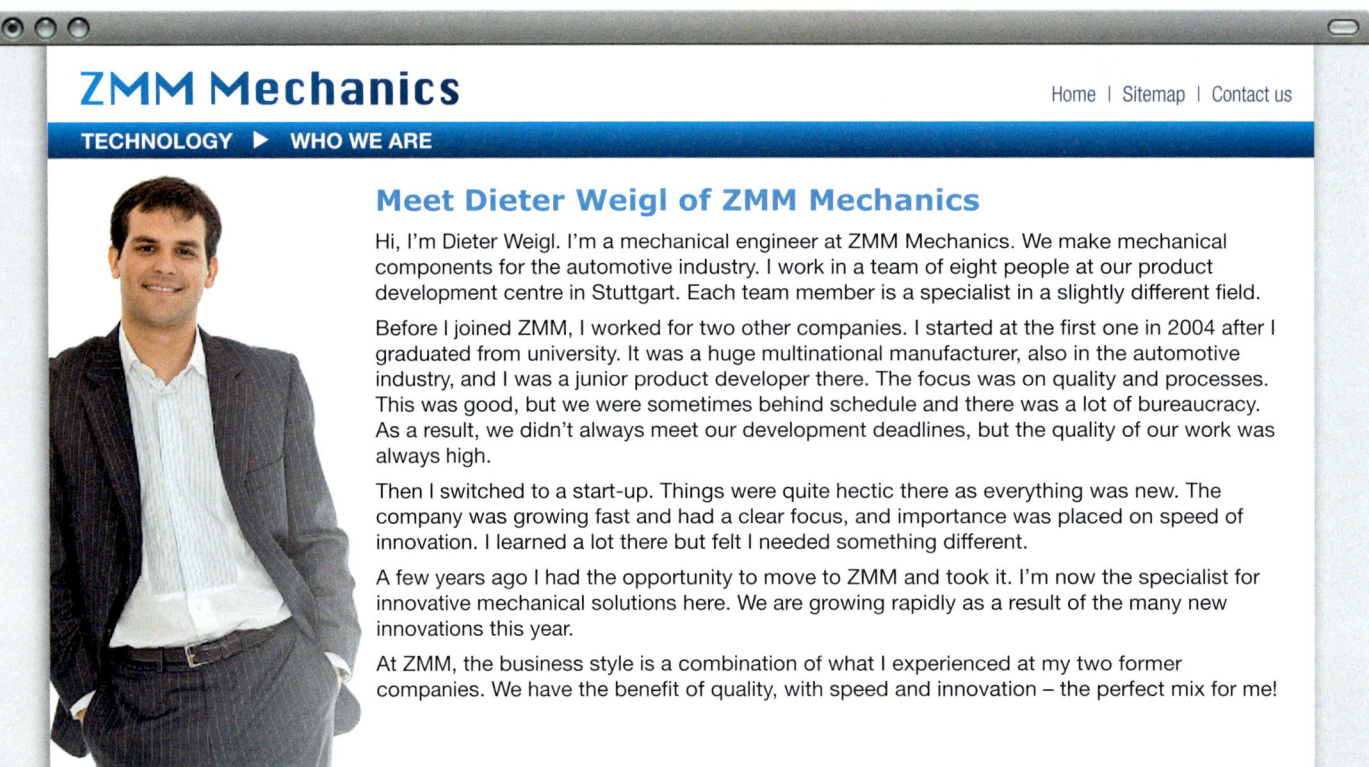

ZMM Mechanics
TECHNOLOGY ▶ WHO WE ARE   Home | Sitemap | Contact us

Meet Dieter Weigl of ZMM Mechanics

Hi, I'm Dieter Weigl. I'm a mechanical engineer at ZMM Mechanics. We make mechanical components for the automotive industry. I work in a team of eight people at our product development centre in Stuttgart. Each team member is a specialist in a slightly different field.

Before I joined ZMM, I worked for two other companies. I started at the first one in 2004 after I graduated from university. It was a huge multinational manufacturer, also in the automotive industry, and I was a junior product developer there. The focus was on quality and processes. This was good, but we were sometimes behind schedule and there was a lot of bureaucracy. As a result, we didn't always meet our development deadlines, but the quality of our work was always high.

Then I switched to a start-up. Things were quite hectic there as everything was new. The company was growing fast and had a clear focus, and importance was placed on speed of innovation. I learned a lot there but felt I needed something different.

A few years ago I had the opportunity to move to ZMM and took it. I'm now the specialist for innovative mechanical solutions here. We are growing rapidly as a result of the many new innovations this year.

At ZMM, the business style is a combination of what I experienced at my two former companies. We have the benefit of quality, with speed and innovation – the perfect mix for me!

Part A

2

3 Use the correct form of the verbs in the box to complete these questions.

be · do · focus · ~~go~~ · ~~graduate~~ · leave · move · work

1 Dieter, you .went. to university, didn't you? When .did. you .graduate.?
2 Where .... you .... before you joined ZMM?
3 What .... you .... on in your first job?
4 What .... your second job like?
5 You .... the start-up a few years ago, right? Why .... you .... to ZMM?
6 So, tell me, what .... you .... at ZMM now?

Now use information from the article to answer the questions for Dieter.

4 👥 Ask your partner questions about his/her past professional experience.

5 🔊 1.14 Listen to Dieter talking about his past and current jobs. Which pictures (A–F) show the past? Which show what he does now?

A

C

E

B

D

F

Use the prompts to summarize what Dieter used to do and how things are now.

He used to get up early but now he goes to work a bit later.

1 get up early
2 drive to work
3 first in the office
4 open-plan office
5 temporary contract
6 job security

6 What things did you use to do but don't do anymore? Use the words in the box or think of your own examples.

live in the country/city · drive / cycle / take public transport to work · work in a large/small office · send faxes/letters · deal with bureaucracy

👥 Tell a partner.

Simple past

I **switched** to a start-up in 2009.
We **didn't** always **meet** our deadlines.
When **did** you **leave** your last job?
I **left** there three years ago.

Used to

Dieter **used to live** in the city centre but he doesn't anymore.
Now I have my own office but I **didn't use to**.

Für Ereignisse, die nur einmal passiert sind, kann „used to" nicht verwendet werden:
• *Dieter changed jobs two years ago.*

23

2 Then & now — Part A

7 Link the words in boxes A and B and use them to complete Dieter's profile on a professional networking site.

A automotive, product, training, ~~innovative~~, permanent, university, mechanical

B contract, division, degree, developer, industry, opportunities, ~~solutions~~

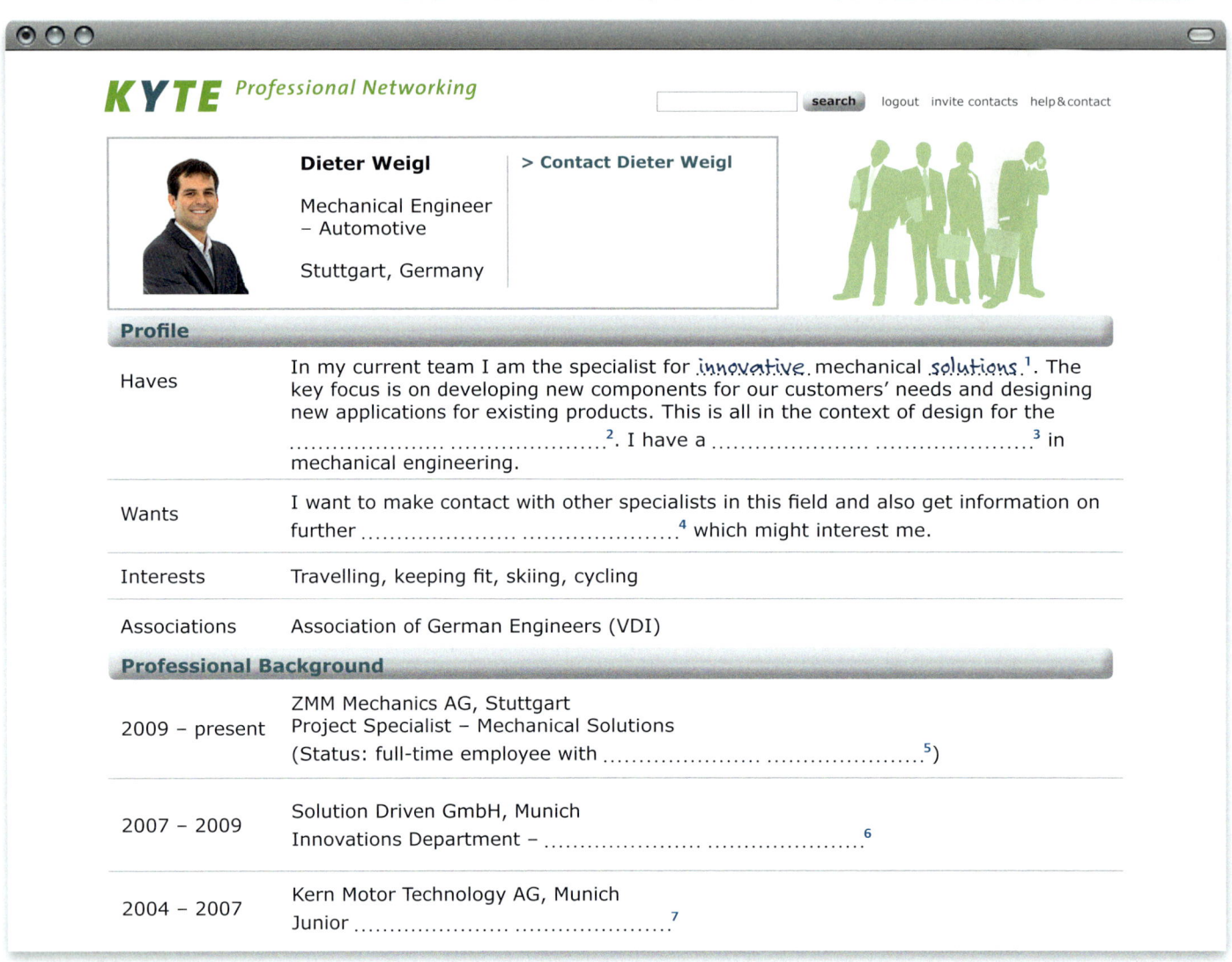

KYTE Professional Networking

Dieter Weigl
Mechanical Engineer – Automotive
Stuttgart, Germany

> Contact Dieter Weigl

Profile

Haves — In my current team I am the specialist for _innovative_ mechanical _solutions_.¹ The key focus is on developing new components for our customers' needs and designing new applications for existing products. This is all in the context of design for the .... ². I have a .... ³ in mechanical engineering.

Wants — I want to make contact with other specialists in this field and also get information on further .... ⁴ which might interest me.

Interests — Travelling, keeping fit, skiing, cycling

Associations — Association of German Engineers (VDI)

Professional Background

2009 – present — ZMM Mechanics AG, Stuttgart
Project Specialist – Mechanical Solutions
(Status: full-time employee with .... ⁵)

2007 – 2009 — Solution Driven GmbH, Munich
Innovations Department – .... ⁶

2004 – 2007 — Kern Motor Technology AG, Munich
Junior .... ⁷

8 What information should be included in a CV or an online profile? Discuss with your group.

associations · your sex · qualifications · languages · references · educational/academic background · certificates · maternity/paternity leave taken · photo · children · interests · age or date of birth · nationality · ethnic background · complete job history · marital status · relevant work experience

CV = résumé (US)

Part B Old job, new job

▶ Think of your tasks at work. What do you do now that you didn't do five years ago?

1 🔊 1.15 Julia Klein is having an internal job interview. What job does she have now? What's the new job? Does she get it?

Match 1–10 and a–j to make expressions from the dialogue. Then listen again to check your answers.

1. _e_ deal
2. ___ optimize
3. ___ integrate
4. ___ delegate
5. ___ lead
6. ___ manage
7. ___ source
8. ___ get
9. ___ communicate
10. ___ create

a into a team
b budgets and deadlines
c good working relationships
d a team
e ~~with large orders~~
f a process
g the best deals
h with suppliers
i components
j tasks

2 Complete the sentences using the correct form of the verbs in the box. Sometimes more than one answer is right.

> communicate · deal · delegate · handle · lead · learn · manage · meet · optimize

When Julia started her current job, she was able to ....¹ the job quickly, and after a very short time, she could ....² most of her tasks successfully. A year later she was also able to ....³ the ordering process for her department.

Now she ....⁴ regularly with the sales team, and it is clear that she can ....⁵ with large orders.

Team leaders in her department need to ....⁶ a team successfully and be able to ....⁷ tasks. They also are expected to ....⁸ budgets and make sure the team members ....⁹ deadlines.

Can, could, be able to

I **can use** these contacts now.
Can you **lead** a team?
I **could handle** my last job easily.
She **was able to create** good relationships from the beginning.

2 Then & now — Part B

3 Write about your past and present job skills and abilities.

In the past	Now
I could(n't) …	I can …
I used to …	I can't …
I was(n't) able to …	I'm (not yet) able to …
I was responsible for …	I'm responsible for …

👥 Tell a partner.

> **Talking about your skills, abilities and responsibilities**
>
> I can delegate tasks / manage projects / meet deadlines / …
> I'm responsible for placing orders / sourcing components / …
> I can deal with everything that comes my way.
> In my last job, I was able to manage / handle …
> I used to be responsible for …
> When I first started, I couldn't …, but now I can …

Zeigen Sie, dass Sie aktiv zuhören:
- Oh, really?
- That's interesting.
- Tell me some more about that.

4 👥 Which of the working conditions below would you prefer? Why? Discuss the pros and cons of each in your group.

1 You need to work from home four days a week. You can only come into the office on Fridays because we have a hot-desking policy. You get your own company smartphone and laptop.

2 You have to work five days a week. You can take 40 holiday days per year, but you also need to work two weekends a month (Saturday and Sunday). You get a company car. Childcare is provided.

3 You work seven days a week with only one day off per month. You live in furnished accommodation with your co-workers. Every six months you get three months off. Pleasant working environment where teamwork is encouraged.

4 You are able to work flexi-time, but you need to be in the office between 9 a.m. and 3 p.m.: that's our core time. Christmas bonuses are standard; summer bonuses are not.

■ **Did you know?**
Hot-desking: flexible Arbeitsweise, wobei Arbeitsplätze von Kollegen/Kolleginnen geteilt werden, je nachdem wer im Büro ist.

5 Before reading this article about changes in the book publishing industry, do a quick class survey. How many prefer to read books …

- online? • using an e-book reader? • while holding an actual book?

Then & Now

Books, e-books and beyond in the American market

In 1990, most books were bought in shops or from mail-order companies. Multinational online retailers like Amazon didn't exist and most people didn't have Internet at home.

In 2000, people started to use the Internet more and more to purchase books because it was convenient. An order could be placed online in minutes, and a couple of days later the books were delivered to your home.

Today, online sales of books are growing faster than ever before. The popularity of this method of shopping can be seen in the number of customers who visit Amazon.com – more than 65 million every month!

In addition to how books are purchased, how they are read is also undergoing a revolution. A couple of years ago, very few people could imagine reading a whole book from a computer screen: they wanted to hold something solid in their hands. The introduction of electronic devices on which digital books can be read, such as the Kindle (released in 2007 by Amazon) or Apple's iPad (released in 2010), persuaded many people to change their minds. And now that smartphones can be used to display digital books, e-book fans no longer have to purchase a special device.

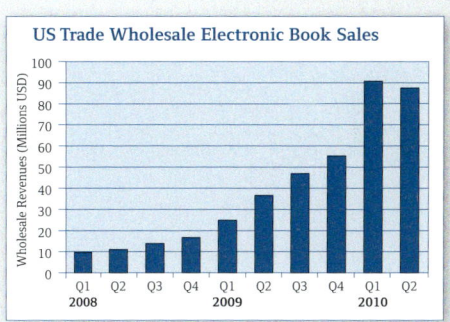

In recognition of the e-book's growing popularity, Apple launched their own online e-book shop called iBookstore in early 2010, and Google followed before the end of the same year with Google eBooks.
US e-book sales increased dramatically between 2008 and 2010 (see graph). But perhaps the strongest indication of the increased popularity of e-books and e-readers was that, in 2010 and for the first time ever, Amazon started selling more digital books than hardcover books in their online shop.

6 What does it say in the text about the following?

1 how things used to be
2 e-readers
3 smartphones
4 e-books

7 Complete the sentences with verbs in the passive voice.

1 In 2007, the first generation Kindle .... (sell out) in five and a half hours.

2 At first, the Kindle 2 .... (criticize) for its high retail price of $359. Later, the price .... (reduce) to $259.

3 The iPad .... (announce) at the beginning of 2010 and .... (release) a couple of months later.

4 Three million iPads .... (purchase) in the first 80 days.

5 From the beginning, e-books .... (can download) wirelessly using either device.

> **Passive: simple past and modals**
>
> Amazon's Kindle **was released** in 2007.
> An order **could be placed** online and the books **were delivered** to your home.
> Books **used to be sold** in that shop but now smartphones are sold there.

2 Then & now

Business file

📁 I'm calling about …

1 🔊 1.16 Karsten Meier calls his colleague Rachel Pennant in the purchasing department. What happens during the call?

1. ☐ Karsten speaks to Rachel and asks her for some information.
2. ☐ Karsten doesn't reach Rachel. He says that he'll call back later.
3. ☐ Karsten doesn't reach Rachel and leaves a message.
4. ☐ The line is bad and Karsten is cut off.

Listen again and tick the phrases that you hear.

1	☐ This is Karsten Meier.	☐ It's Karsten Meier here.
2	☐ Could you repeat that, please?	☐ Could you say that again, please?
3	☐ Could you put me through to …?	☐ I'd like to speak to …
4	☐ I'm afraid she's not here.	☐ I'm sorry, she's not here at the moment.
5	☐ Can she call you back later?	☐ Could you call back later?
6	☐ I need some information from her.	☐ I have some information for her.
7	☐ Can I leave a message?	☐ Can you take a message?
8	☐ Sure, go ahead.	☐ One moment. I need to get a pen.
9	☐ I need to know when …	☐ Can she tell me when …?
10	☐ I'll tell her later.	☐ I'll give her the message when she returns.

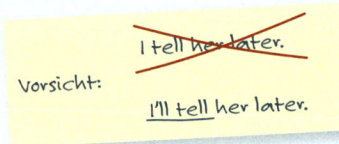

Vorsicht: I tell her later. ~~I tell her later.~~ I'll tell her later.

2 🔊 1.17 Rachel returns Karsten's call. What information does she have for him and how does he react? Listen and take notes.

order update

Business file **2**

3 👥 **Work with a partner to make some phone calls.**

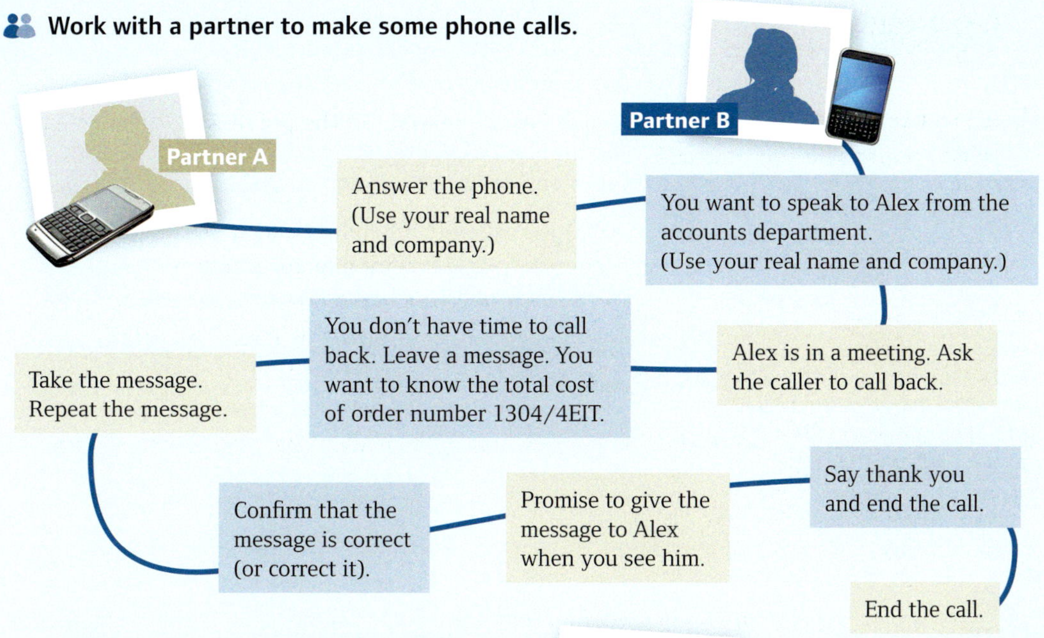

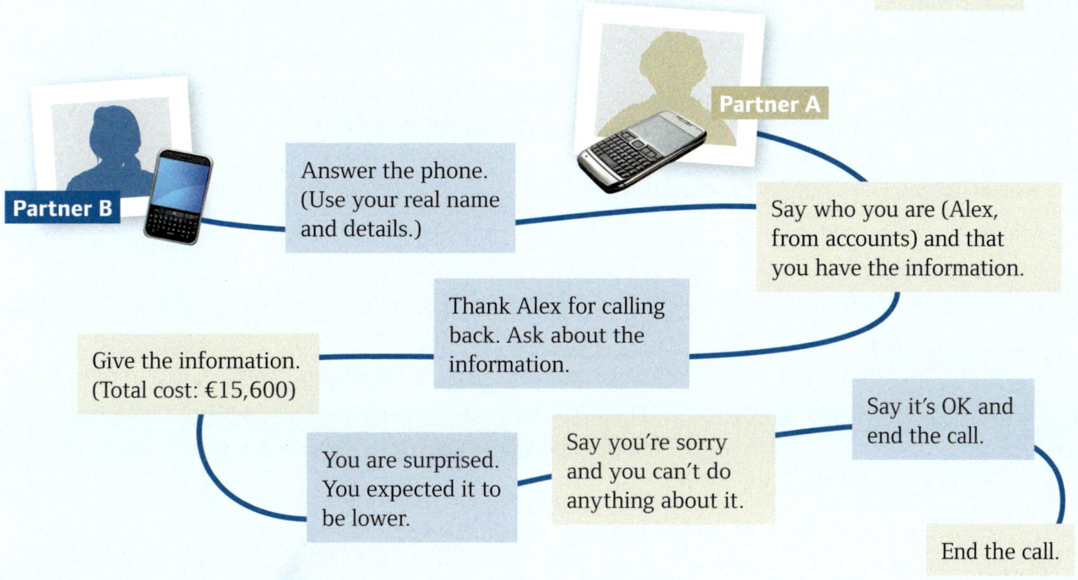

Partner A
- Answer the phone. (Use your real name and company.)
- Take the message. Repeat the message.
- Confirm that the message is correct (or correct it).

Partner B
- You want to speak to Alex from the accounts department. (Use your real name and company.)
- Alex is in a meeting. Ask the caller to call back.
- You don't have time to call back. Leave a message. You want to know the total cost of order number 1304/4EIT.
- Promise to give the message to Alex when you see him.
- Say thank you and end the call.
- End the call.

Partner B
- Answer the phone. (Use your real name and details.)
- Give the information. (Total cost: €15,600)
- You are surprised. You expected it to be lower.

Partner A
- Say who you are (Alex, from accounts) and that you have the information.
- Thank Alex for calling back. Ask about the information.
- Say you're sorry and you can't do anything about it.
- Say it's OK and end the call.
- End the call.

4 👥 **Work with a partner to get some product information.**

→ *Partner A: file 4, page 131;* → *Partner B: file 19, page 137*

5 👥 **Now make a similar call using your own name and company. Invent the necessary details in advance with your partner.**

Giving and getting information

Hello. This is …. You called me earlier?
I have some good news for you.
We can get it to you by the 20th.
Is that OK for you?
I understand. / I see.
I'm sorry, but …
I'm afraid I can't do more / anything else to help you.

Thanks for calling me back.
Can you tell me the status of my order?
That sounds good. Thanks.
Well, to be honest, …
I really need them asap (say: A-S-A-P).
I'm afraid that's unacceptable / won't work for us.
That's OK. It's good to know about it so I can plan accordingly.

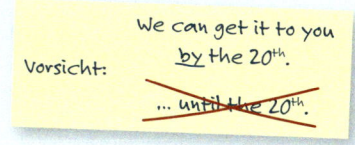

Vorsicht: We can get it to you <u>by</u> the 20th. ~~… until the 20th.~~

2 Grammar summary

Simple past

1 I **left** school **in 2004**.
   A few years ago Dieter **had** an opportunity to move to ZMM and **took** it.
   Did they **go** to university?
   – Yes, they **did**. / No, they **didn't**.

I / he / she / it / you / we / they	worked … / moved … didn't work … / didn't move … had … / drove … didn't have … / didn't drive …

2 Things **were** quite hectic there.
   Was Dieter first in the office every day?
   – Yes, he **was**. / No, he **wasn't**.

Mit dem *simple past* werden abgeschlossene Ereignisse und Situationen in der Vergangenheit beschrieben. Signalwörter dafür sind u. a. *yesterday*, *last month*, *two minutes ago*, *in 2004* (**1**).

Bei regelmäßigen Verben bildet man das *simple past*, indem man *-(e)d* an den Infinitiv anhängt. Viele Verben wie *have* und *drive* sind unregelmäßig.

Die Formen von *to be* im *simple past* sind *was/were* and *wasn't/weren't* (**2**).

> Für eine Liste unregelmäßiger Verben siehe Seite 194.

Passive: simple past

I **was employed** by ZMM **in 2006**.
The components **were produced** yesterday.

I / he / she / it	was / wasn't	given …
you / we / they	were / weren't	

Das *simple past passive* wird mit *was/were* und dem Partizip Perfekt gebildet.

Für die Verwendung des Passivs siehe Seite 18 (Grammar summary, Unit 1).

Used to

1 Mary **used to drive** to work every day.
   You **didn't use to wear** glasses, did you?
2 We **used to have** a team meeting every Monday **but now** it's on Tuesdays.

> Statt *used to* können wir immer das *simple past* verwenden.

Used to + Infinitiv wird verwendet, um über etwas zu sprechen, das in der Vergangenheit über einen längeren Zeitraum hinweg der Fall gewesen ist aber jetzt nicht mehr aktuell ist (**1**).

Bei einem Vergleich mit der Gegenwart wird häufig *but now* verwendet (**2**).

Can, could, be able to

1 I **can** / **am able to meet** deadlines.
   Julia **can speak** English.
2 **Can** you **meet** me tomorrow?
   – No, sorry, I **can't**.
3 She **couldn't** / **wasn't able to do** that in her last job. She didn't have the skills.
   After a four-hour meeting, we **were able to find** a solution.
4 **Can** I **leave** a message?
   Could you **repeat** that, please?
5 Their product range **can be seen** here.
   Back then, books **couldn't be purchased** online.

Mit dem Modalverb *can* (sowie mit seiner Ersatzform *be able to*) kann man sich u. a. zu
- Fähigkeiten (**1**) und
- Möglichkeiten (**2**) äußern.

In der Vergangenheit spricht man mit *could* über allgemeine Fähigkeiten. Mit *was/were able to* spricht man über eine bestimmte Handlung (**3**).

Can und *could* werden verwendet, um eine Bitte oder Aufforderung auszudrücken. *Could* klingt höflicher als *can* (**4**).

Bei Modalverben und ihren Ersatzformen wird das Passiv mit *be* + der dritten Form gebildet. In welcher Zeit das Verb steht, erkennt man am Modalverb (**5**).

Extra practice 2

1 Angela is talking about her career. Complete the text with the simple past form of the verbs in the box.

get · go · graduate · not have · not like · live · move · study · take · work

'I was born in Dresden and I also ....¹ to school there. After school, I ....² for four years at the Technical University in Munich and ....³ in 2004. After that, I ....⁴ a job with a company called Tangelo in Erlangen where I ....⁵ in the marketing department. I ....⁶ in Nuremberg at that time and I ....⁷ a car, so I ....⁸ the train to work. Then, in 2009, I ....⁹ to a company called PTC in Ansbach. I ....¹⁰ PTC at first, but now I'm really happy here.'

Where can you use *used to* above? Rewrite the sentences.

2 Make questions about Angela.

1 Where / she / go / to university? ..Where did she go to university?......................
2 When / she / graduate? ....
3 Where / be / her first job? ....
4 How / she / get / to work back then? ....
5 When / she / move / to PTC? ....

Now look at exercise 1 and answer the questions.

3 Complete the dialogue with the correct form of the simple past.

Ann: Hi, Pete. How ....¹ (be) the meeting? ....² (you/be able to) optimize the ordering process?

Pete: No, we ....³ (not/have) time, unfortunately. But we ....⁴ (begin) discussing options, and the team ....⁵ (make) some good suggestions. Why ....⁶ (you/not/be) at the meeting, by the way?

Ann: Oh, I ....⁷ (not/can) make it after all. My assistant ....⁸ (have) a problem that he ....⁹ (not/can) handle by himself.

4 Business life then and now. Complete the gaps with the passive form of the verbs in brackets.

1 Networking ..used to be done........................ (used to/do) at conferences for the most part, but now it .... (also/do) online.
2 Back then, new products .... (can/see) in brochures and catalogues but now they .... (can/also/see) on the company website.
3 Nowadays, at our company, orders .... (can/place) online, but back then they .... (usually/place) by fax.
4 Our main products .... (used to/produce) in Switzerland, but now they .... (make) at our factory in Hong Kong.

31

2 Extra practice

5 Match the collocations. Then use them to complete the sentences below.

engineering, ordering, developer, member, performance, job, industry, review, department, product, opportunity, purchasing, team, process

1 I optimized the .... in the logistics department last year.
2 I had a .... in a new department, so I moved.
3 In my role as ...., I have to create new products.
4 We got a new .... this week. Her name's Susan Brown.
5 Most departments have to place orders through the ....
6 My yearly .... gives me the opportunity to look back at the past year.
7 The .... is growing in Germany.

6 Match the extracts from an online profile to the headings.

1 Full Name
2 Haves
3 Wants
4 Interests
5 Associations
6 Professional background
7 Educational background
8 Languages

a German Logistics Association (BVL)
b I want to make contact with other specialists in this field.
c Painting, skiing and gardening
d In my current team I am the specialist for managing deadlines and budgets.
e Anna Zimmermann
f German (native speaker), English (good knowledge)
g 2009 – present   Sales assistant, Robert Bosch GmbH, Stuttgart
h 2005 – 2009   Electronic engineering, University of Duisburg-Essen

7 Match person B's replies to what person A says.

Person A
1 How can I help you?
2 Could you spell that, please?
3 Would you like to leave a message?
4 Could you take a message, please?
5 I'm sorry I can't do more to help you.

Person B
a Yes, please.
b Sure, go ahead.
c That's OK. I know you're trying.
d Sure, it's A-L-E-X S-M-I-T-H.
e I'd like to speak to Sue Brown, please.

8 🔊 1.18 Listen and take a message.

Call

Message for: 1

Date/Time: 13 April, 11:50 am

Caller: 2

Message: ....

....

.... 3

Extra practice 2

9 **Translate into English.**

1. Wo sind Sie geboren?
2. Meinen ersten Job habe ich 1997 als Team Assistent bekommen und wurde dann 2002 zum Projektmanager.
3. Wir haben unsere Fristen nicht immer eingehalten.
4. Früher bin ich mit dem Auto zur Arbeit gefahren aber jetzt fahre ich mit dem Bus.
5. Sie hat die Bestellung vor zwei Monaten aufgegeben.
6. Er kann momentan nicht ans Telefon gehen, weil er in einer Besprechung ist.
7. Es tut mir leid. Ich kann Ihnen nicht weiter helfen.
8. Ich gebe ihr Bescheid, wenn sie wieder hier ist.

Typical mistakes

1. Susan **was born** in Bielefeld.
   NOT Susan is born in Bielefeld.
2. I left school **in 2001**.
   NOT I left school 2001.
3. I **got** my first job in 1999.
   NOT I became my first job in 1999.
   (get = *bekommen*, become = *werden*)
4. I **didn't go** to school in Hamburg.
   NOT I didn't went to school in Hamburg.
5. We **used to write** a lot of letters in my department.
   NOT In former times, we wrote …
6. We sent an email **two days ago**.
   NOT We sent an email for two days.
7. I'm sorry, I **can't** help you.
   NOT I don't can help you.
8. **I'll give** her the message.
   NOT I give her the message.

Culture spot

When in Rome …

When you apply for a job in another country, it's important to find out about the cultural norms there, as they may be different to what you are familiar with in your country.

In Germany, for example, it's usual to include the following information in your CV: a photograph, your age and date of birth, and your marital status. In contrast, in the UK and USA it can be illegal for employers to ask you for this personal information. The anti-discrimination laws are very different there, and unsuccessful applicants can accuse a company of discrimination if they don't get the job. For this reason, many companies don't want you to include this personal information when applying.

A common final sentence in a CV is 'references available upon request'. In the UK and USA it's not usually necessary to include copies of references from past employers in your application. Instead, you just need to show them to the potential employer if they are requested. This procedure saves both you and the person reading your application time.

It's difficult to have a 'do's and don'ts' list for what to put on your CV. The best thing is to do some research before sending in your application. Find out what is considered 'usual' in the national and corporate culture of the company you are applying to.

Tip: Have a look at the company's website or do an online search for information on what's appropriate.

anti-discrimination law — Antidiskriminierungsgesetz
applicant — Bewerber/in
When in Rome (do as the Romans do). — Andere Länder, andere Sitten.

3 A company tour

In this unit you will ...

- practise welcoming visitors and socializing
- talk about rules and regulations
- describe a process
- write emails

Business file

- develop small talk tactics

Part A Meeting people

▶ How often do you write emails? How many do you write in English? Are most of your emails formal or informal?

1 Petra Schöder and Tony Marstons work in the marketing department of the German division of the British footwear manufacturer Cantona Ltd. Read the email and match the parts to the descriptions.

	greeting		main reason for writing
	request for a favour		closing
1	header		introductory remarks

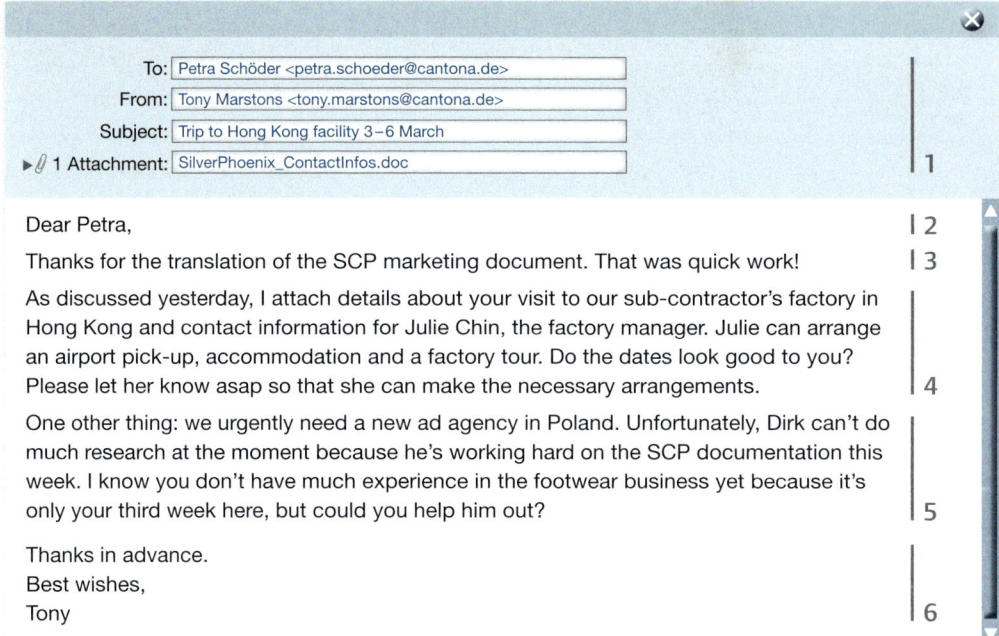

To: Petra Schöder <petra.schoeder@cantona.de>
From: Tony Marstons <tony.marstons@cantona.de>
Subject: Trip to Hong Kong facility 3–6 March
1 Attachment: SilverPhoenix_ContactInfos.doc | 1

Dear Petra, | 2

Thanks for the translation of the SCP marketing document. That was quick work! | 3

As discussed yesterday, I attach details about your visit to our sub-contractor's factory in Hong Kong and contact information for Julie Chin, the factory manager. Julie can arrange an airport pick-up, accommodation and a factory tour. Do the dates look good to you? Please let her know asap so that she can make the necessary arrangements. | 4

One other thing: we urgently need a new ad agency in Poland. Unfortunately, Dirk can't do much research at the moment because he's working hard on the SCP documentation this week. I know you don't have much experience in the footwear business yet because it's only your third week here, but could you help him out? | 5

Thanks in advance.
Best wishes,
Tony | 6

2 Are the following statements true or false?

1. Petra translated the marketing document slowly.
2. Petra doesn't know much about the shoe business.
3. Petra should confirm as quickly as possible that the travel arrangements look good.
4. Cantona needs to find a new advertising agency immediately.

3 Complete the gaps with the adjective or adverb form of the words in the box. You don't need to use all the words.

Adjectives and adverbs

Julie can make the **necessary** arrangements.
Do the dates look **good** to you?
You know Europe **well**.
We **urgently** need a new ad agency.
Unfortunately, he can't manage this alone.

careful · difficult · exact · fast · good · quick · strange

1. How .... can you write an email in English?
2. Which foreign languages sound .... to you?
3. How .... can you walk in the shoes that you're wearing?
4. Did you listen .... to the news last night? If so, what do you remember ....?

👥 Ask your partner the questions.

Part A 3

4 🔊 1.19 It's 3 March and Petra is arriving at the factory in Hong Kong. Listen. What do Petra and the factory manager Julie Chin talk about?

■ **Did you know?**
In China steht der Familienname vor dem Vornamen. Manche Chinesen suchen sich einen englischen Namen aus, den sie im Umgang mit Ausländern als Rufnamen verwenden.

Listen again. What does Julie say to welcome Petra and make her feel at ease?

5 Do you remember what was said? Complete the sentences, then listen again to check if necessary.

1 It's nice to ……………… meet you in ……………… after all the emails.
2 And how was your ………………? Did everything go ………………?
3 We can go to a ……………… Hong Kong restaurant, if you ………………
4 ……………… you like a cup of coffee or something while we're waiting for Li Wen?
5 Whereabouts in Austria, if you don't ……………… me asking?
6 Oh, sorry, would you ……………… me for a minute? I need to take this.

6 👥 Work in groups of three or four. Take it in turns to welcome visitors and introduce them to your 'colleague'. Use the flow chart and follow either the blue or beige arrows.

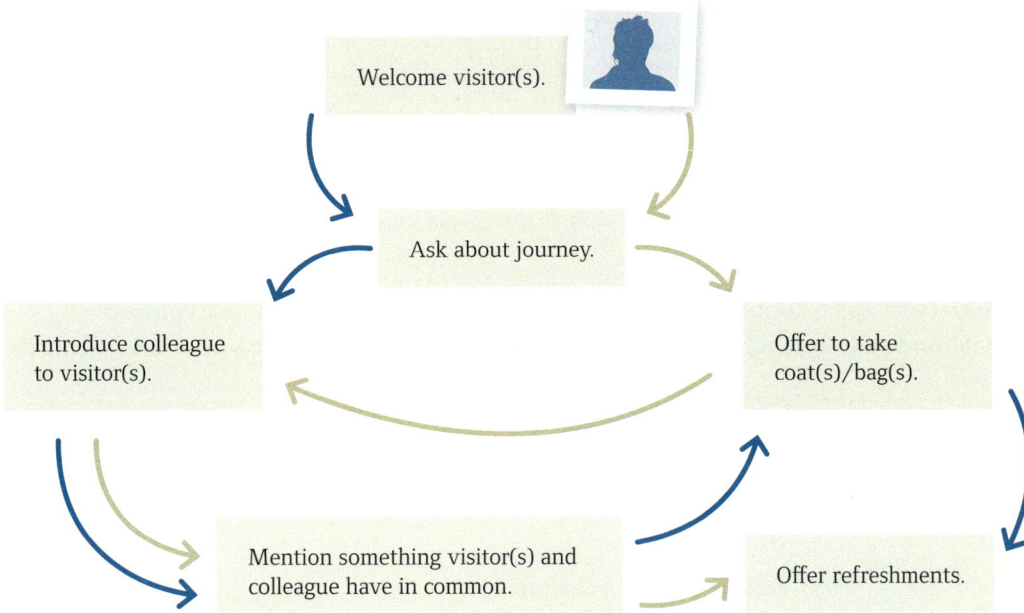

Welcoming a visitor

You must be …
Did you have a good trip?
How was your journey/flight?
I'd like you to meet …
May I introduce …?
Can I take your coat/bag?
Can I get you something to drink?
Would you like a cup of coffee?
Please help yourself to tea and biscuits.
So, what's your first impression of …?

35

3 A company tour — Part A

7 Before reading the extract from Cantona's blog, match these words from the text with their definitions. What do you think the blog article will be about?

1. competitor — a to start selling something (e.g. a product) for the first time
2. market share — b a company that sells a similar product in the same market
3. sabbatical — c the percentage of sales of a particular type of product
4. commuter — d to tell people about something (e.g. a new product)
5. to launch — e a period of time when someone stops work to travel/study
6. to announce — f a person who travels a long distance to work each day

Cantona – Goodbye 'work shoes', hello 'shoes for work'!

posted by: T. Roberts, PR Dept on 22 February

Looking back
About two years ago, things weren't going that well here at Cantona. We were mainly producing 'work shoes' – practical footwear designed for use in the health, manufacturing and agricultural sectors. The shoes were great – and still are! – but sales were slow. At that time our competitors were doing quite well, because they were expanding their ranges and adapting to the market, but we were selling less than usual and rapidly losing market share.

How the SmartCommuter brand was born!
About 18 months ago, our founder and CEO James Nestleton realized something had to change, so he took a four-month sabbatical to Central America to try and figure out what the company was doing wrong. While he was hiking through the highlands of Mexico, he met some local shoemakers who were making simple but elegant leather footwear designed for people who spend long hours on their feet in difficult terrain.

Inspired by the innovative design, we developed our SmartCommuter range, a new line of 'shoes for work'. The first model in this new range was launched six months ago: the SmartCommuter Basic (SCB), a sturdy yet stylish shoe designed for commuters who walk or cycle to work but want a shoe that looks smart in the office too. Now we are pleased to announce our next model in the series, the SmartCommuter Pro (SCP).

8 Match the sentence halves.

1. b Two years ago
2. At the same time, Cantona's competitors
3. The CEO wanted to figure out what was wrong,
4. While he was travelling through Mexico,
5. When he saw the shoemakers,

a. he met some local shoemakers.
b. Cantona was mainly making and selling work shoes and sales were slow.
c. were introducing new product ranges and increasing their market share.
d. they were making exactly the kind of shoe he was looking for.
e. so he took a four-month break.

Which tense (past continuous or simple past) is used to describe the background situation or a longer action in the past? Which is used to talk about a one-time event?

9 Interview a partner. What was he/she doing …

- at this time two years ago?
- when the teacher started the lesson?
- at eight o'clock this morning?
- when …?

Past continuous

Two years ago, they **were making** work shoes.
While he **was travelling**, he met some shoemakers.
What **were** you **doing** this time last year?
I **was working** at the company when they launched the new shoe.

36

Part B **3**

Part B How things work

▶ When did you last have a fire drill at work?
Do you know what to do if there's an alarm?

1 Read this excerpt from Silver Phoenix's online safety guide. What can't you do in the factory?

**Silver Phoenix
Footwear Manufacturers**

General information and safety guidelines for visitors

Click here to access website for Chinese French German Italian Japanese version
During the tour
- All visitors must wear protective headgear. Safety helmets and earplugs are available at the main desk.
- Smoking is strictly forbidden. You mustn't smoke anywhere on the premises except in designated smoking areas.
- Always keep to the minimum safety distance from the machinery as marked in red on the floor.
- Never touch items near or on the machinery.
- Do not attempt to switch machinery on or off.
- Stay close to your guide at all times and follow his/her instructions carefully.
- In case of a fire alarm, head for the nearest exit.

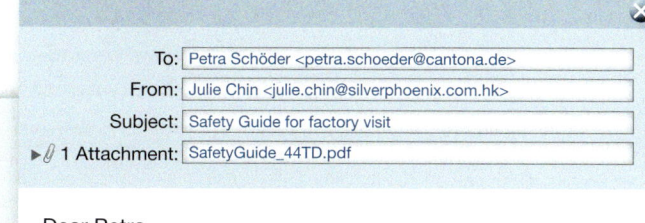

To: Petra Schöder <petra.schoeder@cantona.de>
From: Julie Chin <julie.chin@silverphoenix.com.hk>
Subject: Safety Guide for factory visit
1 Attachment: SafetyGuide_44TD.pdf

Dear Petra,
FYI please find attached our factory safety guide. It's quite long, but don't worry: you needn't print it out because you will get one in your welcome package when you arrive.

Are the following statements true or false?

		true	false
1	A safety helmet must be worn at all times.	☐	☐
2	You need to take these guidelines with you to the plant.	☐	☐
3	You can get several versions of this guide online.	☐	☐
4	You don't have to be careful near the machinery.	☐	☐
5	You mustn't touch any switches.	☐	☐
6	You needn't do as your guide says.	☐	☐

Must(n't), need(n't), (not) have to

All visitors **must wear** helmets. Helmets **have to be worn** at all times.
You **mustn't smoke** on the premises.
You **needn't print out** these instructions.
You **don't have to wear** earplugs.

2 👥 Write a 'welcome leaflet' for the class with rules and recommendations.

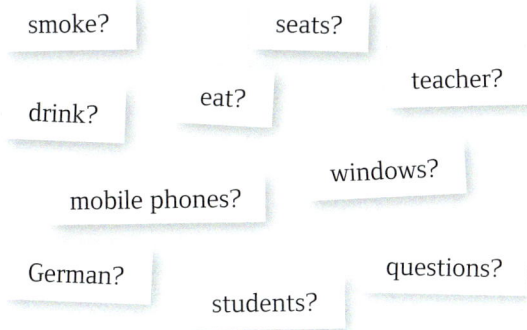

German mustn't be spoken here except in emergencies.

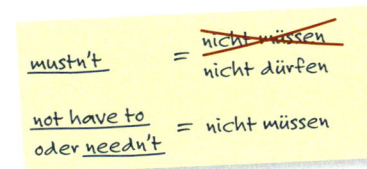
mustn't = ~~nicht müssen~~ nicht dürfen
not have to oder needn't = nicht müssen

👥 Read out your rules. How do they compare with other people's?

37

3 A company tour — Part B

Getting back to the subject

So what was I saying?
As I was saying, …
Anyway, where were we?
Ah, yes. We were talking about …

3 🔊 1.20 Listen. Li Wen, the supervisor of the Silver Phoenix factory in Hong Kong, is talking to Petra and Julie. Tick the areas of the factory that are mentioned.

☐ loading bay ☐ reception area ☐ quality control
☐ unloading bay ☐ conveyor belt ☐ canteen
☐ cutting area ☐ shop floor ☐ assembly line

4 Fill in the missing verbs and put the steps in the manufacture of shoes in the right order. Listen again to check your answers.

attach · cut · ~~deliver~~ · give · inspect · pack · sew · take · take

A ☐ Finally, they ……………………¹ in boxes and ……………………² to the loading bay ready for shipment.

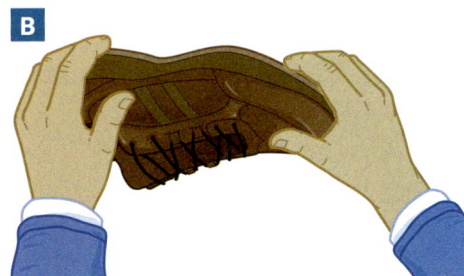

B ☐ Following that, they must …………… ……………………³ for defects by quality control.

C **1** First, material such as leather or synthetic fabric _is delivered_.⁴ to the factory's unloading bay.

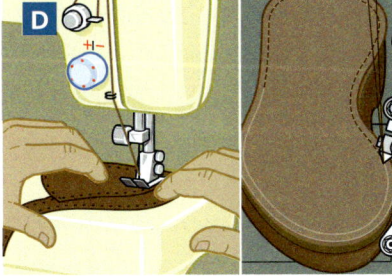

D ☐ Next, the upper parts of the shoe have to ……………………⁵ together, and then ……………………⁶ to the sole.

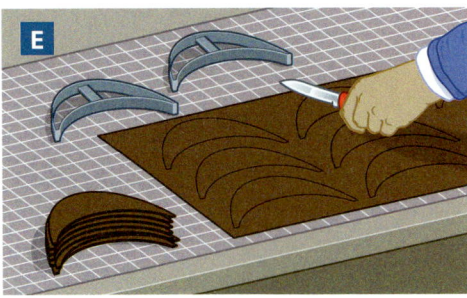

E ☐ Then it ……………………⁷ to the cutting area where it ……………………⁸ into shape.

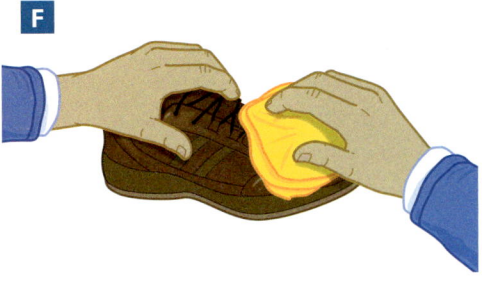

F ☐ During the next stage, the shoes …………… ……………………⁹ an attractive finish.

Part B 3

5 How are goods ordered? Put the different stages in a logical order.

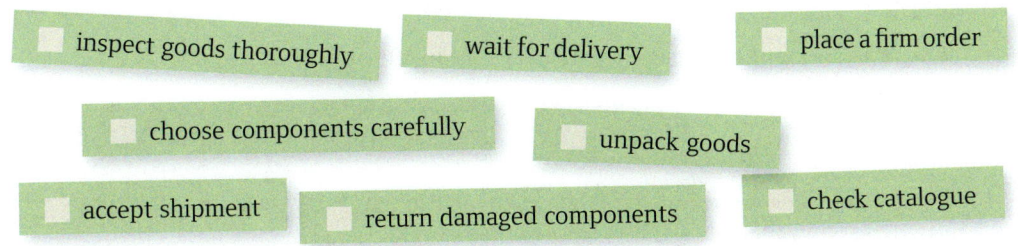

Talking about processes

First / First of all, the material is taken …
Next, the shoes are removed …
During this stage …
After that / Following that, …
Finally, …
To wrap things up, …
This is a very important stage.
It's quite a tricky/complicated process.

6 Take it turns to explain a typical process in your company.

- getting a new ID card?
- eating lunch at the canteen?
- organizing a business trip?
- ordering stationery?

While you are listening to your partner explain the process, use expressions and questions from the phrase box to show interest.

Showing interest

Oh, really? / Yeah.
I see. / Uh-huh.
OK, I get it. / Got it.
What kind of …?
Why is that?
What happens then exactly?

7 Complete the email with the adjective or adverb form of the words below.

fantastic · good · grateful · lucky · quick · recent · thorough

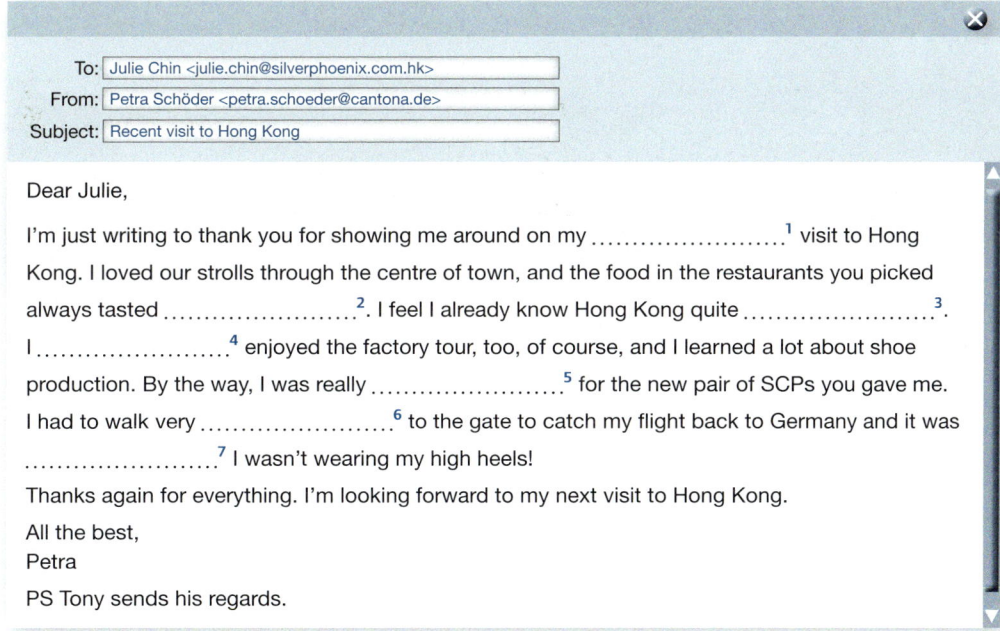

Write a similar 'thank you' email. Choose one of these models.

→ *See the Business Correspondence section for help with writing emails.*

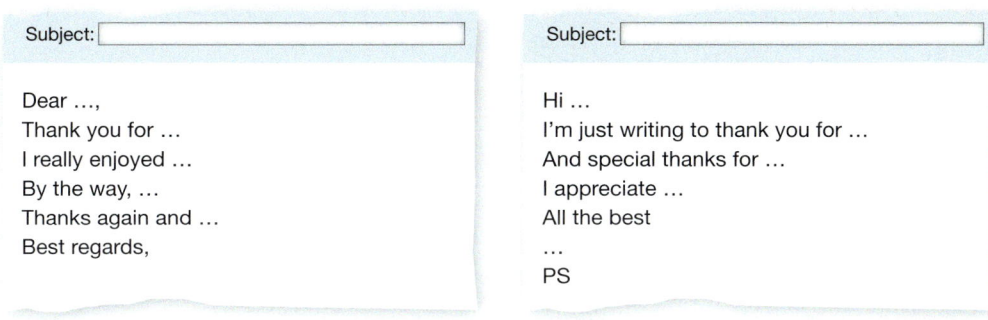

3 A company tour

Business file

📁 Tell me more …

1 👥 Look at these opportunities for small talk. Can you think of any more?

During an interval at a concert

At a restaurant

At the airport

During a coffee break

In a car while sightseeing

2 🔊 1.21-24 Miro Bernatsky works for Alpeo, a home and general merchandise retailer in Switzerland. He is visiting the UK on business.
Listen to the four conversations and complete the table. Where are the speakers and what are they talking about?

	Location	Small talk topic
1		
2		
3		
4		

3 Listen again. Which speakers …

a ask a question about the other person's lifestyle or experience?
b make a compliment about the other person's country or hometown?
c ask a question about the other person's country or hometown?
d ask or talk about something local?
e ask a question about something they see or hear?

Business file **3**

4 You are expecting three visitors. They work for an important customer of yours and are spending a few days in your hometown or city.
Use your own ideas to fill in details on the two blank cards.

Name:
Nationality:
Job:
Interests and preferences:

Name: José Martinez
Nationality: Spanish, from Madrid
Job: works for a clothing manufacturer
Interests and preferences: music, fishing, hiking, likes vegetarian food

Name:
Nationality:
Job:
Interests and preferences:

Pick a location from the collage in exercise 1 and practise making small talk with one of your visitors. Keep the conversation going for at least two minutes, and then swap roles.

Making small talk

Asking questions
Is this your first visit to the UK?
Is there anything in particular that you'd like to try/see/do?
So, what's life like in Zurich?
Yes, I enjoy hiking. What about you?
What's that over there?
What kind of things can you recommend here?

Establishing interests and discovering things you have in common
You know, I just love Switzerland. I was there last year.
What kind of sports do you like doing?
Oh, that's the kind I like too.
What are some of the most interesting places to visit around here?
I know the place well in fact.
Do you like Thai food too?
So, do you spend a lot of time outdoors?

Making, accepting and refusing invitations
Would you like to have dinner / go to a show tomorrow evening?
How about going …?
I'd love to. Thanks.
That would be nice/lovely.
Well, only if we have enough time.
Actually, if it's all the same with you, I'd prefer not to because …

Recommending
I think that's worth a visit.
Is there anything you can especially recommend?
Have you ever tried Swiss food?
Is there anything particular you'd like to try?
How about something local?
I can really recommend this. It's a local speciality.

3 Grammar summary

Adjectives and adverbs

1 They did a **thorough** inspection of the goods.
   Julie is very **quick**.
2 We have to inspect the goods **thoroughly** before shipment.
   The company was **slowly** adapting to the market.
3 **Unfortunately**, we don't have time for a discussion with the new manager.
   Strangely enough, the product didn't sell.

quick	quick**ly**
happy	happ**ily**
careful	careful**ly**
comfortable	comfortab**ly**

4 The company's new product sells very **well**.
   She has to work **late** tomorrow.
   He works so **hard** that he **hardly** ever has fun.
5 The new ads look **good**.
   I feel **great**!

Adjektive beschreiben wie etwas oder jemand ist. Sie beziehen sich auf ein Nomen (**1**).

Adverbien beschreiben, wie etwas geschieht oder getan wird. Sie beziehen sich meistens auf ein Verb (**2**). Sogenannte Satzadverbien beziehen sich auf einen ganzen Satz und geben die Meinung des Sprechers wieder (**3**).

Man bildet die meisten Adverbien, indem man -ly an das Adjektiv hängt.

Achtung! Es gibt auch unregelmäßige Adverbien (good → well) sowie Adverbien mit zwei Formen (late → late/lately [kürzlich] und hard → hard/hardly [kaum]) (**4**).

Auf Verben, die Eigenschaften ausdrücken können, wie z. B. look, feel, smell, taste und sound folgt kein Adverb, sondern ein Adjektiv (**5**).

Past continuous

1 At this time two years ago, the company **was** mainly **producing** work shoes.
2 While our competitors **were adapting** to the market, we **were** rapidly **losing** market share.
3 We **heard** about the opening of the new factory while we **were travelling** through Mexico.
   Cantona **wasn't doing** very well when the CEO **decided** to take a sabbatical.

I	was / wasn't	
he / she / it		travelling …
you / we / they	were / weren't	

Mit dem *past continuous* beschreibt man Situationen oder Handlungen, die zu einem Zeitpunkt in der Vergangenheit andauerten (**1**).

Diese Situationen oder Handlungen können gleichzeitig stattfinden, ohne sich zu beeinflussen (**2**) oder sich überschneiden (**3**). Wenn sich die Situationen überschneiden, wird die Hintergrundsituation im *past continuous* und die Unterbrechung im *simple past* geschildert. In solchen Sätzen finden sich oft die Signalwörter *when* und *while*.

Must(n't), (not) have to, need(n't)

1 All visitors **must register** at reception.
   Until today visitors **had to leave** their mobile phones at reception, but they **won't have to do** that from now on.
2 **Do** I really **have to wear** safety shoes?
3 Headgear **must be worn**.
   Look at the sign. It says I **have to wear** a helmet.
4 We **need to clean** the machine before the weekend.
5 You **mustn't wear** high heels in the manufacturing area. It's not allowed!
6 You **don't have to** / **needn't wear** earplugs, but you can if you want to.

Mit *must* und *have to* drückt man aus, dass etwas absolut notwendig ist. *Must* gibt es nur in der Gegenwart, die Ersatzform in allen Zeiten ist *have to* (**1**). Fragen werden meist mit *have to* geformt (**2**). Nur in der Gegenwart gibt es einen Bedeutungsunterschied: Während *must* ausdrückt, was der Sprecher/die Sprecherin für notwendig hält, drückt *have to* aus, was den Umständen nach notwendig ist (**3**).

Mit *need to* drückt man ebenfalls aus, dass etwas notwendig ist (**4**).

Achtung! *Mustn't* bedeutet „nicht dürfen" (**5**); *don't have to/needn't* bedeutet „nicht müssen" (**6**).

Extra practice 3

1 Fill in the table with the correct forms of the adjective or adverb.

Adjective	Adverb	Adjective	Adverb
bad	...............¹	good	...............⁶
...............²	carefully	...............⁷	luckily
current	...............³	possible	...............⁸
easy	...............⁴	thorough	...............⁹
fast	...............⁵	usual	...............¹⁰

2 Complete the gaps with the adjective or adverb of the word in brackets.

1 He made the shoes quite .... (quick) because he's an experienced worker.
2 Why didn't the design look .... (good)? They didn't work .... (hard) enough to get things .... (right).
3 We .... (urgent) need to change a few things around here.
4 John was .... (lucky). He got to the airport in time to catch his plane.
5 The team didn't do too .... (bad), and their supervisor looked .... (happy) with the result.
6 Why didn't she call us .... (immediate)? She knew it was .... (important).

3 Complete the gaps with the the simple past or the past continuous of the verbs in the box.

announce · expand · introduce · launch · lose · work

1 While they .... in the purchasing department last month, the trainees met a lot of key suppliers.
2 They .... the launch of the latest model in the series last week.
3 Our sales were poor last year. We realized that we .... market share quite rapidly.
4 When we .... the new product last year, we never thought it would be such a great success.
5 Georg arrived in the lobby while his colleague .... the visitors to the head of production.
6 When the company .... its range to include tablet computers, they decided to look for a new advertising agency.

4 Put the verbs in brackets into the passive. Then match the sentence halves and put them in the right order to make a logical sequence.

☐ Next,
☐ Then it
1 First,
☐ After this
☐ Finally,
☐ During

a the material for the shoes .... (cut) by skilled workers.
b .... (deliver) to the factory.
c the material ..is ordered.... (order).
d .... (do), the complete shoe .... (put) together.
e the shoes .... (check) by quality control and then they .... (ship) to the customer.
f this stage, the upper part of the shoe .... (attach) to the sole.

43

3 Extra practice

5 Look at the company guidelines and complete the sentences with *must*, *mustn't* or *don't have to/needn't*.

company guidelines	necessary	not necessary	not allowed
jackets and ties (men)	✔		
personal use of Internet			✔
be able to speak English	✔		
start work at nine		✔	
smoking on premises			✔
show ID cards		✔	

1 Ties .... by male employees.
2 Employees .... the Internet privately.
3 Employees .... English.
4 Employees .... before nine o'clock.
5 Employees .... on the premises.
6 ID cards .... when entering the building.

6 Complete this dialogue with suitable phrases.

> Can I take your coat? | Is this your first visit to London? | You must be | How was your flight? | Nice to meet you.

Host: Hello. ....[1] Jan Tarnowski.
Guest: That's right.

Host: I'm Jenni Andersson. ....[2]
Guest: Nice to meet you, too.

Host: ....[3]
Guest: Oh, yes. Thanks.

Host: ....[4]
Guest: Great. But we were a little late landing.

Host: No wonder with this fog! ....[5]
Guest: Well, it is actually.

7 Which syllable is stressed in these words? Put them in the right columns.

> appointment · arrangement · competitor · compliment · document · information · invitation · sabbatical

•..	.•.	.•..	...•.

🔊 1.25 Listen to check your answers.

Extra practice 3

8 Look at the words in exercise 7. Find …

1. three things you can make.
2. one thing you can take.
3. five things you can give somebody.
4. three things you can attach to an email.
5. somebody you want to be better than.

9 Translate into English.

1. Die Übersetzung der Sicherheitsanweisungen sieht gut aus.
2. Wir haben oft Besucher auf dem Gelände.
3. Unser Geschäftsführer hat letztes Jahr Mexiko besucht.
4. Besucher müssen sich nicht an der Rezeption anmelden.
5. Ich habe Angst vor Feuer.
6. Wir bieten den Besuchern eine zweistündige Werksbesichtigung.
7. Ich hatte gestern einen wichtigen Termin mit der neuen Werksleiterin.

Typical mistakes

1. The arrangements **look good**.
   NOT *The arrangements look well.*
2. We **often adapt** too slowly to new markets.
   NOT *We adapt often too slowly …*
3. Petra visited the factory **last month**.
   NOT *Petra visited last month the factory.*
4. You **don't have to / needn't** wear a helmet.
   NOT *You mustn't wear a helmet.*
5. I'm **afraid of** serious emergencies.
   NOT *I'm afraid for serious emergencies.*
6. He took a **four-month** break.
   NOT *He took a four-months break.*
7. I have **an appointment** with Petra to discuss the trip.
   NOT *I have a date with Petra …*

Culture spot

What is the point of small talk?

The basics
Native English speakers often expect to make a little small talk before getting down to business. After saying hello and asking how you are, the kinds of subjects they like to talk about are ordinary things, like the weather in your part of the world (e.g. during a phone call), your flight (e.g. when picking you up at the airport) or your recent holiday (e.g. when writing you an email). When you start talking shop too quickly, it can come across as abrupt and unfriendly to many native English speakers and can make them feel uncomfortable.

Getting good at small talk
The main thing is to keep the conversation flowing smoothly and to show genuine interest in the other person. Prepare some questions about your partner's home town or country beforehand. Say something like: *Is it true that …?* or *Could you tell me more about …?* or *So, what do you think about …?*

Some people might feel that small talk is superficial and a waste of time. But learning how to get good at small talk is worthwhile because it can help you build relationships with your business partners.

to get down to business	zum Geschäftlichen übergehen
to talk shop	über die Arbeit reden
to come across	auf andere wirken
superficial	oberflächlich

4 Big plans

In this unit you will ...

- talk about plans and projects
- look at graphs and sales figures
- practise taking part in meetings

Business file

- check and compare information
- practise placing an order

Part A Looking ahead

▶ Is your town/city famous for a product or an industry? What about other towns or cities in your region?

1 🔊 1.26 Before you listen to a news report, look at the picture and the text below. What do you think the report will be about? Then listen and see if you were right.

Factfile: Premier Dairies GmbH

Founded in 1918 by Gustav Meier
One of the top five dairy product manufacturers in Europe
Markets: Germany, France, Spain, UK
Employees: 4,300
Net turnover last year: €2.1 bn

++ Premier Dairies reacts to strike – new product line coming ... ++

Answer these questions.

1 What does Premier Dairies GmbH do and where is it based?
2 Who founded the company and who runs it now?
3 Who is on strike and why?
4 How does Premier Dairies plan to react?

2 Now listen again and complete the gaps in the sentences.

1 Wolfgang Meier says the company is going to .... its prices ....
2 They are also going to bring out a new .... line.
3 The strike will probably push .... up again.
4 The new .... is going to be better than anything now on the ....
5 It looks like it'll be an .... for Premier Dairies.

Which of the sentences 1–5 above ...

a describe(s) plans or intentions?
b predict(s) the future based on signs or current information?
c make(s) a prediction or a guess?

3 Complete these sentences so that they show your opinion ...

about Premier Dairies:
1 I think Premier Dairies' plan to launch a new product will ...
2 It looks like they are going to ...
3 I guess their customers will ...

about the future in general:
4 It looks like ... is/are going to ...
5 It's possible that ... will ...

Future: *going to* vs *will*

They**'re going to create** a new product range.
They say it**'s going to be** better than anything else.
Are you **going to eat out** tonight?

The strike **will** probably **push** prices up.
In my opinion, the new product **won't sell** very well.
Sorry, no time now. I**'ll call** you later.

Part A 4

4 Interview your partner. What are his/her plans? (If you don't have any plans, make a spontaneous decision.)

| What | are you going to do | • after the lesson? • at the weekend? | • on your next day off? • on your next holiday? |

I'm not sure. Perhaps I'll …

It depends. Maybe I'll …

Good question. I think I'll …

5 Interview a different partner. When was the last time he/she did these things? When's the next time?

- call a meeting
- attend a meeting
- chair a meeting
- postpone a meeting
- organize a meeting
- cancel a meeting
- bring a meeting forward
- schedule a meeting

6 One of the project teams at Premier Dairies is going to have a meeting to discuss the new product line. Look at the meeting invitation and answer the questions.

1 Who's going to attend the meeting?
2 Who do you think is going to chair the meeting?
3 Where's it going to be?
4 What's the main reason for the meeting?
5 What are the participants going to talk about first?

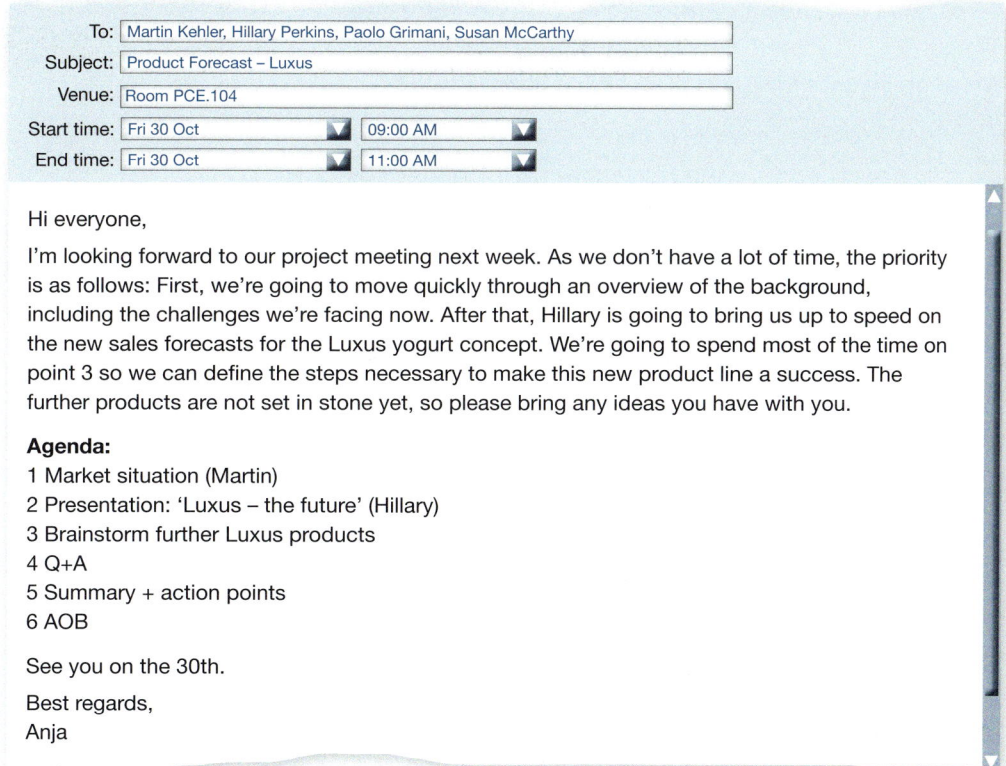

To: Martin Kehler, Hillary Perkins, Paolo Grimani, Susan McCarthy
Subject: Product Forecast – Luxus
Venue: Room PCE.104
Start time: Fri 30 Oct   09:00 AM
End time: Fri 30 Oct   11:00 AM

Hi everyone,

I'm looking forward to our project meeting next week. As we don't have a lot of time, the priority is as follows: First, we're going to move quickly through an overview of the background, including the challenges we're facing now. After that, Hillary is going to bring us up to speed on the new sales forecasts for the Luxus yogurt concept. We're going to spend most of the time on point 3 so we can define the steps necessary to make this new product line a success. The further products are not set in stone yet, so please bring any ideas you have with you.

Agenda:
1 Market situation (Martin)
2 Presentation: 'Luxus – the future' (Hillary)
3 Brainstorm further Luxus products
4 Q+A
5 Summary + action points
6 AOB

See you on the 30th.

Best regards,
Anja

Find words and phrases with the following meanings in the email.

1 the place where an event takes place
2 to update someone
3 to be fixed and finalized (e.g. a decision)
4 the time to ask and answer questions
5 the list of which things must be done before the next meeting
6 a chance for the participants to talk about issues not on the agenda

47

4 Big plans

Part A

7 🔊 1.27 Listen to the beginning of the team meeting. What difference is there to the agenda in the invitation?

> Wir benutzen „will" auch um etwas spontan zu versprechen:
> - I'll send it over to you later today.
> - Will do, no problem.

Match the sentence halves. Then listen again and check.

1. As you can see from the graph, sales in the yogurt segment rose
2. In the second quarter sales continued
3. This caused
4. Early forecasts show that there
5. Sales will probably drop

a. to rise and peaked at €8.5m in June.
b. will be an initial rise in sales.
c. slightly before the second quarter.
d. sales to fall sharply to €6m.
e. steadily during the first two quarters of the year.

8 Which graph does Martin explain? What about Paolo?

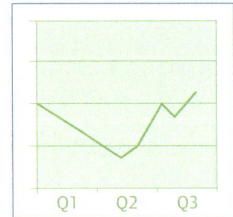 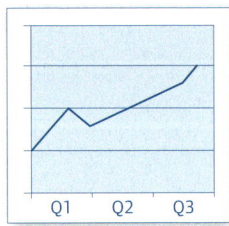 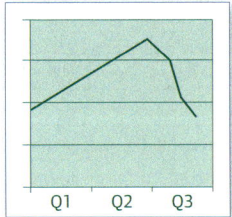

9 Work with a partner. Take it in turns to describe and draw line graphs.

→ *Partner A: file 5, page 131;* → *Partner B: file 20, page 137*

Describing trends			
to rise to go up to increase	a rise an increase ↗	to fall to go down to drop to decrease	a fall a drop a decrease ↘
to remain stable →		to level off ↗	

Sales **rose steadily** during the first two quarters of last year.
This caused sales to **fall sharply** to €6m.
Early forecasts show that there will be an **initial rise** in sales.
Sales will probably **drop slightly** before the second quarter.

Part B | 4

Part B Projects & planning

▶ Think of the last project you worked on. What was it and what was your role? How many other people were involved, and how often did you have to attend project meetings?

1 🔊 1.28 The team from Premier Dairies is meeting again in February to talk about a new production line. Listen to Susan McCarthy and fill in the stages (1–6) in the project timeline.

Optimization · Production (current line) · Training · ~~Installation~~ · Testing · Production (new line)

Stages													
1 Installation													
2													
3													
4													
5													
6													
	Jan	Feb	Mar	Apr	May	Jun	Jul	Aug	Sept	Oct	Nov	Dec	Jan

2 Complete the in-house memo with the missing months. Look at the chart to help you.

> Dear Colleagues,
>
> As you know, we are going to introduce the new Luxus production line at the end of the year. It's very important for all of us that this project runs smoothly. Therefore, I'd like to communicate the key elements of the project schedule to you all.
> 1. The installation phase will start at the beginning of ....
> 2. During the testing phase, which will take place from .... to ...., regular optimization changes will be made.
> 3. Employee training will be started in ....
> 4. Production on the new line will start at the beginning of ....
> 5. Production on the current line won't be stopped until the middle of ....
>
> We all need to work together to make this new production line a success.
>
> Thank you.
> Wolfgang Meier, CEO

Passive: will future

The installation **will be completed** by the end of May. Testing **will be carried out** on an ongoing basis.

3 Write a memo (of about 100 words) explaining the steps in a project you are currently working on.

49

4 Big plans — Part B

4 Interview your partner about his/her future plans and schedules. Use the chart below to ask questions.

What	will has to should must	be done be started be finished be completed be …	by the end of the day/week? tomorrow / the day after tomorrow? next quarter/month? in June/September? by the beginning of March / next month? …?

Tell the class two interesting facts about your partner's future plans.

5 🔊 1.29 Listen to the rest of the meeting from exercise 1. Which one of these statements is true?

a ☐ Everyone agrees with the schedule.
b ☐ They are going to run night and weekend shifts in December.
c ☐ They plan to make the transition from the current production line to the new one in one day.

Listen again and tick the phrases you hear.

1 ☐ I can't agree to that schedule. ☐ I disagree with that point.
2 ☐ In my opinion, we need to … ☐ I think we need to …
3 ☐ I understand how you feel. ☐ I understand your concern.
4 ☐ Wait a minute. Are you saying that …? ☐ Wait a second. Does that mean …?
5 ☐ Paolo, you wanted to say something? ☐ Yes, Paolo?
6 ☐ I agree with you up to a point. ☐ I agree with you on that point.
7 ☐ Is that possible? ☐ Can that be done?
8 ☐ I'll check the figures again. ☐ I'll have another look at the figures.

6 When speaking informally, people sometimes say words together quickly, e.g. *gonna* instead of *going to*.

A two-week changeover period isn't gonna be long enough …

What do you think is meant by the following?

gimme   getcha   lemme   waddaya   wadja   wanna

50

Part B 4

🔊 1.30 Now listen and write the missing words. Use the correct spelling!

1 Do you .... postpone the meeting?
2 .... help you with the projector.
3 .... do after the meeting?
4 .... put on the agenda?
5 .... a call next week.
6 Can I .... something to drink?

7 Work in small groups and choose a person to act as chair. Then select one of the statements below and have a mini-meeting to discuss it.

- The company should block Internet access to sites such as Facebook, Twitter or YouTube.
- The perfect number of participants at a meeting is …
- Listening to the radio at work is good for morale.
- Work and private life should be kept separate.
- Presentations shouldn't be longer than … minutes.
- It's important to socialize with colleagues.

Taking part in meetings
Let's get started.
Let's move on to the next point.
Could you tell us about / explain …?
What's your opinion?
In my opinion, …
I agree.
I agree with you up to a point.
I'm sorry, I'm afraid I (have to) disagree.
With respect, I can't agree to …
I don't mind. / I'm easy.
Wait a minute. / Excuse me.
Sorry to interrupt.
Can I ask a question?
What exactly do you mean by …?

Present your results to the rest of the class.

8 Make a timeline for a project. Use the ideas below or think up your own project.

Present your chart to the rest of the class. Take notes when it's your turn to listen, then ask questions to clarify.

4 Big plans

Business file

📁 Have I got that right?

❶ 👥 The Dutch company GIVE-IT supplies promotional giveaways to companies across Europe. Work with a partner to exchange information.

→ *Partner A: file 6, page 132*
→ *Partner B: Call your partner and ask him/her for the missing prices, order numbers, and minimum order quantities on the catalogue page below. If you have a problem understanding, use the phrases in the box. Then answer your partner's questions.*

GIVE-IT Corporate Gifts
Promo items and printed merchandise are our speciality!
We can print your logo or company slogan on (almost) any item!
Just ask!

OUR PRICE
€ 1
men's T-shirt
order no. 2
women's T-shirt
order no. 3

available in navy, light blue, red and white
sizes: S, M, L, XL
min. order: 200

STAR BUY!!
ONLY € 4
USB memory stick 2 GB
order no. ZSRA8854
min. order: 500

€ 5
umbrella
order no. 6
available in red, blue and black; min. order: 180

ONLY € 7
travel bag
order no. 8
min. order: 160

€ 9
towel
order no. YZXC4887
min. order: 40

€ 10
key ring
order no. AEVW9003
min. order: 11

STAR BUY!!
ONLY € 1.50
mug
order no. 12
min. order: 500

€ 0.60
plastic spoon
order no. IERA8776
min. order: 13

quality pen € 0.22
order no. GJHW5551
min. order: 14

Checking information

Sorry, I didn't catch that.
Could you say it again / repeat it, please?
Was that seventy or seventeen?
– Seventeen, one-seven.
How much does it cost?
If I understand correctly, that means …
Let me read that back to you:
P for Papa, W-4-8 …

52

Business file

4

The international spelling alphabet

A	Alpha	G	Golf	L	Lima	Q	Quebec	V	Victor
B	Bravo	H	Hotel	M	Mike	R	Romeo	W	Whisky
C	Charlie	I	India	N	November	S	Sierra	X	X-ray
D	Delta	J	Juliet	O	Oscar	T	Tango	Y	Yankee
E	Echo	K	Kilo	P	Papa	U	Uniform	Z	Zulu
F	Foxtrot								

2 🔊 1.31 Karl Hempel works in the marketing department at Premier Dairies GmbH. He is interested in ordering promotional giveaways for the new Luxus yogurt range. Listen and take notes. What does Karl order?

> How to supply logo?
>
> Catalogue prices include cost of printing logo?
>
> Terms of payment?
>
> Shipping and handling?

3 Use the catalogue page and your notes from the phone call to complete the invoice.

```
GIVE-IT B.V.                                              INVOICE
Onlandseweg 22
9765 EC Paterswolde        Invoice No. 1001/927
Niederlande                Invoice Date: 18 January 20..

To:   Karl Hempel            Ship to (if different from
      Premier Dairies GmbH   billing address)
      Bayreutherstr. 53
      93047 Regensburg
      Duitsland
```

Qty.	Order no.	Description	Unit price €	Amount €

Terms:		
	Subtotal	
	Shipping & handling	
	Logo development charge	
	Amount due	

Signature:
_____   Thank you for your business

Now work together to compare your invoice with GIVE-IT's. Theirs has a number of mistakes in it. Can you find them all?

→ *Partner A: Look here;* → *Partner B: file 21, page 138*

4 Practise placing and taking orders. First decide on the items you want to order from the catalogue page in exercise 1. Then call a partner to place the order.

53

4 Grammar summary

Will future

1. Prices **will** probably **rise** in the next quarter.
2. I think I**'ll eat** out tonight.
3. We**'ll start** the installation phase tomorrow as planned.
   I**'ll send you** the overview tomorrow.
4. The new product **won't sell** well in Asia.

I he / she / it you / we / they	will ('ll) will not (won't)	give …

5. Something is wrong with the line. I'm afraid we **will have to** stop production.
   I hope we**'ll be able to** take Friday off.

Mit *will*
- macht man Vorhersagen oder stellt Vermutungen über eine unvorhersehbare Zukunft an (**1**). Signalwörter hier sind z. B. *probably, I hope, I'm afraid*.
- drückt man spontane Entschlüsse aus (**2**). Signalwörter hierfür sind z. B. *I think, I guess*.
- macht man eine feste Zusage oder ein Versprechen (**3**).

Die Verneinung von *will* in der Kurzform lautet *won't* (**4**).

Will kann mit *have to* und *be able to* genutzt werden. *Will have to* beschreibt, was in der Zukunft geschehen muss. *Will be able to* beschreibt wozu man in Zukunft in der Lage oder fähig sein wird. (**5**).

Going to future

1. We **are going to launch** a new product line in June.
   I**'m not going to have** lunch today. I'm too busy.
2. It**'s going to rain**. Look at those clouds!

I	'm / 'm not	
he / she / it	's / isn't	going to change …
you / we / they	're / aren't	

3. The sales team **was going to have** a meeting this afternoon, but then it was cancelled.

Mit *be going to* spricht man über Absichten oder Pläne (**1**) oder Aktivitäten in der Zukunft, für die es schon Vorzeichen gibt (**2**).

Die Vergangenheitsform von *be going to* ist *was/were going to*. Die Vergangenheitsform wird verwendet, um zu beschreiben, was vorgesehen oder geplant war, dann aber nicht durchgeführt werden konnte (**3**).

Passive: *will* future

The training **will be finished** by the end of March.
The meeting **won't be cancelled**.

I he / she / it you / we / they	will be asked … won't be given …

Das *will future passive* wird mit *will be* und dem Partizip Perfekt gebildet.

Für die Verwendung des Passiv siehe Seite 18 (Grammar summary, Unit 1).

Word order with adverbs of manner

1. Sales fell **slightly** in the third quarter but increased **sharply** in November.
2. We'll have to **steadily** increase production in the new year.
3. They **slowly** raised the prices last year.
   They raised the prices **slowly** last year.
   (Nicht: They raised slowly the prices last year.)

Adverbien der Art und Weise beschreiben wie etwas geschieht. Sie stehen im Satz meistens nach dem Hauptverb (**1**) oder nach dem Modalverb (**2**).

Manche Adverbien können je nach Betonung unterschiedliche Positionen im Satz einnehmen. Wichtig ist es jedoch zu bedenken, dass sie – im Gegensatz zum Deutschen – fast nie zwischen dem Verb und dem Objekt stehen können (**3**).

Extra practice 4

1 Each sentence has a mistake. Correct them.

1. ~~We going~~ to start a new project next week. — we're going
2. He are going to look for new clients. ....
3. Do will it be more expensive? ....
4. The goods will to arrive tomorrow. ....
5. They're not going make a profit this year. ....
6. The meeting will be not on Saturday. ....
7. Who will be ask to attend the meeting? ....
8. We will given more information tomorrow. ....

2 Complete the dialogue. Use words from the box and the *will* future.

arrive • be • not be • collect • come • do • email

Helen: Hi Ian, this is Helen from SCD GmbH. I have a small problem. One of our customers wants some spare parts by eight o'clock tomorrow morning. Can you deliver them for us?

Ian: Sure. That ....¹ a problem. With our 'early bird' service, the parts ....² at your customer's by 8 am.

Helen: That's great. When .... you ....³ the parts?

Ian: Let me see. It's 4 pm now. Our courier ....⁴ to your office at six, if that's OK.

Helen: That ....⁵ fine. And .... you ....⁶ me the invoice as usual?

Ian: Yes, I ....⁷ that, no problem.

Helen: Thanks very much, Ian. Bye now.

Ian: You're welcome, Helen. Bye.

3 Complete the sentences with the *will* or *going to* future. Sometimes both are possible.

I'm quite happy because I ....¹ (be) away for two weeks on a training course in Spain. My flight's tomorrow. John, a colleague of mine in Barcelona, promises that he ....² (meet) me at the airport when I arrive. I need to upgrade our systems, and that is what I ....³ (learn) how to do on the course. It ....⁴ (not be) all work though. I hope I ....⁵ (be able to) visit some museums in the evenings. Plus John and I ....⁶ (go) hiking in the mountains on Sunday: we planned this last time I was there. According to weather.com it ....⁷ (be) very warm and sunny during my visit. A postcard? Yes, of course I ....⁸ (send) you one!

4 Extra practice

4 Complete the sentences with the future passive form of the words in the box.

> complete · ~~discuss~~ · give · present · send · serve · not tell

1. The details of the launch ..will be discussed.... at the meeting tomorrow.
2. .... we .... more information about the production schedule?
3. Yes, I'm sure a project timeline ....
4. It looks like the project .... by the end of August.
5. I'm afraid that we .... the name of the product.
6. Where's the agenda? When .... it .... to us?
7. I hope refreshments .... at the meeting.

5 Find collocations to complete the sentences below.

> market   average   pressure   range
> high-end   luxury   products
> product   consumers   forecasts
> sales   consumer

1. The .... cares more about price than anything else.
2. Most companies need a wide .... so they can sell to many different consumers.
3. The latest .... show that this will be the best year ever for the company.
4. .... normally have a high price and are mostly bought by ....
5. Many companies are going to reduce their prices this year due to ....

6 Look at the graph and complete the sentences with the correct form of words from the box.

> drop slightly · decrease steadily · fall sharply · peak ·
> rise · an increase · forecasts · from the graph

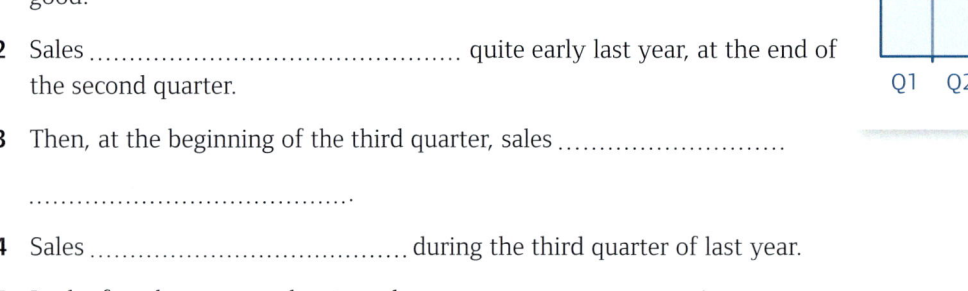

1. As you can see ...., last year was not so good.
2. Sales .... quite early last year, at the end of the second quarter.
3. Then, at the beginning of the third quarter, sales ....
4. Sales .... during the third quarter of last year.
5. In the fourth quarter, sales started to .... again.
6. Early .... show that there will be .... in sales in the first quarter this year.
7. Sales will probably .... in the second quarter.

Extra practice **4**

7 🔊 1.32 Listen and take notes.

Caller: ....
Company: ....
Order: ....
1 ....
2 ....

8 Translate into English.

1 Ich freue mich darauf, das neue Produkt zu testen.
2 2010 gab es einen Verkaufsrückgang von 10 %.
3 Ich habe einige wichtige Informationen für Sie.
4 Meine Meinung ist, dass wir auch am Wochenende arbeiten könnten.
5 Was genau meinst du mit „Wochenendschichten"?
6 Die Installation wird bis Ende Januar fertig gestellt.
7 Marketing will das Meeting verschieben.
8 Mach dir keine Sorgen. Ich rufe den Projektleiter morgen an.

Typical mistakes

1 I'm looking forward to **chairing** the meeting.
NOT *I'm looking forward to chair …*
2 There was a **rise**/an **increase in** sales.
NOT *There was a rise/an increase of sales.*
3 I'm calling to check some **information**.
NOT *… to check some informations.*
4 That's my **opinion**.
NOT *That's my meaning.*
5 What exactly do you **mean by** free Internet access?
NOT *What exactly do you mean with …*
6 The report will be completed **by** the end of the week.
NOT *… will be completed until the end …*
7 I **want to** attend the meeting, but I can't.
NOT *I will attend the meeting, but I can't.*
8 **I'll see** you tomorrow.
NOT *I see you tomorrow.*

Culture spot

Being polite

In some cultures and languages, politeness is connected with how direct or indirect you say something. English is one of these languages, and politeness and indirectness often go hand in hand.
Here are some tips on how to be polite in English.

- When complaining, state the problem (*I'm afraid the delivery is late*) rather than focusing on who is to blame (*You didn't deliver on time*). Use words like 'I'm afraid', 'it seems' or 'apparently' to soften your complaint. The passive form is useful here (*A mistake was made*), and you can also use a positive word negatively (*I don't/can't agree*) rather than a negative word (*I disagree*).
- If you want someone to do something for you, ask a question (*Could you please check this again?*). Don't give an order (*Check this again*) or focus on what you want (*I want you to check it again*): this can sound too direct and 'bossy' in English.
- Use words like 'maybe' and 'possibly' to make your request more polite. *Could you possibly bring the project schedule forward?* is more polite than *Could you bring the project schedule forward?*
- When asking for something, avoid the word 'kindly' (*I kindly ask you to reply to this email by the end of the week*) or questions starting *Would you be so kind as to …* . These expressions are so polite that they can sound ironic. Generally, 'Please' or 'Could you please …?' is polite enough.

> I'm afraid there might be a slight delay with the delivery.

apparently	anscheinend/scheinbar
bossy	rechthaberisch

5 It's a deal

In this unit you will ...

- discuss terms and negotiate a deal
- talk about differences and make comparisons

Business file

- compare prices and terms

Part A Terms & conditions

▶ Do you always pay the price on the list or tag? When and where do you bargain and try to negotiate a better deal?

1 Link words from boxes A and B to make collocations.

A		B	
work-life	to get	discount	form
bulk			an order
	order	to place	balance		terms
delivery		a discount	

🔊 1.33 Now listen to Sigrid Petík and Bob Wales from the HR department at Scopicon AG. Which of your collocations do you hear?

2 These statements are incorrect. Listen again and correct them.

1 Scopicon plans to buy employee memberships at a local gym.
2 Sigrid and Bob don't know how much equipment they want.
3 If they pay the full price for the gym equipment, they won't have the money for a drinks machine.
4 The supplier normally doesn't charge for delivery.
5 Scopicon is willing to pay a little more if the supplier delivers to the top floor.

3 👥 Choose appropriate endings for these sentences. Do you and your partner agree?

1 If employees exercise regularly, …
2 People are less likely to injure themselves …
3 Employee motivation will rise …
4 If the gym is in the company, …

a employees won't lose time travelling to it.
b they'll feel better and work harder.
c if they are trained how to use the equipment.
d they might injure themselves.
e if the staff is given more money rather than a gym.
f employees might work out instead of doing their work.
g if the staff sees that management cares about their well-being.
h if they don't work out.

First conditional

It**'ll look** like we're only half trying **if** we **buy** used equipment.
We **won't use up** our entire budget **if** we **get** a discount.
If he **agrees**, we **can order** some more equipment.
There **might be** safety and insurance issues **if** the equipment **isn't** new.

Part A 5

4 Complete these sentences so they are true for you.

If the company offers a free yoga class next month, I …
If I have time this weekend, …
I won't … if …
There might be … if …

👥 Tell a partner.

5 🔊 1.34 The team from Scopicon meets the supplier. What is agreed at the meeting?

discount
quantity
- weights machines

- other fitness machines

- drinks machines

delivery terms
- free delivery?

Listen again for phrases which you can use to …

1 say you don't quite understand something: 'I'm a bit ……………………………….'

2 say something's not possible / won't work: 'That's just not ……………………………….'

3 show you're going in the direction of agreement, but not yet: 'I might …………………… ……………………………….'

4 tell somebody he/she is a tough negotiator: 'You drive ……………………………….'

5 offer something extra for free: 'I can ……………………………… mats ….'

6 ask for someone's opinion/approval: 'How does ………………………………?'

7 show you agree with a suggestion/proposal: 'OK, that ……………………………….'

6 👥 Try to sell your partner something you have, e.g. your watch, pen, mobile phone. Use phrases from the box and the flow chart below to help you.

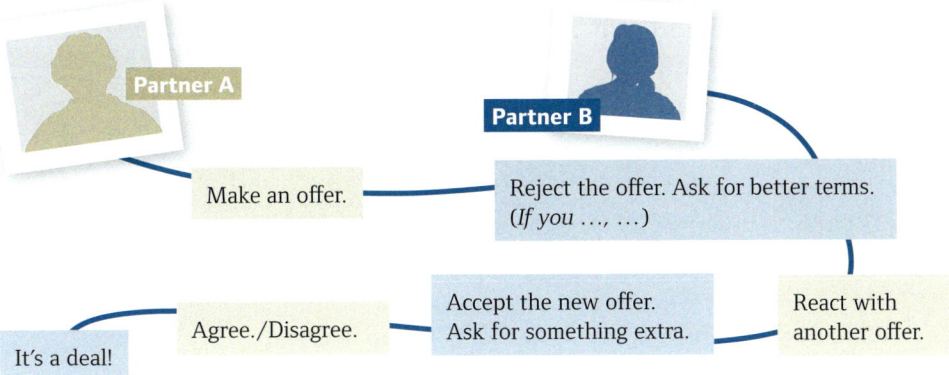

What did you try to buy/sell? For what price? Are you happy with the result? Now exchange roles.

Negotiating a deal

We might be able to … if you …
I'll tell you what: if you can …, I'll …
How about if we …?
Will you …?
What do you think?
How does that sound?

Yes, that sounds fair/acceptable.
I might be able to agree to that.
OK, now it's getting interesting.
You drive a hard bargain, but I can agree to that.

I'm sorry, that's not possible.
I'm afraid that's not feasible.
I can't increase the discount / lower the price.

5 It's a deal — Part A

7 Match the words to their meanings.

- win-lose (negotiation)
- flexibility
- walk-away point
- win-win (negotiation)
- vice versa

a a negotiation in which all parties are successful
b the point when a negotiation becomes impossible and one party ends it
c a negotiation in which there can only be one winner
d the other way round
e when there is room for a range of results

Use the words above to complete the gaps in the article below.

Mark McGovern's Tips for Successful Business

Negotiating to win!

The key to a successful negotiation is preparation. So what's important when preparing for a negotiation? Well, first, it's good to know if this is a ....¹ negotiation. This means that if I win, you lose, and ....². In that case, just try to get the best deal you can and don't think about long-term relationships.

The best result for a long-term relationship is when both parties can benefit, for example, when the seller and the buyer agree on a result that is acceptable for them both. The seller's ....³ is reached when their terms are negotiated so low that a deal is no longer worthwhile for them, so they stop negotiating and walk away. For the buyer, this point is reached when the seller goes higher than the buyer is willing to pay.

The area of possible agreement is then between the buyer's and the seller's walk-away points: this is where both will be happy with the result and we have a ....⁴ situation. Of course, this area might have ....⁵ within it, so that while both parties will leave with a winning feeling, one could be more of a winner than the other!

A key question to ask yourself is: How important is my relationship with my negotiating partner compared with the result of the deal? This, of course, should greatly influence your style and goal. Good luck, and don't forget to prepare thoroughly for the negotiation. Remember, as they say, 'failing to prepare is preparing to fail!'.

8 What do you think is happening below? In which dialogue 1–3 …

☐ is there a win-win situation?
☐ is there a win-lose situation?
☐ does somebody reach his/her walk-away point?

1
A I'm sorry, but that's the lowest I can go.
B But that's still much too high for me.

2
A How about if I reduce the price by 10 %?
B Yes, I think I can agree to that.

3
A We need to make a decision now. Time is running out.
B Well, I'm sorry. We can't both get on the flight.

🔊 1.35-37 What do you think the As will say next? Listen and see.

9 Negotiate with your partner.

→ *Partner A: file 15, page 135;* → *Partner B: file 29, page 141*

Part B Work-life balance

▶ How do you try to maintain a good work-life balance?

1 🔊 1.38 Listen to two colleagues talking during a coffee break. How important do they think a healthy work-life balance is?

2 🔊 1.39 Now listen to the rest of their conversation. What do they decide to do?

👥 Tell your partner about a sport or activity you like to do. Try to persuade him or her to join you.

3 Make comparisons. Complete the sentences with the correct form of words from the box. (You don't need to use all the words.)

bad · big · difficult · easy · fast · (un)important · long · short · useless

1 Sports are the .... way to improve your job performance.
2 My working hours are .... than they were five years ago.
3 One of the .... problems with my job is the workload.
4 It's .... to manage all my tasks now than it was in my last job.
5 The .... thing is to have a healthy work-life balance.
6 Communication is .... now than before email and text messaging.

👥 Compare your answers with a partner's. Are there any differences?

4 👥 Interview a partner. How is his/her workload different than in the past?

- Are you busier than you used to be?
- Well, things aren't as hectic as they were in my previous job.

Persuading

How about going …?
Why don't you try it / come with me?
Come on!

Oh, I don't know. I'm not as fit as I used to be.
OK, fine. I'll give it a go.

Making comparisons

Our processes are **not as simple as** they used to be.
I'm **busier** now **than** I was at the beginning of the year.
Ute's office is **more organized than** John's.
It's becoming **more and more important**.
Jogging is one of **the easiest** sports to start.
They have **the highest** workload but also **the best** results.

Vorsicht: ~~things aren't so hectic than …~~ things aren't as hectic as …

5 It's a deal — Part B

■ Did you know?
SMS steht für *Short Message Service*. Im Englischen schickt man aber keine „SMS", sondern *text messages* oder *texts*. *Text* wird auch als Verb verwendet, wie z. B.: *I'll text you later*.

5 Dirk has second thoughts. Put the text messages in the correct order and add the times.

~~Wednesday 21:18~~ · Wednesday 21:22 · Wednesday 21:45 · Thursday 18:52 · Thursday 18:54 · Thursday 18:55

A ....

Sry. Need to snd few mails quickly. C u in 20mins. Front door. OK?

B ....

Hi Dirk. Ready 2 go? S.

C *1 Wednesday 21:18*

Hi Sue. Just in. v.tired. Need to wrk late 2mrw nite. Sry. Can't make jogging. Maybe next week? Dirk

D ....

Better late than never ;-)

E ....

OK. Fair point. C u at 7.

F ....

Hi Dirk. FYI. Exactly what work-life blnce is about – lol! C'mon. Pack ur sports gear. C u at 7… or u choose burnout? ;-)

True or false? Discuss with a partner and find examples in the text messages above.

1 In texts, words are often shortened by removing some of the vowels.
2 Words are written as they sound rather than how they are really spelt.
3 Numbers are only used as numbers and for talking about the time.
4 Fixed expressions are often shortened to just the first letters of each word.

6 Match the people and what they say.

A I use my smartphone in the evenings to communicate with my boss when he's travelling. It's more convenient than staying late in the office.

Claudia works in PR.

Jonathan is a P. A.

David owns a small business.

B I use email to communicate with my staff. I try not to use any abbreviations, though. They're too confusing.

C I use Twitter to send information to my company's followers. I have to use abbreviations to keep the messages short.

Discuss in a small group.

1 Do you prefer communicating by email, phone or text message? Why? Which is most effective when?
2 Do abbreviations help or hurt communication? How appropriate are they in a business context?

Part B   5

7 How do some companies help their staff deal with stress? Read the advertisement. Does Work-Life offer anything new?

Get the balance right!

Do any of these sound familiar?

The economy is better than it was a few years ago, but …
- ☑ you have a bigger workload than before.
- ☑ you need to complete more tasks faster than in the past.
- ☑ you are more stressed and have less free time than you used to.
- ☑ your work-life balance is still out of balance!

You can't ignore these signs – it's the fastest way to burnout!

Are you nodding your head? Don't worry – help is on the way!

A company's most valuable assets are its employees. This is why many companies now have a greater focus on workplace well-being and try to reduce counterproductive workplace stress. We can help you and your team both in and outside the office with walking lunches, business yoga, stress management seminars and much, much more …

"I'm not as stressed at work and can concentrate better now thanks to Work-Life's help."
Paul P., IT Auditor

If you want to know more, call Work-Life on 0208 2893971.

What do you think of the advertisement? What's your opinion of such offers?

8 Look at the data on working conditions in different European countries. Complete the sentences with country names.

Working time and work-life balance in European companies (by country)

Companies with some kind of flexitime arrangement (%)
- SE 65
- IE 55
- ES 43
- PT 23

Companies with overtime work (%)
- IE 87
- IT 78
- PL 57
- HU 44

Companies with male employees taking parental leave (%)
- SE 69
- BE 49
- FR 39
- IT 22

Companies with phased (step-by-step) retirement schemes available (%)
- NL 64
- UK 53
- CZ 33
- IT 10

Source: European Foundation for the Improvement of Living and Working Conditions

Fewer/fewest, less/least, more/most

Fewer people work flexitime in Portugal **than** in Ireland.
Italy is the country with **the fewest** men who take parental leave.
I have **less** time to do sports **than** I used to.
Most people at my company start work before 8 am.

1 More people in ………………… than in ………………… have a flexitime option at work.

2 People in ………………… work less overtime on average than employees in ………………… .

3 Fewer men take parental leave in ………………… than in ………………… .

4 ………………… is the country with the fewest companies offering phased retirement schemes.

How do you think the situation in your country compares? Discuss in your group, then look at the file for more data.

→ *Information file 30, page 142*

5 It's a deal

Business file

📁 What are your terms?

1 🔊 1.40 Andrea Duff runs a small company in Frankfurt that supplies and stocks vending machines. Today she's meeting with the sales rep from an English company called Refresh to talk about purchasing new vending machines. Listen and tick the correct answer or answers.

1 The prices of the vending machines …
   a ☐ are ex works.
   b ☐ include delivery to Andrea's logistics centre in Frankfurt.

2 The terms of payment are …
   a ☐ payment in advance.
   b ☐ COD (cash on delivery).
   c ☐ payment in full within 30 days.

3 Brian prefers that Andrea pay by …
   a ☐ credit card.
   b ☐ bank transfer.
   c ☐ cheque.

4 Andrea can return the vending machines if she changes her mind about the size, …
   a ☐ but she must pay the transport costs.
   b ☐ and Refresh will pay the transport costs.

5 If Andrea is unhappy with the quality of the machines, …
   a ☐ she will get a refund.
   b ☐ she will be given a discount on the next order.
   c ☐ she won't have to pay the transport costs.

6 Brian offers Andrea …
   a ☐ no discount.
   b ☐ a 10% discount.
   c ☐ a rebate of 5% after six months.

7 Andrea …
   a ☐ places her first order straight away with Brian.
   b ☐ decides against Refresh vending machines.
   c ☐ will place her order next week.

2 After the meeting, Andrea makes notes of what they agreed. Write her notes (or a short summary) of the most important points.

Business file 5

Talking about prices and terms

What do your prices include?
Are these the ex works prices?
Do these prices include delivery/taxes?
What are your terms of payment?
What method(s) of payment do you accept?
What discount(s) can you offer us?
What do I do if I have a problem with …?
Can you let me have that in writing?

The prices are ex works. They (don't) include delivery/taxes.
Our terms of payment are 30 days / payment in full within 30 days.
We ask for payment in advance. / Payment is COD (Cash On Delivery).
You can pay by credit card but our preferred method of payment is bank transfer.
We can give/offer you a 5% bulk discount.
I'm sorry, we never give discounts on a first order.
We can give you a rebate after six months.
If it's our fault, we'll refund the money and pay the transport costs.

3 Work in groups of four to eight to discuss terms at a trade fair.

1 First find a partner and choose one of the companies in file 31 on page 142. (But make sure you choose a different company from the others in your group.) Look at the role card, decide your prices and terms, and complete the notes on the right.
2 Then find a place in your classroom and set up your 'stand'.

→ *Partner A: Stay on the stand and answer the visitors' questions.*
→ *Partner B: Go round the 'trade fair' and find out about the other companies and their products. Make careful notes about prices and terms.*

4 Discuss as a class.

1 Check with the companies that you visited. Did you get the correct information?
2 Are there two (or more) companies with the same products? Who has the best prices and terms?

Company:
Products:
Prices:
Prices include:
Terms of payment:
Discounts:

5 Grammar summary

First conditional

1 If we **buy** used equipment, we **will have** problems with our insurance.
(Nicht: If we ~~will buy~~ used equipment, …)
2 If he **agrees**, we **can order** some equipment.
If we **reject** this offer, we **might not be able to get** another one.
3 You**'ll lose** weight if you **visit** the gym regularly.
There **may be** a problem if she **forgets**.

Kein „will" im if-Satz!

Mit dem *first conditional* drückt man aus, was unter bestimmten Voraussetzungen geschehen wird. Dann steht im *if*-Satz das *simple present* und im Hauptsatz das *will future* (**1**).

Um auszudrücken, was unter bestimmten Voraussetzungen geschehen könnte, benutzt man im Hauptsatz Modalverben wie *can*, *may* und *might* (**2**).

Beginnt der Bedingungssatz mit dem Hauptsatz, folgt kein Komma (**3**).

If vs when

1 **If** you drive a hard bargain, you'll probably win.
The staff will be healthier **when** we have the new gym.
2 Everybody wins **when**/**if** there is a win-win situation.

If bedeutet „falls"; *when* bedeutet „wenn" im zeitlichen Sinne (**1**).

If und *when* sind austauschbar, wenn sie „immer, wenn" bedeuten (**2**).

Comparison of adjectives

1 Company A is (much) **bigger** than Company B. In fact, it's one of **the biggest** and the **most successful** companies in Europe.
2 This negotiation was **easier than** the last one.
3 Our competitors are **as successful as** we are.
My new job is not **as hectic as** my last one.

adjective	comparative	superlative
fresh	fresher	freshest
large	larger	largest
big	bigger	biggest
easy	easier	easiest
careful	more careful	most careful
good	better	best
bad	worse	worst

4 This job is **more interesting** and **less stressful** than my previous one.
My colleague has **the least demanding** job but **the most difficult** boss.

Menschen und Dinge können mithilfe der Steigerungsformen von Adjektiven verglichen werden (**1**).

Werden zwei Personen oder Dinge als unterschiedlich beschrieben, verwendet man *-er*/*more* … *than* (**2**). Setzt man zwei Personen oder Dinge gleich, so werden sie mit (*not*) *as* … *as* verglichen (**3**).

Adjektive steigert man wie folgt:
- einsilbige Adjektive (z. B. *fresh*, *large* und *big*) sowie zweisilbige Adjektive auf *-y* (wie *easy*) durch Anhängen von *-er* und *-est*.
- mehrsilbige Adjektive (wie *careful*) mit *more* und *most*.

Manche Adjektive (wie *good* und *bad*) haben unregelmäßige Steigerungsformen.

Mit *more* und *the most* drückt man eine positive Steigerung aus, mit *less* und *the least* drückt man eine negative Steigerung aus (**4**).

Comparison of nouns

1 **Fewer people** go on long holidays now than used to.
The manufacturing industry offers **the fewest sabbaticals**.
2 Employees who do sport usually have **less stress** than those who don't.
People with a good work-life balance have **the least stress**.
3 **More employees** than before work flexitime, nevertheless **most people** don't have a good work-life balance.

Zählbare Nomen (z. B. *people*, *jobs* oder *sabbaticals*) vergleicht man mit *fewer* und *the fewest* (**1**).

Unzählbare Nomen (also Nomen, die keinen Plural haben wie *stress*, *information* und *money*) vergleicht man mit *less* und *the least* (**2**).

Zählbare und unzählbare Nomen vergleicht man mit *more* und *most* (**3**).

Vorsicht: most people / ~~the most people~~

Extra practice 5

1 Rearrange the words to make sentences starting with *if*.

1 if / give / the contract / I'll / I see her / her *If I see her, I'll give her the contract.*
2 be able to / we hurry / by 5 pm / we might / if / finish ....
3 a discount / you / give me / if / I'll / the order / increase ....
4 order / the quality / good / if / is / I'll / more ....
5 a problem / have / the delivery / we may / if / is late ....

2 Match the sentences halves to make a logical sequence.

1	The delivery date of our new product range	a	we'll beat them to the market.
2	If we don't deliver before the summer starts,	b	the new product line will be a success.
3	However, if we do,	c	our competitors will beat us to the market.
4	If we beat them to the market,	d	we'll sell more products.
5	If we sell more products,	e	will be very important.
6	If the new product line is a success,	f	everyone will be happy.

3 Write the correct word: *if* or *when*. In one sentence both words are possible.

1 He's coming here at 4 pm. .... he does, I'll give him the information.
2 They drive a hard bargain, but we'll celebrate with champagne .... we get a good deal. I hope we do.
3 Sales are always good .... the weather's bad.
4 We'll reach our targets this quarter .... the customer orders soon.

4 Six of the comparative and superlative forms below are incorrect. Can you correct them?

1 more interesting ✔
2 more new *newer*
3 largest ....
4 easyest ....
5 importanter ....
6 most complicated ....
7 famousest ....
8 more small ....
9 harderer ....
10 most effective ....

5 Complete the sentences with the correct form of the adjectives in brackets.

1 ManagTec AG is our .... supplier. (old)
2 This deal isn't as .... as the last one. (interesting)
3 The CEO is often the .... person in the company. (important)
4 Google is one of the .... online companies. (big)
5 Communication is .... with email than with letters or faxes. (fast)
6 It's .... to work with the new software than it was before. (easy)
7 Last year was .... year ever for the company. (bad)
8 My new smartphone is definitely .... than my old mobile. (useful)

67

5 Extra practice

6 Complete the sentences about the graph with words from the box below. You won't need them all.

fewer · the fewest · less · the least · more · the most

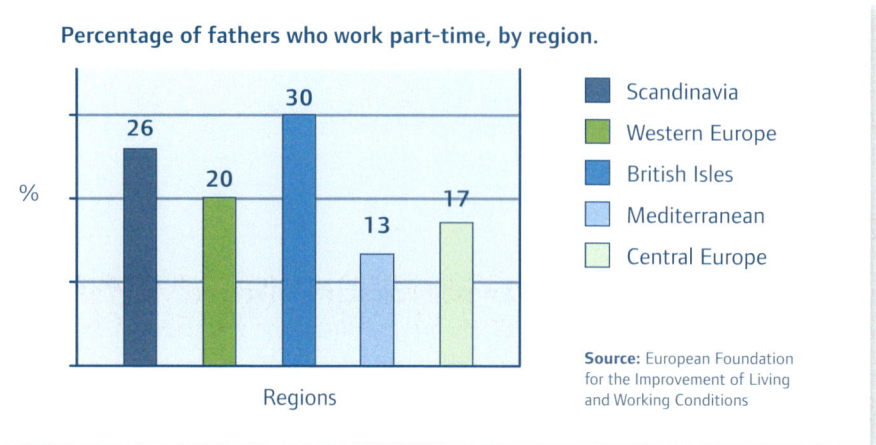

1 By percentage, ... fathers in Scandinavia work part-time than those in Western Europe.
2 The Mediterranean region has .... number of fathers in part-time work.
3 The percentage of fathers in part-time work in Central Europe is .... than in Western Europe.
4 The British Isles has .... fathers in part-time work.
5 There are .... fathers in part-time work in Scandinavia than in the British Isles.

7 Which word or phrase doesn't collocate with the word in the circle? Cross it out.

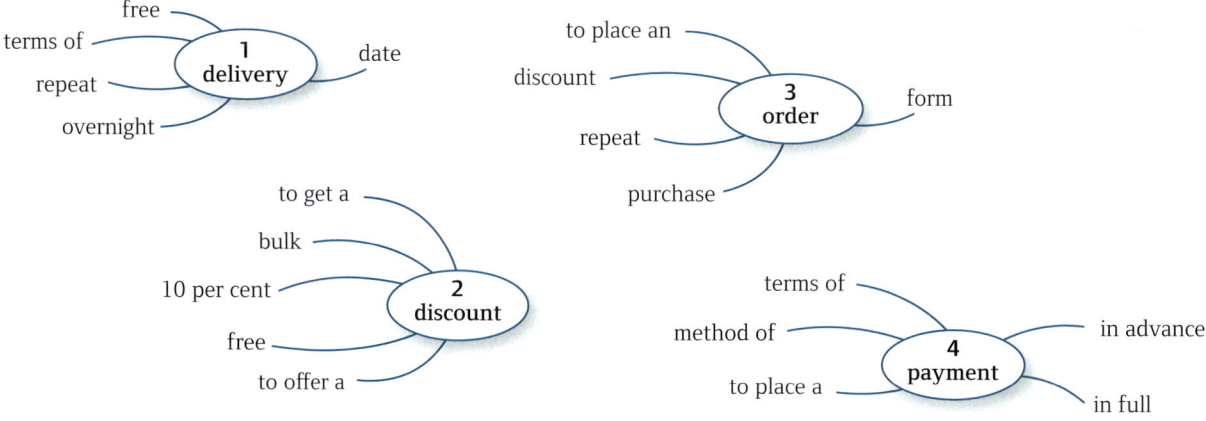

8 Match the questions and answers.

1 What do your prices include?
2 What are your terms of payment?
3 What discounts can you offer us?
4 How does that sound?
5 How about if I throw in some free units?
6 Can you send me the order overnight?

a I'm sorry, we don't normally give a discount on a first order.
b I'm afraid that's not feasible. We can't deliver before the end of the week.
c We ask for payment within 30 days of delivery.
d Well, that's a start, but a discount is better than more units. How about that?
e Insurance, delivery and installation.
f That sounds reasonable. I think I might be able to agree to that.

Extra practice 5

9 Complete the email with items from the box. If you need some help, check the Culture spot below.

am · asap · BTW · e.g. · FAQ · IMO · re · RSVP

Be careful: this email is OTT (over the top), i.e. it is exaggerated!

Hi Jack,

............¹ the new software: ....² it's too expensive.

Can you find an alternative, ...³ an update of the current version?

............⁴, can you send the new ....⁵ list for the help desk. I need it ....⁶.

And don't forget to ....⁷ before 11 ....⁸. That's when I need to update my team leader.

Cheers, Mark

10 Translate into English.

1 Wenn der Zulieferer einen Rabatt anbietet, werden wir eine Bestellung aufgeben.
2 Wir nehmen möglicherweise zwei zusätzliche Maschinen, falls die Ausstattung gut ist.
3 Ruf mich an, wenn du ankommst – ich hole dich ab.
4 Die meisten Mitarbeiter nehmen gerne an Skype Meetings teil.
5 Eine schlechte Verhandlung ist viel schlimmer als keine Verhandlung!
6 Es gibt heutzutage mehr Seminare zur Stressbewältigung als vor 15 Jahren.
7 Die Arbeitsabläufe hier sind nicht so kompliziert wie in meiner alten Firma.
8 Ich benutze mein Handy oft, um Termine mit Kollegen zu machen.

Typical mistakes

1 We'll get a discount if we **order** more.
   NOT ... *if we will order more.*
2 We can offer you free delivery **if** you order today.
   NOT ... *when you order today.*
3 It's great that you can come today. Let me know **when** you arrive.
   NOT *Let me know if you arrive.*
4 **Most** people like taking holidays.
   NOT *The most people like taking holidays.*
5 Jogging is **much worse** than yoga.
   NOT ... *is much more worse than yoga.*
6 His workload is **heavier than** before.
   NOT *His workload is heavier as before.*
7 Some negotiations are **not as difficult as** they seem to be.
   NOT ... *are not so difficult than they seem to be.*
8 I often use my credit card **to order** online.
   NOT *I often use my credit card for to order online.*

Culture spot

'What does that stand for?'

Abbreviations, acronyms and other short forms are quite usual in English, especially in email communication. Here are some common ones that are often used in a business context:

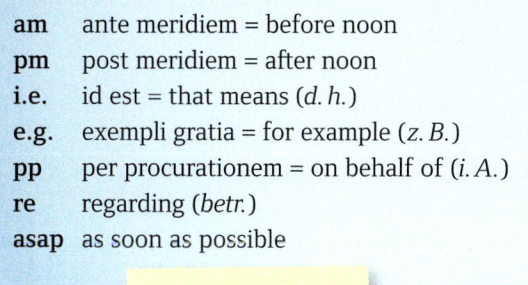

IMO...

am	ante meridiem = before noon	**approx.**	approximately
pm	post meridiem = after noon	**VAT**	value added tax (*MwSt.*)
i.e.	id est = that means (*d. h.*)	**FAQ**	frequently asked questions
e.g.	exempli gratia = for example (*z. B.*)	**RSVP**	French for 'please reply' (*u. A. w. g.*)
pp	per procurationem = on behalf of (*i. A.*)	**BTW**	By the way
re	regarding (*betr.*)	**FYI**	For your information (*z. K.*)
asap	as soon as possible	**IMO**	In my opinion
		ATB	All the best

say it: A-S-A-P

6 Changing times

In this unit you will …
- talk about your experiences
- discuss and make arrangements
- check and report progress

Business file
- update a diary
- write emails to make and change appointments

■ Did you know?
Sowohl im direkten Gespräch als auch bei E-Mails bevorzugen viele Frauen die neutrale Anredeform *Ms* statt *Mrs* oder *Miss*.

Part A A new job

▶ Name three people – famous or not – who have interesting jobs. What do you know about their companies and their careers?

① Which adjectives go with each noun? Cross out the one that doesn't fit.

1 a   pioneering / polite / creative / leading   company
2 a(n)   industrial / medical / challenging / sharp   field
3 a(n)   cheap / rewarding / long / interesting   career
4 a(n)   successful / adaptable / innovative / rewarding   manager

② 🔊 2.2 Listen to this excerpt from an American podcast about the business world. Which collocations above did you hear?

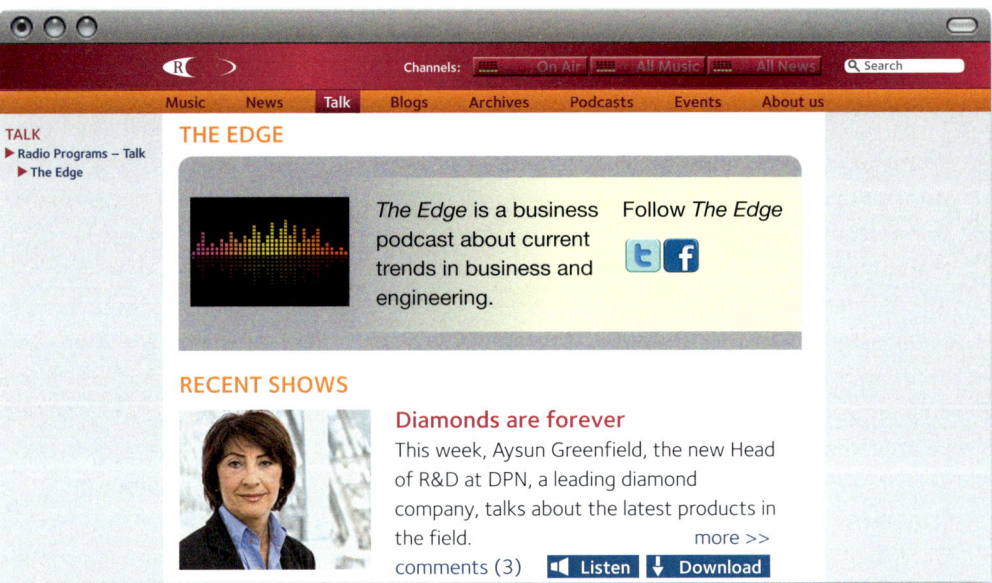

Are the following statements true or false? true false

1 DPN was founded in the nineties.
2 Aysun Greenfield is new to the company, but this isn't her first job in management.
3 She once had a job in Africa.
4 She can't speak French very well.
5 She is unfamiliar with YouTube.
6 She knows quite a few successful businesswomen.

③ Look at these statements. Which ones are true for Aysun? Which ones are true for you?

1 I have learned at least two foreign languages.
2 My family hasn't travelled much.
3 I have worked in more than one company.
4 I've never posted any videos on YouTube.
5 I've met a lot of people from different backgrounds.
6 I haven't had to work very hard in my career so far.
7 My spouse or partner has lived in Turkey.

👥 Compare your answers with a partner's.

Part A   6

4 What are the adjectives connected with these verbs? Complete the tables.

Verb	Adjective
challenge	a ....
create	b ....
extend	c ....
impress	d .impressive.................

Verb	Adjective
reward	e ....
succeed	f ....
value	g ....

Read this extract from the DPN company magazine introducing Aysun to the staff, and use the adjectives above to fill the gaps.

Meet Aysun Greenfield

Aysun, a mechanical engineer with an .impressive........... ¹ track record, is a .... ² addition to our company. She now lives here in Dortmund but she has lived and worked in a number of different countries all over the world, including the USA and Australia, and thus has .... ³ knowledge of all aspects of our industry. From 1998 to 2005, she worked as a plant manager in a very .... ⁴ diamond company in Western Australia, and then from 2006 to last January, she ran another plant in Dar es Salaam, Tanzania. She met Patrick Heilbronner at this year's Antwerp Diamond Trade Fair and, a short time afterwards, she was offered the .... ⁵ post of Head of R&D here at DPN. Aysun is eager to improve her German and has just signed up for a language course. She is very .... ⁶ and even has a YouTube channel, which she started in 2010. So far she has made ten videos featuring women with very .... ⁷ careers. Strangely enough, she's never made one about herself, but maybe that's next on the agenda! If you want to see what Aysun does behind the camera, check out the link below.

5 Match the questions and the answers. Why are some questions in the simple past and others in the present perfect?

1 Where was Aysun born?
2 Has she lived in Germany all her life?
3 Has she ever worked in Australia?
4 What did she do there?
5 When did Aysun start making videos?
6 How many videos has she made so far?

a She was the plant manager of diamond company.
b Yes, she has. She worked there from 1998 to 2005.
c She's made ten.
d She was born in Turkey.
e She made her first one in 2010.
f No, she's lived in lots of different countries, including Tanzania.

Now make questions to fit these answers.

1 At the Antwerp Diamond Trade Fair.
2 Shortly after the fair.
3 Yes, she has. She's lived in Tanzania and South Africa.
4 From 2006 to January this year.
5 No, never! But she might some day.
6 Yes, she has. She'll start German lessons soon.

Present perfect

I **have had to** work hard (all my life).
Aysun **has made** several videos.
She**'s** never **worked** in Germany.
I**'ve learned** three languages so far.
Have you ever **managed** a company?

6 Changing times — Part A

Asking follow-up questions about past experiences

Oh, really. So, when exactly were you there?
Wow! And what kind of things did you do there?
That sounds intriguing. Was it a business trip or were you just there for fun?
And tell me … was it useful?

6 Use verbs and noun phrases from the collage below to ask each other questions. If the answer is yes, ask a follow-up question. Otherwise ask a new question.

- Have you ever taken part in a breakfast meeting?
- Yes, I have actually.
- No, luckily not.
- No, I'm afraid I haven't.

to write
a report in English · a three-page email · a letter to the editor

to post
a video on YouTube · a comment on a blog

to take part in
a video conference · a webinar · a breakfast meeting · a stand-up meeting

to listen to
a podcast in English · a complete audiobook · an American radio programme

to work
in an open-plan office · from home · for a multinational company · until 9 pm

to go
on a business trip to Asia · to Australia · to the US on business · bowling with a colleague

Report your findings to the class.

Jan has been to Australia twice. He was last there in September last year.

Brigitte has never taken part in a stand-up meeting, but she has taken part in a breakfast meeting. It was in Munich two years ago and she ate Weißwurst and drank Bavarian beer.

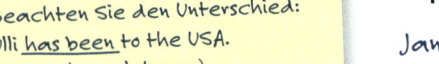
Beachten Sie den Unterschied:
Ulli <u>has been</u> to the USA. (Now he's back home.)
Uta <u>has gone</u> to the USA. (She's still there.)

Part B Making arrangements

▶ Describe an interesting workday last week. What meetings did you have, and when? Which day was the most interesting?

1 Wiebke Rick and Anton Schubert both work in the R&D department at DPN's headquarters in Dortmund. Before listening to their conversation with David, a British colleague who's new to the team, look at Wiebke's diary and answer the questions.

1   What day(s) does Wiebke have free?
2   When does she have a personal appointment and when does she have a date?

■ **Did you know?**
In *Business English* werden oft Redewendungen aus der Welt des Sports verwendet.
I just wanted to **touch base**.
(I just wanted to see what you're doing.)
Good luck with **the pitch**!
(Good luck with the (sales) presentation!)
She has a **good track record**.
(She has been successful in her career.)

🔊 2.3   Now listen. What arrangements do Wiebke and Anton make with David? Fill in the gaps in the diary.

Week 14

	Monday, 3 April	Tuesday, 4 April	Wednesday, 5 April	Thursday, 6 April	Friday, 7 April	Saturday, 8 April	Sunday, 9 April
9.00	9.30 Meeting with Aysun	9.15 Presentation at potential 2	8.30 Morning off	8.30 Doctor's appt	9.00 All-day Workshop 5		
10.00							
11.00	11.15 Write report						
12.00							
1.00							
2.00	1.30 Taxi to airport		2.00 Test XS 3	2.35 Meeting .... 4 (Appraisal!!!)			2.00 Taxi to airport
3.00	3.05 Flight to 1						
4.00		4.40 Return flight					
5.00							5.00 Fly to 6
6.00			5.30 Meet Jens at T.O. Café (+ film?)				
7.00							

6 Changing times — Part B

2 🔊 2.3 Listen again for phrases that fit the definitions, and fill in the gaps.

1. to talk to someone briefly: 'I just wanted to ……………………………….'
2. to be difficult: 'I hope it won't …………………………… to convince them.'
3. to wish someone luck: 'I'll …………………………………………… for both of you!'
4. to say you're unhappy about something: 'It's ………………………… you're not coming.'
5. to ask if something was successful: 'Did that …………………………?'
6. to say something is necessary: 'Don't worry! It can't ……………………….'
7. to go someplace with somebody: 'Would you like to ……………………?'

3 👥 Work with a partner. First write five questions about Wiebke's and Anton's arrangements this week. Then ask your partner your questions.

> What is she / are they doing on … at …?

> When/Where is she / are they …?

> When does the plane for … leave?

4 👥 Look at your diary and tell a partner what you're doing next week/month.

5 🔊 2.4 Listen to Aysun talking to Bettina, her PA. They're checking the arrangements for the trip to Cape Town.

Present continuous for future arrangements

Wiebke and Anton **are flying** to Berlin this afternoon.
When **are** they **coming** back?
We**'re** not **leaving** until Sunday now.

„not ... until" = erst
We're <u>not</u> leaving <u>until</u> Sunday.

„by" = bis spätestens
Please finish it <u>by</u> Monday.

Simple present for future schedules

The flight **leaves** at 5 pm.
When **do** you **arrive** in Cape Town?

What has Bettina already done? Listen and put ticks ✔ or crosses ✘ on her 'to do' list.

- reschedule flight to Cape Town ☐
- order taxi to airport on Sunday afternoon ☐
- talk to Philip ☐
- pick up the new data projector ☐
- find an extra cable ☐

Part B 6

Complete these sentences from the dialogue, then listen and check.

1 **Aysun:** I .... just .... that it's almost five o'clock.
2 **Bettina:** I .... already .... your flight to Cape Town.
3 **Aysun:** Great, and .... you .... a taxi to the airport?
4 **Bettina:** I .... him several messages but he .... yet.
5 **Aysun:** .... you .... the new projector yet?
6 **Bettina:** I'm afraid I .... to find one yet.

When do we use 'already'? When do we use 'yet'?

> **Present perfect with *already*, *not ... yet* and *just***
>
> I**'ve** already **sent** the email.
> **Have** you **done** that yet?
> Yes, I **have**. I picked it up yesterday.
> They **have**n't **learned** it yet.
> I**'ve** just **noticed** that it's quite late.

6 🔊 2.5 Bettina confuses the words 'chairing' and 'sharing'. Listen to these pairs of words and say what order you hear the words in. Write 1 or 2 in the boxes.

[ʃ] ☐ ship   ☐ shoe   ☐ shoes   ☐ shop   ☐ she's
[tʃ] ☐ chip   ☐ chew   ☐ choose   ☐ chop   ☐ cheese

🔊 2.6 Now listen and fill in the missing letters on the business cards.

..........arles ....en

..........ester Silicon ....ip Company

165 ....utter Court

..........elsea, England, UK

..........irley and

..........ane ....elton

Luxury ....ips

7283 ....attleford Drive

..........elltown, Maryland, USA

7 👥 Next week you and your partner are having a meeting with five important clients from around the world.

1 Look at the pictures below and make a 'to do' list for the meeting. Invent the details yourselves: Where are the clients from? (Shanghai? Chile?) How long are they staying? What's on the agenda?
2 Tick two or three things on your list (but not all).
3 Check the arrangements with your partner. Have a conversation like Aysun and Bettina's in exercise 5.

> **Checking and reporting progress**
>
> Have you been able to ...?
> Have you done that yet?
> By the way, did you remember to ...?
> How much progress have you made so far?
>
> Well, we've done ..., but we haven't ... yet.
> I'm afraid there's still quite a bit to do.
> Actually, there isn't much left to do.
> We've made excellent progress.
> We've done practically everything.
> It's been tough, but I think we're almost there.
> I think the end is in sight.

6 Changing times — Business file

📁 Can we find a time?

1 🔊 2.7-10 Malcolm Minsky works for an insurance company in Melbourne Australia. It's 8.30 on Monday morning and he has to change some of his appointments. Listen and update the page from his diary.

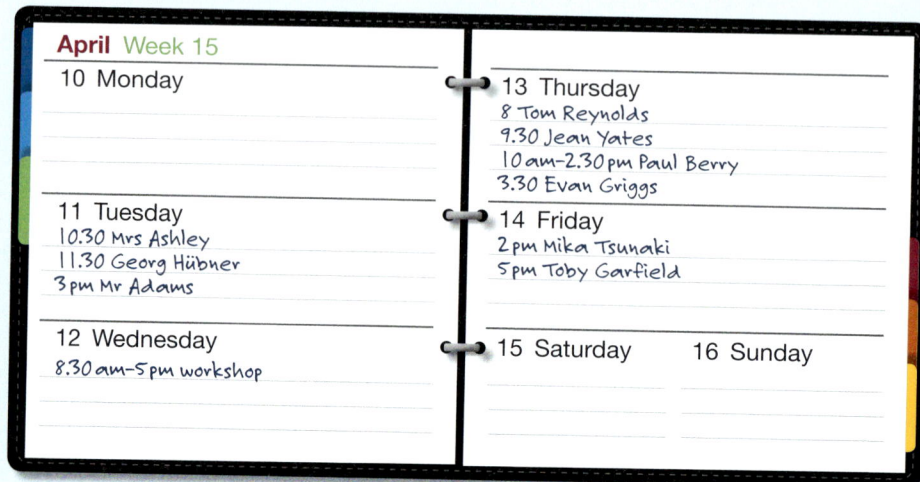

April Week 15

10 Monday

11 Tuesday
10.30 Mrs Ashley
11.30 Georg Hübner
3 pm Mr Adams

12 Wednesday
8.30 am–5 pm workshop

13 Thursday
8 Tom Reynolds
9.30 Jean Yates
10 am–2.30 pm Paul Berry
3.30 Evan Griggs

14 Friday
2 pm Mika Tsunaki
5 pm Toby Garfield

15 Saturday   **16 Sunday**

Listen again. In which conversation (1–4) does Malcolm …

a ☐ make a new appointment?
b ☐ cancel an appointment?
c ☐ postpone an appointment?
d ☐ bring forward an appointment?

Dealing with appointments

Unless otherwise indicated, you can use these phrases both for emails and on the telephone.

Making an appointment
What time would suit you?
When is it convenient for you?
Are you free tomorrow morning?
I was wondering if you could make it later this morning.
Can you make it tomorrow?
– I'm very sorry but I'm afraid I can't manage tomorrow.
– Sorry, but Thursday afternoon is inconvenient for me.
– Next Wednesday would be fine. How about at around ten o'clock again?
Shall we make a provisional appointment for Wednesday? @
Well, shall we pencil that in? 📞

Changing an appointment
Just a quick note to say that unfortunately I can't manage Thursday. @
I'm so sorry! I can't make it on Thursday. 📞
Can't we just cancel this one and deal with everything next week?
Unfortunately, something unexpected has come up, and I'm afraid I won't be able to make our appointment next week.
I'm really sorry for the inconvenience.
I apologize for this.
Can we find an alternative time?

Confirming an appointment
Tomorrow at 9.30 is fine with me.
Fine, so that's tomorrow at 9.30 then. 📞
I can confirm our appointment on Tuesday at 9.30. @
Yes, that should work out. 📞
I'm looking forward to seeing you next week.
See you next week then. Bye now. 📞

> Die Vergangenheitsform wirkt weniger direkt und somit höflicher als die Gegenwartsform.
> • I <u>was wondering</u> if you could make it …
> • I <u>wanted</u> to phone you this morning, too.

Business file

6

2 It's 9.30 am and Malcolm's email inbox is full. Look at these extracts from four of his emails. Which email is from one of the callers in exercise 1?

A
I really appreciated your phone call last week and think your idea for a workshop on Wednesday is great. The times you suggested suit me fine, so go ahead and finalize the arrangements.

B
Just a quick note to inform you that ADELAIDE (the room you booked for the meeting on Wednesday) is too small for the numbers you have given us. We are putting you in MELBOURNE instead. Sorry for any inconvenience caused. Attached are details …

C
Just tried to get through but I couldn't. I'm very sorry, but my assistant just got in and I'm afraid I can't manage tomorrow after all! I'm double-booked. How about later in the week? I'm available all day on Friday. Can you make it at 2 pm? Let me know!

D
Could you get back to me as soon as possible about the proposed change to the seminar room? We sent you an email about it on Friday afternoon but we haven't heard back yet. Does MELBOURNE suit you? I need to know asap for the final booking …

Which email …

1 ☐ postpones an appointment?
2 ☐ confirms an arrangement?
3 ☐ asks for confirmation of arrangements?
4 ☐ announces new arrangements?

3 Work in groups of three to find a time for a meeting, and to write emails.

A British construction firm is building a new factory for your company, and you and your partners are your company's 'project team'. You need to find a time next week (Wednesday, Thursday or Friday) when the three of you can meet three colleagues from the British firm – all six of you together. You'll need about two hours for the meeting.

1 First look at your file where you'll see an extract from your diary and an email from a member of the British team. Work together to find the best time for the meeting.

→ *Partner A: file 7, page 132;* → *Partner B: file 22, page 138;* → *Partner C: file 32, page 143*

2 Now write an email to the British colleagues to confirm the arrangements.
3 What about the appointments you had in your diary before? Do you have to cancel or postpone any appointments now? If so, write emails to say you are sorry and to suggest alternative times.

Grammar summary

Present perfect

1 I **have posted** three videos on YouTube.
  She**'s lived** in Africa.
  They**'ve interviewed** some innovative people.
2 I**'ve learned** three languages so far.
  Have you **visited** the new factory recently?
  – Yes, we **have**. It looks much better!
3 **Have** you ever **had** a job in Morocco?
  – No, I**'ve** never **worked** in Africa.

I	have ('ve) haven't	
he / she / it	has ('s) hasn't	worked … had … been …
you / we / they	have ('ve) haven't	

Mit dem *present perfect* drückt man aus, dass etwas bereits irgendwann in der Vergangenheit geschehen ist. Dabei wird der Zeitpunkt in der Vergangenheit nicht genannt (**1**). Häufig wird jedoch ein Zeitrahmen impliziert, der bis in die Gegenwart reicht. Signalwörter dafür sind beispielsweise *so far*, *not yet*, *already*, *lately*, *recently* (**2**).

Auch *ever* (jemals) und *never* (nie, niemals) sind Signalwörter für das *present perfect*. Sie stehen vor dem Partizip Perfekt (**3**).

Das *present perfect* wird mit *have* oder *has* und dem Partizip Perfekt gebildet. Für die Liste der unregelmäßigen Verben und deren dritten Formen, siehe S. 194.

Already / yet / not … yet

1 We've **already** made excellent progress.
  The assistant has **already** downloaded the podcast.
  Have you booked the flight **yet**?
2 I have**n't** confirmed the appointment **yet**.
  Why have**n't** you signed up for the webinar **yet**?

Already und *yet* entsprechen dem deutschen „schon". *Already* verwendet man meist in Aussagesätzen und *yet* in Fragen. *Already* steht vor dem Partizip Perfekt, *yet* am Ende des Satzes (**1**).

Not yet entspricht dem deutschen „noch nicht". Auch hier steht *yet* meistens am Ende von Aussagesätzen und Fragen (**2**).

Present perfect vs simple past

1 My colleague **has lived** in many countries.
  She **lived** in India from 2006–2007.
  Have you **met** the new Head of R&D?
  – Yes, I **met** her yesterday evening.
2 When **did** you **move** into the open-plan office?
  – We **moved** there last week.
  (Nicht: When have you moved …?)

Mit dem *present perfect* wird ausgedrückt, dass etwas irgendwann geschehen ist. Mit dem *simple past* wird ausgedrückt, dass etwas zu einem bestimmten Zeitpunkt passiert ist. Der Zeitpunkt wird im Satz genannt (oder impliziert) (**1**).

Fragen zu Geschehnissen an einem bestimmten Zeitpunkt in der Vergangenheit stellt man im *simple past* (**2**).

Present continuous for future arrangements

1 We**'re flying** to Cape Town on Monday.
  I**'m having** an appraisal interview at 3 pm.
  Are you **doing** anything on Sunday morning?
2 We **are going** to a seminar on Monday.
  (Besser als: We are going to go to a seminar on Monday.)

Das *present continuous* wird auch verwendet, um über feste Verabredungen oder Zeitpläne in der Zukunft zu sprechen (**1**).

Bei Aussagen mit *go* oder *come* wird häufig das *present continuous* anstelle des *going to future* verwendet (**2**).

Simple present for future schedules

The flight **leaves** for Milan at 8.35 am.
The hotel bar **doesn't open** until 6 pm.
Where **does** the team meeting **take place**?

Das *simple present* wird verwendet, um zukünftige Geschehnisse zu beschreiben, die durch Zeitpläne, Kalenderabläufe o. ä. terminiert sind.

Extra practice 6

1 Use the prompts below and a verb from the box to make questions with *Have you ever …* .

apply · be · do · give · ~~post~~ · use

1 a video on YouTube *Have you ever posted a video on YouTube?*
2 SAP software ....
3 late for an important meeting ....
4 for a visa ....
5 business with the Chinese ....
6 a presentation in English ....

Now match these answers to the questions above.

a ☐ Yes, three years ago in Manchester. It was quite challenging!
b ☐ Actually, I did that last week. It's quite a funny one and a lot of people have watched it.
c ☐ Yes. I went to a trade fair in Shanghai last year and made a lot of contacts there.
d ☐ Not yet. But my company is planning to install it on all our computers.
e ☐ Yes, when I went to Azerbaijan last year. And you need an invitation too!
f ☐ No. But sometimes I've had to rush to get there on time.

2 Complete the sentences using the present perfect.

1 .... (Mary/ever/work) in R&D?
2 I .... (never/be) to Turkey but I'd like to go.
3 They .... (not/test) the prototype yet.
4 .... (we/be able to) contact Aysun yet?
5 He .... (have to) book a bigger room for the meeting.
6 You .... (not/attend) a training course recently, have you?
7 She .... (just/upload) a video onto the intranet.

3 Complete the text with the present perfect or simple past form of the verbs in brackets.

I ....¹ (travel) a lot in my life. I ....² (be) to many 'exotic' countries, including Malta, Nigeria and Vietnam. And I ....³ (work) in two different countries. In 2009, I ....⁴ (work) in Venezuela for a British company. I ....⁵ (learn) Spanish while I was there. Then, in 2011, I ....⁶ (have) a job in France, in Paris to be exact. But I'm afraid I ....⁷ (not/try) to learn French – I ....⁸ (speak) English all the time! But my dream is to go to Australia again – I ....⁹ (be) there once when I was a child and I ....¹⁰ (never/forget) it!

6 Extra practice

4 Complete the sentences with *already* or *yet* in the right position (a or b).

1 Have you booked ....ᵃ the hotel room ....ᵇ?

2 I have ....ᵃ sent ....ᵇ the email to Tom.

3 He hasn't seen ....ᵃ the new website ....ᵇ.

4 Have ....ᵃ they picked up the brochures ....ᵇ?

5 I've ....ᵃ applied ....ᵇ for a new job.

6 The company hasn't launched ....ᵃ the new bicycle ....ᵇ.

5 Complete this dialogue with the present continuous or simple present forms of the verbs in brackets.

David: So Wiebke, what are your plans for tomorrow?

Wiebke: Let me see – first of all, I 'm meeting ....¹ (meet) a client at 9 am in Hamburg. The plane ....² (leave) at 6 am so I'll have to get up quite early.

David: That's tough. How long ....³ (you/stay) in Hamburg?

Wiebke: Just a couple of hours. I ....⁴ (see) another client back here tomorrow afternoon.

David: Oh, so, when ....⁵ (your plane/get) back to Dortmund?

Wiebke: At four. And the meeting with the client is at five, with dinner afterwards!

David: Oh, so a late evening. What about Friday? Are you free then?

Wiebke: Yes, I think so. As far as I know, I ....⁶ (not/do) anything on Friday.

David: Fantastic. Would you like to have dinner with me?

6 Complete this email with these phrases.

get back to me · I'm afraid · I really appreciated · just a quick note · otherwise

Dear Jan

..................¹ to say that I enjoyed our last meeting very much.

..................² the opportunity to meet you all in person. But I have some bad news about our next meeting. ....³ I can't manage Wednesday after all. Can we meet on Thursday at the same time instead? ....⁴ we could meet on Friday. Which day suits you best? Could you ....⁵ as soon as possible, please?

Best wishes
Katrin

7 🔊 2.11 Listen and cross out the incorrect information in the message.

Message for Mr Shufford/Chufford¹

Please check the shares/chairs².

Shirley/Charlie³ can't make it to the next meeting.

(She's hurt her shin/chin⁴.)

80

Extra practice 6

8 Find collocations to complete the sentences below.

A pioneering, extensive, impressive, rewarding

B career, track record, company, knowledge

1 Let's hire him! He's the one with the most ....
2 I really like my job. Few people have had such a ....
3 To do this job properly you need .... of marketing and logistics.
4 As a .... in the field of energy, we have a unique portfolio.

9 Translate into English.

1 Ich musste hart arbeiten, um Werksleiterin zu werden.
2 Ich war eben auf einer internationalen Konferenz.
3 Meine Kollegin nimmt heute Nachmittag an einem Stand-Up Meeting teil.
4 Ich habe mich gefragt, ob du den Flug umlegen könntest?
5 Hast du das Kabel für den Beamer schon gefunden?
6 Ich habe mir mehrere Termine notiert.
7 Können Sie den Termin bitte bis morgen um 11 Uhr bestätigen?
8 Ich hole die Broschüren morgen um 9 Uhr ab.

Typical mistakes

1 I had to work **hard** in my last job.
  NOT I had to work ~~hardly~~ …
2 She **has been** to our supplier on a business trip but now she's back.
  NOT She ~~has gone~~ to our supplier … but now she's back.
3 We're flying to Berlin **this afternoon**.
  NOT We're flying to Berlin ~~today afternoon~~.
4 I **was wondering** if we could postpone the meeting.
  NOT I ~~ask me~~ if …
5 Please make sure the conference room is equipped with a **projector**.
  NOT … equipped with a ~~beamer~~.
6 I've **noted down** several business appointments for you.
  NOT I've ~~noticed~~ several …
7 Marketing needs the new schedule **by** Monday morning.
  NOT … ~~until~~ Monday morning.
8 They **are travelling** to India soon.
  NOT They ~~travel~~ to India soon.

Culture spot

Time matters

According to a recent survey of 2,700 chief executives released by the American consulting firm Proudfoot, CEOs are late for meetings 60 per cent of the time. In another survey in Britain, only 30 per cent of people think that it's unacceptable to arrive late for a business meeting and 14 per cent think it's OK to leave colleagues or clients waiting for up to 20 minutes. How acceptable is it to be fifteen minutes late for a meeting in your country?

What can you say when you arrive late for a meeting?
- In a formal workplace, apologize to the chair quietly when you come in, or wait for an appropriate pause in the discussion. Often a simple explanation such as *Sorry I'm late, our client in Milan called* is enough, and doesn't disturb the progress of the meeting.
- In an informal workplace, perhaps you can add some humour. You can smile and shrug, and give a quick and amusing account of what delayed you. A one-liner like *You wouldn't believe the traffic this morning* may be appropriate. But try not to overdo it and be ready to get straight down to business.

| progress | Vorwärtskommen |
| to shrug | mit den Achseln zucken |

81

7 Out of the office

In this unit you will ...

- talk about recent activities and new developments
- practise small talk and saying goodbye
- learn how to communicate successfully in hotels and restaurants

Business file

- structure and give presentations

Part A Presenting ideas

▶ What's the best way to propose improvements within a company?

- a suggestion box?
- a regular meeting?
- a spontaneous meeting with your boss?
- your company's intranet?

1 Stefan Altmann works in the banking sector. Before listening, match these financial terms with the definitions.

1. money given to somebody which has to be paid back after a certain period of time
2. the cost of borrowing money
3. the money a company receives from selling goods or services
4. the total value of goods or services sold by a company over a period of time, e.g. one year
5. money a bank lends customers so they can buy property with it

☐ revenue ☐ interest rate ☐ mortgage ☐ turnover ☐ loan

> There's normally <u>interest on</u> a loan (Zinsen), but someone <u>is interested in</u> or <u>shows interest in</u> sth. (Interesse).

🔊 2.12 Listen. What does Stefan do and why is he in Italy today?

Present perfect with *for* and *since*

Max **has lived** in Munich *since* 2010.
I**'ve worked** here *for* many years now.
We**'ve spent** a lot of time *since* our first meeting working out the details.

True or false? Tick the correct box.

		true	false
1	Stefan has worked for the Credmasse Group since 1995.	☐	☐
2	The group has two main business units operating out of Munich.	☐	☐
3	SAOR Financing specializes in lending money.	☐	☐
4	Stefan and Max Baker have spent over four months working on their proposal.	☐	☐
5	Stefan's been in Milan for two days.	☐	☐
6	He hasn't seen Max for over a week.	☐	☐

Part A 7

2 Complete these present perfect sentences with the correct form of the verbs in brackets and *for* or *since*.

1. The revenue from Credmasse's loans .... (be) disappointing .... the last two years.
2. Stefan .... (work) for Credmasse .... 13 years now.
3. Max and Stefan .... (be) in Milan .... around 10 am.
4. They .... (know) each other .... SAOR was acquired.
5. Many new financial products .... (create) .... the beginning of the year.

Passive: present perfect

SAOR Financing **has** recently **been taken over** by Credmasse.
The proposal **hasn't been presented** yet.
A number of new branches **have been opened** this year.

3 Match the sentence parts. Which sentence is about a situation that is finished? Which one is about a situation that is ongoing?

1. We worked on the project for one year …
2. We've worked on the project for one year …

a. but we're not working on it anymore.
b. and we're still working on it.

Now decide which words or phrases below signal the simple past (sp) and which signal the present perfect (pp). (Note that some can be used with both tenses.)

- ☐ already
- ☐ at that time
- ☐ for five years
- ☐ just
- ☐ last week
- ☐ never
- ☐ recently
- ☐ since 2003
- ☐ so far
- ☐ two days ago
- ☐ yesterday
- ☐ yet

👥 Ask your partner questions with the words above.

> How many hours did you work last week?

> Have you seen your company's CEO recently?

4 The meeting went well and Stefan sent the following email to everyone involved. Read the message and select the correct form of the verbs.

Dear All,

Here's a quick summary of our discussion, also for the benefit of those in cc.

At the start of the meeting **we gave / we've given** ¹ a review of the situation and **followed / have followed** ² this with an overview of what **was done / has been done** ³ over the past two months. Then we **presented / have presented** ⁴ our ideas for a new range of loans for the Consumer Banking Business Unit.

As we explained, the Consumer Banking Unit **was / has been** ⁵ the most successful unit two years ago. Unfortunately, its market share **decreased / has decreased** ⁶ by a large amount around six months ago when our competitors **got / have got** ⁷ some of our market share. It is obviously time to increase our offer, which is why we **developed / have developed** ⁸ this new range of consumer loans. We expect these new products to give us an increase in turnover of around 6–8 %. (See attached .ppt document with details, market information and forecasts.)

Best regards,
Stefan

Present perfect vs simple past

SAOR Financing **has been** part of the Credmasse group **for three months**.
Stefan **has finished** his part of the presentation and now it's Max's turn.
We **met** about **six weeks ago**.
At that meeting we **decided** to create a new series of loans.

7 Out of the office — Part A

5 Use the correct form of words from the box to complete these sentences about company performance.

> decrease in · fall · increase by · increase of · reduce · rise · stable

1. Three years ago turnover .... €1.2m and ended that year at €9.6m. This represented an .... around 14%.
2. That was after we .... our product range by 20% so we could focus on our main products.
3. Then two years ago there was a slight .... revenue when sales .... to €8.9m.
4. Last year sales were ....
5. Turnover this year .... and things are looking good.

6 Work with a partner. Use the information in your file to talk about the recent activities and performance of different companies.

→ *Partner A: file 8, page 133;* → *Partner B: file 23, page 139*

Take turns telling your partner about recent developments at your company or a company you know well.

7 2.13 Stefan and Max are leaving the Credmasse office. Listen and match the sentences.

1. Let me get your coats.
2. Is this your first time in Milan?
3. I'm sorry I can't join you tonight.
4. When are you coming back?
5. Would you like me to call you a taxi?
6. Have a good trip home and keep in touch.

a. No, I've been here once before.
b. In around three months, I think.
c. Mine's the black one.
d. We will, Maria. Thanks a lot.
e. No, that's not necessary, thanks.
f. That's OK. Maybe it will work out next time.

Saying goodbye

Thanks for coming.
It's been good seeing you.
Let me get your coat / the door for you.
Do you know when you'll be coming back?
Please say hello / give my best/ regards to …
Would you like me to call you a taxi?
Enjoy the rest of your time here.
Have a good trip home.
Take care. Let's keep in touch (about …).

8 What do you talk about when you say goodbye to business partners or colleagues from other places?

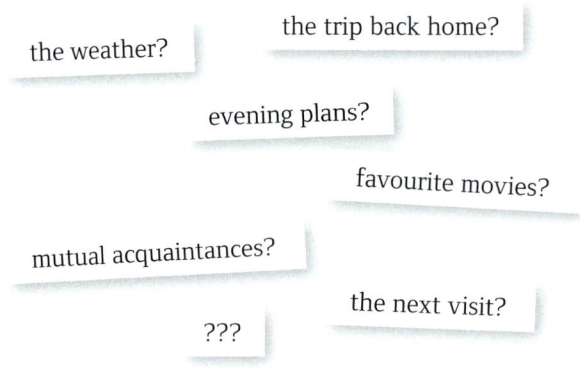

the weather?
the trip back home?
evening plans?
favourite movies?
mutual acquaintances?
the next visit?
???

Work with a partner and think of a situation that is realistic for you. Then act it out.

Part B Travelling on business

▶ Do you sometimes go on business trips? What are the advantages and disadvantages of being on the road?

1 🔊 2.14-16 After a walk around the city, Stefan Altmann and Max Baker went back to their hotel. Listen and answer the questions.

In the hotel room
1. What problem did Max have?
2. When does the hotel serve breakfast?
3. What time did Max order the taxi for?

In the hotel bar
4. What did Stefan and Max order?
5. What didn't the barman have and what alternative did he suggest?

In the restaurant
6. Did they have trouble finding a table?
7. What did Max order?
8. What doesn't Stefan eat?

2 What did they say? Complete these sentences from the dialogues, then listen and check.

1. I'm .... there aren't any .... in my room.
2. I'll send some up ....
3. Can I get you .... to drink?
4. I'm sorry. We don't have any .... left.
5. Is there .... sitting at this table?
6. Do you have any .... dishes?

Look at the sentences above. When do we use *some* and when do we use *any*?

3 Complete the sentences with *some(thing)* or *any(thing)*.

1. Did you have .... drinks from the minibar?
2. Can you give me .... to write with, please? I need to take a message.
3. You'll find .... nice restaurants in this 'What's On?' brochure.
4. I'm sorry, we won't have .... free tables until around 9.30 pm.
5. Are there .... non-smoking rooms in the hotel?
   – Yes, there are .... on the first floor.
6. Excuse me, could I have .... mineral water, please?
7. I'm sorry, the restaurant has closed early. We don't have .... left in the kitchen.

Some and any

I'll send **some** towels up straight away.
There's **something** on my chair.
Would you like **some** crisps?
Can you recommend **somewhere** local to eat?
Do you have **any** vegetarian dishes?
Is there **anyone** sitting here?

7 Out of the office — Part B

Communicating at the hotel

Can I help you?
Could you order me a taxi for 7.15 am, please?
Could I have a glass of wine, please?
Do you have any vegetarian/vegan/regional dishes?
I'll have … for my starter.
I'd like some/a … to start and … for my main course.

4 🔊 2.17-19 Listen to these three restaurant conversations, and complete the table.

Customer	Problem	Solution
1		
2		
3		

What did they say? Match the sentence halves.

1 I'm afraid that's not
2 Could you please
3 Would it be possible
4 I'm sorry to say
5 I'm afraid that

a to move tables?
b that we had to wait a very long time.
c bring me a new set of cutlery?
d what we ordered.
e my meal is overcooked.

Making polite requests and complaints

Excuse me. I've just … . Could you please …?
I was wondering if we could …
Would it be possible to …?
I'm afraid that's …
I'm sorry to say that …

5 👥 Use information in your file to make some conversations. Then write down one conversation and read it to the class.

→ Partner A: file 9, page 133; → Partner B: file 24, page 139

What else might go wrong in a restaurant and how would you deal with it? Brainstorm with a partner and then act out the scenario.

neighbours too noisy

music too loud

portions not big enough

dirty cutlery

???

6 As business travelling has become more expensive, many companies now use virtual meeting software. Read the interview on the next page and make notes under the following headings:

Pros and cons of …

travelling to a meeting	virtual meetings

86

Meetings: Face-to-face or virtual?

As a member of a number of project teams and a leader of some, Anita Bauer has a lot of meetings. We caught up with her before a flight to Warsaw to speak to her about the pros and cons of different ways to conduct meetings.

Manager Today: So Anita, you're on your way to Warsaw this time. How much travelling have you done so far this year?

Anita Bauer: Well, that's difficult to say. I've been on a lot of trips to various places for team meetings this year. I've had around two meetings a month somewhere offsite. But we've also increased the number of virtual meetings we have, so we can cut down on the time and costs involved in travelling to face-to-face meetings.

Manager Today: Virtual meetings. OK, that's interesting. Why are you actually going to Warsaw now for your meeting then?

Anita Bauer: Well, you don't actually physically meet the other people in the meeting if you have a virtual meeting. This can be a disadvantage if it's a kick-off meeting for a new project, for example. It's important to have some relationship-building activities at such a meeting. You can't really do that in a virtual meeting.

Manager Today: So, today's meeting is a kick-off meeting?

Anita Bauer: Unfortunately not. A number of mistakes have been made in this project, so we are having a so-called crisis meeting. It's where we put out the fire and get the project back on track. There's been some conflict within the team so it's important we meet face-to-face to sort things out.

Manager Today: Right. So face-to-face meetings are good for relationship building as well as for dealing with sensitive issues and problems.

Anita Bauer: Exactly. But they do cost a lot of money and also mean time away from the office. Normally, when things have been set up and the project is running well, we communicate via virtual meetings. It saves a lot of time and money.

Manager Today: So how exactly does it work?

Anita Bauer: Well, the project leader schedules the meeting within the virtual meeting software, and then invitations are automatically sent to the attendees via email. Each of the attendees then logs on at the agreed time. We can all hear each other as we're wearing headsets, and some of us have webcams. We normally just use the webcams at the beginning of a meeting to say hello, though, and then turn them off.

Manager Today: Why do you do that?

Anita Bauer: Well, the webcam uses a lot of bandwidth and this can have a negative effect on the sound quality. When we turn off the sound, it's normally better for people who are in areas that don't have a lot of bandwidth.

Manager Today: And what makes a virtual meeting better than a teleconference?

Anita Bauer: Well, they're the same in that you can all talk together at the same time, but with a virtual meeting you can all look at the same documents by screen sharing. It makes discussing and working on project documents a lot easier if we know we're all looking at the same thing.

Manager Today: That sounds great. Well, thanks a lot for talking to us, Anita, and we hope your meeting today goes well so you can get back to your office and virtual meetings.

7 Find words in the text which fit the definitions.

1. a meeting you have at the beginning of a project
2. things you do to bring a new team together
3. equipment you need to hear and be heard when using the computer
4. equipment you need so the participants can see you
5. the speed at which you can upload and download information, sound or video
6. when others can see what you see on your monitor during a virtual meeting

8 Have you ever taken part in a virtual meeting? What kind of meetings do you think are most effective when? Discuss in small groups, then present your ideas to the rest of the class.

7 Out of the office — Business file

📁 I'd like to begin with …

1 👥 What makes a good presentation? What makes a bad one?
Brainstorm two lists with your partner and present them to the class.

Good

Bad

2 Match the presentation techniques to the reasons for using them.

A good presenter …

1 *f* states the purpose of the presentation
2 ___ reformulates,
3 ___ uses pauses
4 ___ gives lists in groups of three
5 ___ asks rhetorical questions
6 ___ refers to the audience's knowledge or experience
7 ___ uses the names of the people in the audience
8 ___ outlines the benefits for the audience
9 ___ prepares 'extra' slides for anticipated questions

a to get the audience thinking about the answer before he/she says it.
b to put more attention on the word(s) just before or after.
c so that they feel involved and included.
d so that they feel that they're not wasting their time.
e to make them feel that he/she is speaking directly to them.
f so that the audience knows what the presentation aims are.
g because this number of items is easier to remember.
h so that it is easier to spontaneously react to questions.
i which means saying the same thing again but with other words in order to stress a point.

3 🔊 2.20 Now listen to a presentation about the installation of new software for conducting virtual meetings. Which techniques above does the presenter use?

Business file 7

Presenting

Introduction
Good morning/afternoon …
I'd like to tell you about / explain …
In the next hour, there are three main points I'd like to make.
My presentation will take around 20 minutes.
By the end of this presentation, you'll have a better understanding of …
If you've got any questions, just ask.
Feel free to ask any questions.
I'll take questions at the end.

Main part
I'd like to begin with …
That brings us to the next point …
As you remember from last year, …
Well, in other words, …

Visuals
This slide gives you an overview of …
I'd like to draw your attention to …
As you can see on the right/left …
Here you can see …

Ending
That brings me to the end (of my presentation).
Are there any questions?
Thanks, that's a good question.
I thought you might ask that. I have an extra slide here which will help answer your question.

4 Use the notes in your file to present a new product to your partner.

→ *Partner A: file 10, page 133;* → *Partner B: file 25, page 139*

5 Prepare a five-minute presentation about your department, a project you're working on or anything that interests you.

```
Beginning
..........................................................
..........................................................

Middle
..........................................................
..........................................................

End
..........................................................
..........................................................
```

Now get into groups and take turns giving each other your presentations. When it's your turn to listen, think of two questions to ask each presenter, and ask them either during or at the end of the talk.

```
Questions?
..........................................................
..........................................................
```

89

7 Grammar summary

Present perfect with *for* and *since*

1. She's **lived** in Milan for many years.
   We**'ve been** part of the group for ten years now.
2. Interest rates **have been** high since April 2011.
   I**'ve worked** hard since our last meeting.
3. How long **have** they **had** this hotel?
   They**'ve had** this hotel for many years.
   (Nicht: They ~~have~~ this hotel for many years.)

Das *present perfect* beschreibt Geschehnisse, die in der Vergangenheit begonnen haben und bis in die Gegenwart andauern. Mit *for* wird die Zeitspanne benannt, in der das Geschehen anhält (**1**). Mit *since* verweist man auf den Anfangszeitpunkt, an dem das Geschehen begonnen hat (**2**).

Auch wenn die Situation für die Gegenwart immer noch relevant ist, kann im Gegensatz zum Deutschen die Gegenwart nicht verwendet werden (**3**)!

Present perfect vs simple past

1. They **launched** a new product last summer and **have** already **increased** their market share.
   I **started** here when I was 22, so I **have been** with the company for 15 years now.
2. We **worked** on the product line for two months last year.
3. I **worked** on the project two months ago.

> Im US-Englisch wird oft das <u>simple past</u> in Sätzen mit den Signalwörtern <u>already</u>, <u>yet</u> und <u>just</u> usw. verwendet.

Mit dem *present perfect* wird ausgedrückt, dass etwas zu einem implizierten Zeitpunkt geschehen ist. Signalwörter sind u. a. *recently, already, just, since* und *for*. Mit dem *simple past* wird ausgedrückt, dass etwas zu einem bestimmten Zeitpunkt passiert ist. Der Zeitpunkt wird meist im Satz genannt (**1**).

Auch im *simple past* kann *for* verwendet werden, wenn die beschriebene Zeitspanne eindeutig in der Vergangenheit liegt (**2**).

Das deutsche „vor" wird mit *ago* ausgedrückt. *Ago* steht am Ende des Satzes und nicht vor der Zeitangabe (**3**).

Present perfect passive

1. The mortgage **has** already **been paid**.
   The new branches **haven't been opened** yet.
2. **Has** the proposal **been accepted**?
   Have they **been given** the loan?

I	've / haven't	
he / she / it	's / hasn't	been asked …
you / we / they	've / haven't	been given …

Das *present perfect passive* wird mit *have/has been* und dem Partizip Perfekt gebildet (**1**).

Bei der Fragebildung steht das Objekt vor *been* (**2**).

Für die Verwendung des Passivs siehe Seite 18 (Grammar summary, Unit 1).

Some and *any*

1. I have **some** messages for you.
   I think there's **someone** sitting here.
2. Could I have **some** peanuts, please?
   Would you like **something** to eat?
3. I don't have **any** time at the moment.
   I can't find my ticket **anywhere**.
4. Have you been on **any** business trips lately?
   Do you know **anyone** in Milan?

Some wird verwendet in bejahten Aussagesätzen (**1**), in Angebotsfragen und Fragen, auf die eine positive Antwort zu erwarten ist (**2**). *Any* wird verwendet in verneinten Aussagesätzen (**3**) und offenen Fragen (**4**).

Dies gilt ebenso für alle weiteren Verbindungen wie *someone/anyone, something/anything, somewhere/anywhere*.

Extra practice 7

1 Select the correct verb forms to complete the sentences.

1. Sales were / have been bad again last year; in fact they weren't / haven't been good since 2010.
2. Sales rose / have risen five per cent so far this year.
3. I gave / I've given a new product presentation yesterday and 50 people attended / have attended.
4. The loans were introduced / have been introduced three years ago.
5. Revenue last year was / has been around one million euros.
6. The new products were already launched / have already been launched; they were / have been on sale for five months now.
7. We had / have had our first meeting the day before yesterday. It went / has gone very well.

2 Complete the sentences with *for*, *since* or *ago* and the words in brackets.

1. I've worked here .... (ten years)
2. She left the company about .... (three months)
3. He's been on holiday .... (two weeks)
4. I've lived in a small town near Nuremberg .... (1996)
5. Did you try to call me ....? (five minutes)
6. She's been my boss .... (last May)
7. We've been married .... (six years)
8. Fiona has worked in our department .... (January last year)

3 Complete the sentences with *some/any*, *someone/anyone*, *something/anything* or *somewhere/anywhere*.

1. Would you like .... tea or coffee? Or can I get you .... cold to drink?
2. Oh, there isn't .... sugar in this. Could I have ...., please?
3. Do you have .... empty folders? I can't find one .... in my office.
4. There are .... good apps for this. Has .... here tried one of them yet?
5. Are there .... good restaurants near your office? I need to take .... out for a meal.
6. How nice! I don't have .... important to do today.
7. I'm sorry, but she doesn't have .... time this month. Can .... else help you?

4 Match the sentences and responses.

1 We think you're on the right track.	a Yes, I'll do that.
2 Is this your first time in Barcelona?	b No, I've been here a couple of times already.
3 I'm sorry I can't join you this evening.	c Yes, please. I need to go back to my hotel.
4 Please give my regards to Karl.	d Thank you and take care.
5 Would you like me to call you a taxi?	e That's good to hear. I'm happy you think so.
6 Have a good trip home.	f That's OK. We can go out together next time.

7 Extra practice

5 Complete the dialogue with phrases from the box.

> I'll have that. · I'll bring them straight away. ·
> Do you have any vegetarian dishes? · Is there anyone sitting here? ·
> Could I have a glass of wine, please? · Can I get you anything to drink

Waiter: Good evening, sir.

Peter: Good evening. ....¹

Waiter: No, it's free. Here you go. ....² while you're looking at the menu?

Peter: Yes, please. ....³ Let me see … yes, the Bordeaux, and also some mineral water.

Waiter: Of course. ....⁴ (*two minutes later*) So, here are your drinks. Are you ready to order?

Peter: I think so. ....⁵

Waiter: Yes, we do. You might like today's special: it's a vegetarian lasagne, made with aubergine.

Peter: That sounds nice. ....⁶

Waiter: Certainly.

6 Rearrange the words to make presentations phrases.

1 I'd like / next hour / three main things / in the / there are / to show you

   ....

2 my / 20 minutes / around / take / presentation / will

   ....

3 by the end / new consumer products / presentation, / a better understanding / of this / you'll have / of our

   ....

4 just / if / ask / any questions, / got / you've

   ....

5 attention to / to draw / I'd like / results / your / last year's

   ....

6 presentation / that brings / end / to the / me / of my

   ....

7 which / slide here / will / I have an extra / answer your question / help

   ....

7 Choose the correct words.

1 We lost **revenue / mortgage** last year because our competitor introduced two new products.

2 When **loans / interest rates** went up, the number of new **loans / interest rates** dropped.

3 Banks in some countries offer as high as 100% **mortgages / loans**. Almost anybody can buy a property now.

4 **Turnover has / Interest rates have** increased since we introduced the new range of **revenue / loans**.

5 Could I **borrow / lend** some money? The bank won't **borrow / lend** me any.

Extra practice 7

8 Translate into English.

1. Ich brauche die neue Tagesordnung für das Kick-off Meeting.
2. Wir sind an einem Seminar zu Hypothekendarlehen interessiert.
3. Unsere Filiale bietet diesen neuen Service seit zwei Wochen an.
4. Vor drei Monaten ist der Umsatz um 13 % gestiegen.
5. Mein Kollege wird Ihnen eine Übersicht über unsere neuen Kredite geben.
6. Der Service war furchtbar! Wir haben nichts zu essen bekommen.
7. Könnte ich vielleicht dieses Wochenende dein Auto ausleihen?
8. Können wir ein paar extra Stühle im hinteren Teil des Konferenzraums aufstellen?

Typical mistakes

1. We will **need** about 30 minutes.
   NOT We will use about 30 minutes.
2. I'm **interested in** your interest rates.
   NOT I'm interested for your interest rates.
3. She **has worked** in sales for many years.
   NOT She works … for many years.
4. We opened this branch **three months ago**.
   NOT We opened this branch for three months.
5. I can give you an **overview of** our products.
   NOT … an overview about our products.
6. They were closed. I didn't get **anything** to eat!
   NOT … didn't get something to eat!
7. Can I **borrow** some chairs from you?
   NOT Can I lend some chairs from you?
8. Can we have a table at the **back** of the restaurant?
   NOT … the backside of the restaurant?

Culture spot

Doing business in other countries

Every country – and every company – has different ways of doing things. It's not that one way is right and the other wrong; in many cases, the right way is just 'the way we do things around here'. This can put business travellers or those working in international teams in an awkward or uncomfortable position if they don't know much about the (corporate) culture of the people they're doing business with.

Think about these questions:

When you go to a meeting, do you
a dress more formally than usual?
b dress the same as usual?
c call someone and ask how formally you should dress?

How do *you* feel when you are dressed much more or less formally than the other participants? How do you think *they* feel?

In your company/department, are decisions
a made in a team?
b made by one individual?
c discussed in a team and then made by an individual?

How do *you* feel when other business partners are used to a different way of deciding than you? How do you think *they* feel?

It's important to remain open to other ways of doing things. You never know, maybe you'll learn a better way of doing something from another culture. In any case, it's always a good idea to find out about specific cultural traits when doing business with someone from another culture.

awkward — ungünstig
trait — Merkmal

8 At a trade fair

In this unit you will ...
- describe features and benefits of products
- write short memos and do a series of office tasks
- practise writing formal and informal emails

Business file
- analyse data and write a report

Part A The eco trade fair

▶ Have you ever been to a trade fair? Where was it? When did you go?
Name three things companies do at trade fairs.

1 Your company has a stand at a forthcoming trade fair. Make a list of what you'll need.

> display stands · projector · brochures · giveaways · ???

👥 Tell a partner why you'll need the things on your list.

2 Match these environmentally friendly products with the slogans below.

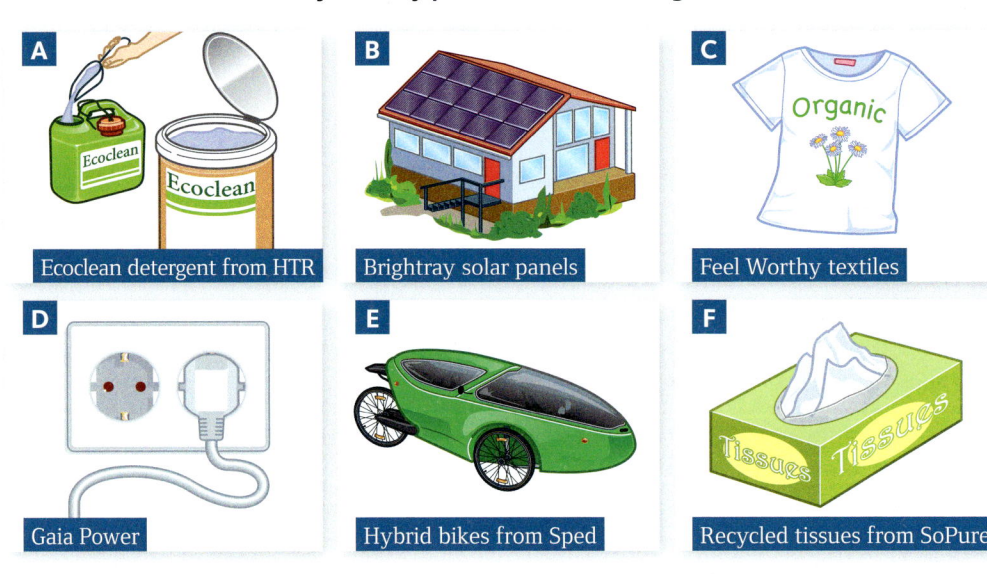

A Ecoclean detergent from HTR
B Brightray solar panels
C Feel Worthy textiles
D Gaia Power
E Hybrid bikes from Sped
F Recycled tissues from SoPure

1 Beautifully made from cotton that is sustainable and biodegradable ... and soft on your skin.

2 Goodbye pre-packaged goods! Hello reusable containers!

3 Power from renewable resources. We are your green provider.

4 Less water, less pollution and no trees needed.

5 Homeowners: Interested in cutting your electricity bills by 10% a year? We provide the solution!

6 Easy to use – roomy, comfortable and dry. It will take you anywhere!

■ **Did you know?**
Providers are companies that offer a service, e.g. utilities.
Suppliers deal more in products, goods, etc.
Wholesalers deliver stock to retailers from their **warehouses**.
Retailers sell goods to the public.

👥 Discuss the benefits and drawbacks of these products. What other environmentally friendly products do you know?

Part A

8

3 ♪2.21 Uli Rietz is talking to Mary Burton, a buyer visiting the Natexpo in Paris. Listen. Which product from exercise 2 is Uli selling?

What do Uli and Mary say? Fill in the gaps, then listen again and check.

1 I .... at your range of ....
2 .... we sit over there? It's .... quieter.
3 What kind of .... did you have .... ?
4 That .... the price, of course.
5 At the ...., I suppose it's .... just a question of price.

4 ♪2.22 Which of the product's features and benefits does Uli mention in the second part of their conversation? Listen and tick the ones he refers to.

1 ☐ superior performance   4 ☐ quality
2 ☐ sustainability   5 ☐ lower price
3 ☐ brand image   6 ☐ promotional giveaways

5 Which linking words does Uli use to describe the benefits of the products?

1 Well, `although / thus` Ecoclean seems expensive, it is better value for money.
2 Ecoclean sets the standard for laundry detergents and `due to that fact / thus` I'm sure you'll see your sales improving over a longer period of time.
3 It's the most environmentally friendly detergent around `due to the fact that / although` there is no packaging and over 60 % of the ingredients come from renewable resources.

What other benefits does Ecoclean have? Match the sentence halves.

1 Ecoclean detergents are great for young families due to the fact that …
2 Our detergent is technologically advanced and therefore …
3 Customers are loyal to this product because …
4 Although it's a bit more expensive than its competitors, …

a it's effective and the benefits are clear to see.
b it's safe to use because it has no toxic ingredients.
c it's actually quite reasonably priced when you consider all the benefits.
d stains are more easily removed than ever before.

6 👥 Are you a good salesperson? Pick a product (or service) you like and describe its purpose and appearance. What special features does it have? Sell it to your partner.

Linking the features and benefits of products

This line is at the bottom/top of the range **and so** appeals to price-conscious/well-off/ high-end consumers.
It is made of steel/plastic/… **and thus** it is durable/stylish/ recyclable/light.
Due to the fact that it's made from the best available materials / the finest ingredients, it is very good quality / value for money / cost-effective.

Adjective + infinitive

It's **safe to use** because it has no toxic ingredients.
We've made sure that our instructions are **easy to understand**.

Adverb + past participle

It's actually quite **reasonably priced** when you consider all the benefits.
All of our products are not only **technologically advanced**, they are also **beautifully made**.

8 At a trade fair — Part A

Linking words

Addition
also / and / besides / moreover / furthermore / in addition

Example
for example / for instance / such as

Contrast
although / but / however / still / despite the fact that / nevertheless / nonetheless / on the other hand

Cause and effect
as a result (of) / because (of) / so / thus / due to (this fact)

Conclusion
as a result / consequently / in conclusion / to sum up / to summarize

Past perfect

Unfortunately, he **had talked** to our competitors **before he met** me.

When they got to the airport, the plane **had** already **left**.

I **had finished** most of my tasks **by 2 pm yesterday**, so I took the rest of the day off.

How many emails had you written by the end of work yesterday?

I think I'd written …

---

7 Uli is writing a memo to his boss at Ecoclean's head office. Was his experience at the Natexpo a complete success? Read the extract from the memo and decide.

> I've been to trade fairs in the UK many times. However[1], I had never been to the one in Paris before, so[2] I wasn't sure quite what to expect. When I arrived there on Monday, the organizers had already set up most of our stand, and furthermore[3] they had given us extra lighting equipment. As a result[4] we were able to use a light show to highlight our product range and thus[5] managed to attract a lot of interest. Although[6] there weren't as many visitors to the fair as we had hoped, our stand was well attended, and we handed out a lot of samples. Unfortunately, we didn't contact as many buyers as expected. But[7] there were exceptions, like, for example[8], Mary Burton, a buyer from Value It, who has placed a substantial order with us. Customers didn't always know as much about eco cleaning products as I had expected. As a result[9] I recommend doing more research in the future into customer awareness issues. Nonetheless[10], the fair was an interesting experience and I managed to do a lot of networking.

Replace the underlined words with alternatives from the phrase box on the left. You might need to rephrase some of the sentences.

8 Look at this sentence from the memo. What happened first: Uli arriving at the fair or the organizers setting up the stand?

> When I **arrived** there on Monday, the organizers **had already set** up most of our stand.

Complete these sentences using either the simple past or past perfect of the verbs in brackets.

1 There ………………………… (not/be) as many visitors at the fair as we ………………………… (hope).

2 Unfortunately, we ………………………… (not/see) Paul at the fair, as he ………………………… (already/go) home by the time we arrived.

3 I ………………………… (not/realize) it at the time, but my boss ………………………… (set up) my appraisal interview without asking me.

9 Use the following framework to write a short memo about a recent visit to a trade fair, a customer or a factory you hadn't visited before.

> I've visited customers / factories / trade fairs many times over the years. However, I had never visited this one before so I wasn't sure quite what to expect. When I arrived there, …………… (*What had already happened?*) and furthermore ……………… (*What else had happened?*). As a result ……………… (*What did you/they do?*) and so ……………… (*What was the consequence?*).
> As a result of this experience, I recommend ……………… (*What have you learned?*).

10 Who in your group had done the most by the end of the day yesterday?

emails · phone calls · meetings · reports · coffee breaks · ???

Part B Back in the office

▶ What do you think is the easiest to do in English: speak to someone face-to-face, talk on the phone, or write an email? What's the hardest? Why?

1 🔊 2.23-26 Uli Rietz's assistant Tracy Roberts is taking care of things in the Bremen office while Uli is travelling. Listen and match the voicemail messages to the descriptions.

- an enquiry about a representative
- a query about an invoice
- a request for a delivery
- a complaint about a delivery

What does each person want? Which messages are formal and which are informal?

2 Listen to the messages again and complete Tracy's 'to do' list.

To do:

- Check Pauline Dubois' ....¹ and phone her back ....² tomorrow at the latest.
- Contact Ms ....³ about replacing the stand-alone ....⁴ stands.
- Send Giovanni Ponzi ....⁵ company brochures (..................⁶ version) asap.
- Phone Svenja Karlsson on ....⁷.

8 At a trade fair

Part B

3 **Work with a partner. Look again at Tracy's 'to do' list in exercise 2 and complete the four office tasks below.**

1 Checking an invoice

Check Pauline's email attachment against Ecoclean's price list and Pauline's last invoice.

→ *Partner A: file 11, page 134;* → *Partner B: file 26, page 140*

Then work together to finish Tracy's email.

From:	Tracy Roberts <tracy.roberts@htr.de>
To:	Pauline Dubois <p_dubois@lareine.fr>
Subject:	

Thanks for your phone message of 31 May. I've just checked your invoice and here are my answers to your queries.

1) Ecoclean Extra Powder

2 Reacting to a complaint
Write Mary a formal email and promise to replace the counter displays with stand-alone displays.

3 Responding to a request
Send Giovanni in Milan an informal email. You've just sent the brochures. They should arrive in about two days.

4 Responding to an enquiry
Call Svenja and leave a message which includes the following points:
- EcoAngels (a wholesaler for organic and environmentally friendly products in Lund) stock Ecoclean (tel: 046 - 32 99 30; email: info@ecoangels.se).
- Or Uli Rietz (the Western European sales manager) can get in touch with her directly and set up an appointment. He will be in Sweden for a few days next month.

Writing formal and informal emails

Use of abbreviations	Use of slang or colloquial expressions
Formal:	*Formal:*
Could you please send the information **as soon as possible**?	Could we arrange an appointment soon to discuss the fair?
By the way, our sales manager would like to set up an appointment with you.	Mr Rietz will be in Sweden next month.
Informal:	*Informal:*
Could you please send the information **asap**?	Can we **touch base** about the preparations for the fair soon?
Btw, Uli would like to meet up with you.	Uli will **be in your neck of the woods** next month.
Use of simple vs complex language	**Leaving words out**
Formal:	*Formal:*
I'd appreciate it if you could send the brochures by Monday at the latest.	**I'm** looking forward to meeting you.
Will you be able to attend the meeting?	**I** hope this helps.
Informal:	*Informal:*
Please send the brochures by Monday.	Looking forward to meeting you.
Can you come to the meeting?	Hope this helps.

Business file

8

④ 👥 **Work with your partner to find the missing information in your sales performance chart.**

→ *Partner A: file 12, page 134;*
→ *Partner B: Look below and ask your partner questions.*

> How many did we sell last year?

> How many have we sold so far this year?

> What was the customer rating last year?

> What's the customer rating this year?

Model	Units sold last year (000s)	Customer rating last year	Units sold this year (000s)	Customer rating this year
PW1710	10	●●●●		
PW2340			9.5	●●●●
PW3500		●●●●●		●●●●●
PW4500	3		1.8	
PW5340			11	●●●
PW6240	11	●●●		

Customer rating key*

very poor ●
poor ●●
average ●●●
good ●●●●
very good ●●●●●

* in terms of reliability and price

⑤ 👥 **Write a report to Joan Winters about the Gemini range. Make sure that you cover all the points in her email. Organize your report into four sections:**

- **Aim:** why you are writing
- **Findings:** the facts and the figures
- **Speculation:** what you think the reasons could be for the success or failure of some of the different models.
- **Conclusions and recommendations:** your opinion and suggestions

Writing a report

Terms of reference
Joan Winters requested this report on the performance of the Gemini range of electric bikes.

Aim
The aim of this report is to compare/review/ examine/contrast/recommend …

Findings
Our findings are as follows: …
We found that …
 … customer ratings (for…) have risen/ fallen compared to last year.
 … sales/customer ratings have remained the same/stable.
 … two/three/… out of six products …
 (but two products …)
 … problems were encountered with some models.

Speculation
This might be due to … the economic situation / the old-fashioned design / …
Perhaps this is because of changes in taste / the high price / …

Conclusions and recommendations
It is clear from these findings that progress has been made…
The most common suggestion for improvement was …
The best-selling / least successful product is / products are …
On the one hand, … . On the other hand, …
Based on the above findings we recommend that … should be considered.
In the light of these findings we suggest that …

> *Das Passiv wird oft in Berichten verwendet:*
> - *Progress <u>has been made</u>.*
> - *We found that problems <u>were encountered</u> …*

8 Grammar summary

Adjective + infinitive

1. The electrical bike is **safe to use**.
   The instructions aren't **easy to understand**.
   The benefits are **clear to see**.
2. This year's report is **more difficult to understand** than last year's.
   The video was **easier to watch** in English than in German.

beautiful	to look at
comfortable	to hold
difficult	to access
easy	to eat
good	to handle
hard	to beat
impossible	to forget
simple	to operate

Nach bestimmten Adjektiven kann der *to-infinitive* benutzt werden (**1**).

Das Adjektiv kann dabei auch gesteigert werden (**2**).

> Die Verbindung von Adjektiven und to-Infinitiven wird häufig in Produktbeschreibungen oder Verkaufsgesprächen verwendet. Sie wird im Deutschen auch mit „lässt sich" übersetzt:
> - The rucksack is easy to handle. (Der Rucksack lässt sich leicht handhaben.)

Adverb + past participle

1. Our customers are **satisfied** with the new, **improved** engine.
2. The trade fair tickets are **reasonably priced**.
   The goods were **nicely packaged**.
   The display stands were **badly damaged** so we couldn't use them.
3. The new product was **well received**.
   The meeting was **well organized**.

Das *past participle* (oder Partizip Perfekt) kann als Adjektiv verwendet werden (to satisfy → satisfied; to improve → improved) (**1**).

Adjektive können durch Adverbien verstärkt werden. Das Adverb steht dann vor dem Adjektiv (**2**).

Achtung! Aus *good* wird auch hier *well* (**3**).

Past perfect

1. When I got there, the meeting **had begun**.
   As I **hadn't seen** John at the stand, I rang him up later to see why he **hadn't stopped** by.
   Why **had** they **set up** the stand before the marketing director arrived?
2. The sales rep **had left** the stand **by the time** I got there.
   They **had** already **unpacked** the equipment **when** I arrived.
   The fair lasted till Sunday afternoon but most people **had gone** home **by Saturday evening**.

I		
he / she / it	had ('d)	worked …
you / we / they	had not (hadn't)	done …

3. It **started** to rain when we **left** the fair.
   I **arranged** an appointment and then **told** my PA to confirm it.

Das *past perfect* wird verwendet, um zwei oder mehrere Handlungen zu beschreiben, die in der Vergangenheit aufeinander folgten. Die Handlung, die zeitlich am weitesten zurückliegt, steht im *past perfect* (**1**).

Häufig verwendete Signalwörter sind *already*, *by*, *by the time* und *when* (**2**).

Das *past perfect* wird mit *had* und dem Partizip Perfekt gebildet. Für die Liste der unregelmäßigen Verben und deren dritten Formen, siehe S. 194.

Wenn zwei Handlungen direkt aufeinander folgen, können beide im *simple past* stehen. Häufig ist dabei die zweite Handlung eine Folge der Ersten (**3**).

Extra practice 8

1 Rewrite these sentences as in the example. Use an adjective + infinitive.

1. Manufacturing mobile phones is expensive.   *Mobile phones are expensive to manufacture.*
2. Understanding his English was easy.

   His English ....
3. Using this detergent is safe.

   This ....
4. Transporting these goods has been difficult.

   ....
5. Organizing the meeting is going to be complicated.

   ....
6. Answering his queries was hard.

   ....

2 Link words from the two boxes to complete these sentences.

> beautifully   perfectly   completely   technologically   reasonably
>
> priced   made   advanced   designed   safe

1. The solar panels are .... – much cheaper than I had expected.
2. Our factory is .... We use the latest production technology.
3. This sports equipment is .... Nothing bad can happen.
4. Can you see how this bike is ....? You won't get tired when you use it.
5. What a nice T-shirt you're wearing. It's so ....

3 Complete the product review with suitable linking words.

> although · for example · however · nonetheless · as a result

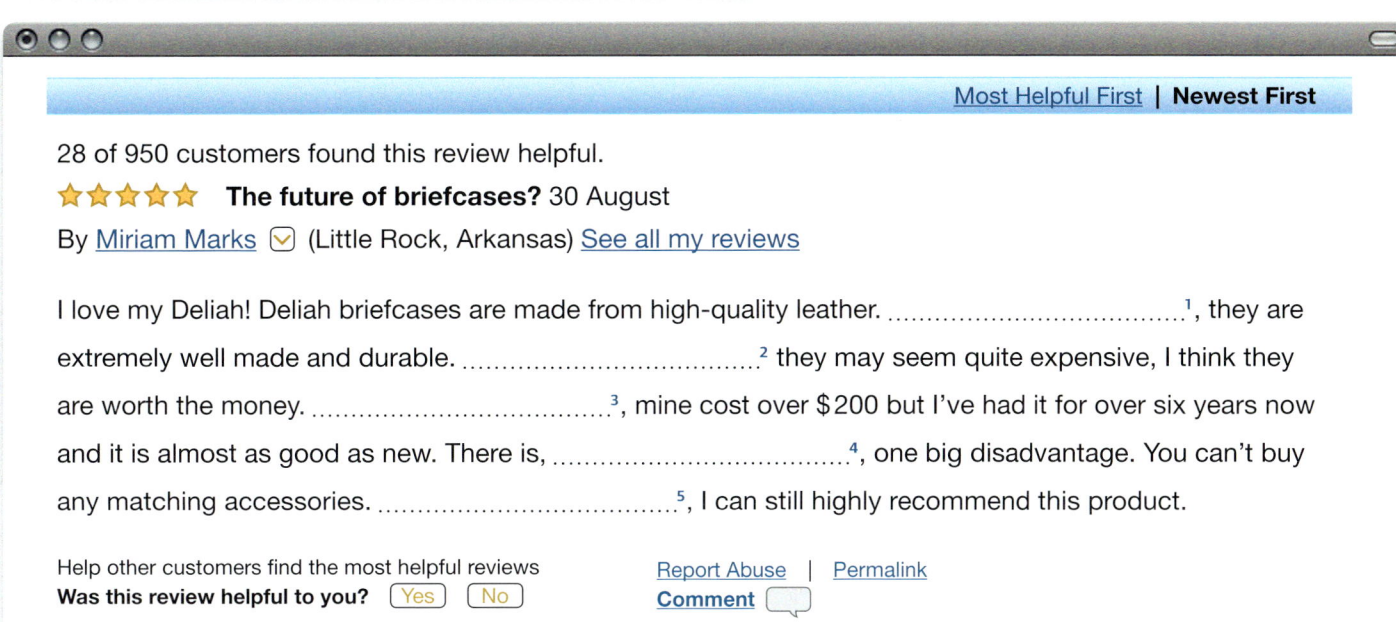

Most Helpful First | **Newest First**

28 of 950 customers found this review helpful.

★★★★★   **The future of briefcases?** 30 August

By **Miriam Marks** (Little Rock, Arkansas) **See all my reviews**

I love my Deliah! Deliah briefcases are made from high-quality leather. ....¹, they are extremely well made and durable. ....², they may seem quite expensive, I think they are worth the money. ....³, mine cost over $200 but I've had it for over six years now and it is almost as good as new. There is, ...⁴, one big disadvantage. You can't buy any matching accessories. ....⁵, I can still highly recommend this product.

Help other customers find the most helpful reviews   Report Abuse | Permalink
Was this review helpful to you? Yes No   Comment

8 Extra practice

4 Complete the sentences with the past perfect form of the verbs in brackets.

1 It's been a busy day. I think I **'d already read** (already/read) 100 emails by nine o'clock this morning.
2 They .... (see) our website on the Internet by the time they contacted us.
3 She .... (already/phone) him to ask about the order when I arrived in the office yesterday.
4 We .... (try) to solve the problem many times before, so it was a relief when we finally found a solution.
5 How many reports .... (you/write) by the end of last week?
6 Why .... (his boss/not/be) in touch before today?

5 Select the correct verb forms to complete the text: simple past or past perfect.

We cleared / had cleared ¹ up everything at the stand after the last customers left / had left ², and then we had / had had ³ some champagne to celebrate a successful three days. Later, a friend who works for a different company joined / had joined ⁴ me, and we walked / had walked ⁵ out of the building together. At that moment it started / had started ⁶ raining. Unfortunately, I left / had left ⁷ my umbrella back at the stand and I didn't feel / hadn't felt ⁸ like running back for it, so I got / had got ⁹ wet.

6 Fill in the gaps with words from the box and decide if these email phrases are formal (F) or informal (I).

appreciate · asap · Btw · hope · speaking of which · touch base

1 ___ Great that your holiday worked out. ...., who's my contact while you're away?
2 ___ I'd .... it if you could send the documents by Monday.
3 ___ Let's .... sometime next month.
4 ___ Please send the documents ....
5 ___ We can discuss this at our next meeting ...., which date would suit you best?
6 ___ .... this helps. If not, give me a ring.

7 Complete the sentences with the correct noun form of these verbs.

complain · complete · fail · offer · perform · prepare · respond · succeed

1 The trade fair was a big .... We managed to to talk to a lot of buyers.
2 We had to do a lot of .... before the fair but it was worth it.
3 These figures show this year's sales ....
4 The .... date for the project is May next year.
5 He got a great job .... but he said no and stayed with his company.
6 How many .... did you receive to our email?
7 Excuse me, I'd like to make a .... about your service.
8 Why hadn't they prepared? The whole thing was a complete ....

Extra practice 8

8 Match these sentence halves from a report.

1. ☐ Bob Carr requested this report
2. ☐ The aim of this report
3. ☐ We found that
4. ☐ This might be due
5. ☐ Or perhaps this is because
6. ☐ Based on the above findings

a. sales increased significantly from May to July.
b. to our innovative sales campaign.
c. is to decide whether to continue our sales campaign.
d. we recommend continuing with the campaign.
e. on sales performance in the last two quarters.
f. of the poor performance of our competitors.

9 Translate into English.

1. Die Waren auf der Rechnung sind nicht die, die wir erhalten haben.
2. Die Besucher auf der Messe waren sehr preisbewusst.
3. Unsere neue Produktreihe bietet ein gutes Preis-Leistungsverhältnis.
4. Wir sollten den Prospekt ins Englische übersetzen.
5. Die Verkaufszahlen von dem neuen KX-Model sehen gut aus!
6. Meine Kollegin hatte die Broschüren am Stand vergessen.

Typical mistakes

1. I think the **goods** from Italy are reasonably priced.
   NOT ... the ~~wares~~ from Italy ...
2. We did a lot of networking **at/during** the trade fair.
   NOT ... networking ~~on~~ the trade fair.
3. This new detergent is good **value for money**.
   NOT This new detergent is good ~~worth for money~~.
4. The new **brochure** looks quite good.
   NOT The new ~~prospect~~ looks quite good.
5. Let's have a look at the **sales figures for** the lighting equipment.
   NOT ... the ~~sales figures of~~ the equipment.
6. I have **left** the giveaways in the office!
   NOT I have ~~forgotten~~ the giveaways ...

Culture spot

Email etiquette

Emails are key relationship-building tools, so it is important to choose your words carefully in order to strike the right tone. This is especially true when writing to people from other cultures. The message you think is just quick and to the point might come across as cold and unfriendly.

- Start off with a warm greeting before you ask your question or make your request. Begin with a comment like *How's it going?* or *Hope you had a nice weekend*. In more formal emails, you can make a reference to why you are writing before making your request: *As you know we are conducting a customer survey, and we'd really appreciate your input*.
- At the end of the email, try to include a friendly comment before signing off: *Thank you for your time and consideration, Thank you very much in advance* or *I look forward to hearing from you*.
- If you need to ask someone for a favour, make sure it doesn't sound like a demand. In formal emails, you can soften your request: *I was wondering if you could provide me with some information*. In informal ones it's a good idea to indicate clearly that you know this is a favour: *Could you do me a favour?*
- When you are late replying to an email, it's important to acknowledge this fact. In informal emails, you could begin by saying *Sorry for my late reply*; in more formal ones, *I apologize for the delay in replying to your email*.

to strike the right tone	den richtigen Ton treffen
to the point	sachdienlich
to sign off	sich verabschieden

9 Culture matters

In this unit you will ...

- talk about a company's history
- discuss international management styles
- explain a menu

Business file

- practise making and handling complaints

Part A New management

▶ What kind of training programmes does your company offer? How many have you attended? What did you learn at the last one?

1 Read this page from the website of an American company called Sutton Associates, and answer the questions.

1 What services does the company offer?
2 How successful has it been compared to other companies in this industry?
3 Where did the company begin and where is it located today?

Sutton Associates
Changing the way companies do business globally

• Home   • About us   • Intercultural Service   • References   • News   • Links   • Contact

For over 30 years we have been changing people's lives and the way they do business.

In 1980, Eric James Sutton began a mission to revolutionize the way people learn and communicate with the help of technology. His mission continues today.

Sutton Associates is one of the world's leading corporate and cross-cultural training providers, and specializes in intercultural team building programs. We also offer relocation training and consulting to organizations that want to help their employees on global assignments make a smooth transfer and adapt quickly to local cultures.

New ideas, competitive prices and useful products: these key words define Sutton.

Global presence – local roots

With 9% of the global market in intercultural team training both online and on site, Sutton is active in North and South America, Europe and Asia. But, true to our roots, we are still based in Cleveland, Ohio, the city where Eric James Sutton brought experts in management and diversity together to launch our first intercultural business seminar.

Find words in the text that have the same or similar meanings to the words below. (Sometimes there is more than one answer.)

1 task
2 to completely change
3 advising
4 international
5 without problems
6 moving to a new place
7 to fit in with
8 variety

■ Did you know?

Relocation services begleiten Geschäftsprozesse, bei denen Mitarbeiter und deren Familien oder auch ganze Abteilungen umsiedeln. Dieser Service wird entweder intern oder durch externe Dienstleister durchgeführt.

Part A   9

2 Look at this sentence from Sutton Associates' website:

'For over 30 years we **have been changing** people's lives and the way they do business.'

Which question does this sentence answer best?

1 ☐ How have they changed people's lives?
2 ☐ How long have they been in business?
3 ☐ How do they do business?

> **Present perfect continuous**
>
> How long **has** Sutton **been providing** cross-cultural training?
> It's **been providing** cross-cultural training for over 30 years / since 1980.
> How long **have** you **been learning** English?
> I **have been learning** English (ever) since I started school.

3 Complete the sentences about the history of Sutton Associates. Use the present perfect continuous.

1 Sutton .... (sell) its products in the UK since 1985.
2 They .... (offer) programmes for international team building since 1995.
3 The company .... (send out) its newsletter to subscribers for over a decade.
4 The staff .... (provide) courses on cross-cultural and diversity training since 2002.

👥 Look at the timeline below and ask each other questions.

- How long have they been offering relocation consulting services?
- How long has Tony Alda been president?
- When did they open a sales office in Munich?

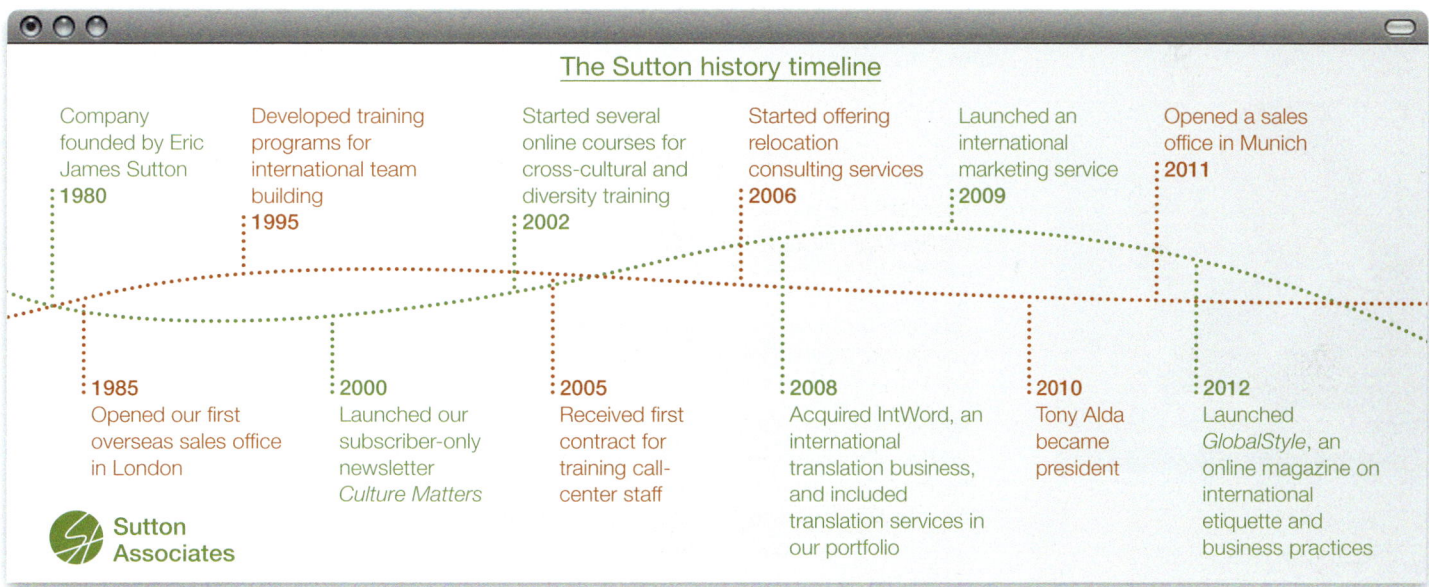

4 👥 Interview your partner. Find out how long he/she has been doing certain things.

> your current address · your job ·
> English or other languages · current sports or interests

Georg, how long have you been living here in Munich?
Oh, I'm not sure exactly. About five years, I think.

9 Culture matters — Part A

5 Kurt Müller writes an enquiry to Sutton Associates. Read the email and decide whether the statements below are true or false.

> Dear Ms Carstons
>
> I have been reading Culture Matters ever since it began and am a big fan.
>
> I am the HR Training Manager at Krüger GmbH, a financial services provider in Munich. We're being taken over in October this year by a large insurance company based in Atlanta, Georgia. Ever since our staff found out about the takeover, they have been very concerned about the future change in management style and are not sure how they will be able to work together with the new colleagues.
>
> I've only been in Munich since the beginning of the year, so I'm not sure if you offer on-site trainings here. If so, we would definitely be interested in your terms and conditions, etc. As soon as I hear from you, I'll gladly provide you with details about our requirements.
>
> Thank you very much in advance.
>
> Best regards
>
> Kurt Müller
> HR Training Manager

		true	false
1	Kurt already knows Amy Carstons quite well.	☐	☐
2	Kurt's company has been taken over by a US firm.	☐	☐
3	He has been looking for a suitable relocation programme for a couple of months.	☐	☐
4	The staff will have to work with American colleagues in the future and is worried about the takeover.	☐	☐
5	Kurt's been living in Munich ever since he began working for Krüger.	☐	☐

6 Amy immediately writes an email to Tony Alda. Select the correct word: *if* or *when*. What does Amy offer to do?

> Hi Tony,
>
> Not sure where you are exactly but fingers crossed you've already arrived in Munich. Just wanted to forward you this email. Interesting, isn't it? If/When ¹ you are still on a plane somewhere in Europe, I know you can't answer immediately, but asap would be good. Can you give Herr Müller from Krüger GmbH a call if/when ² you get to Munich? I googled his company and they seem to be a very interesting potential client. If/When ³ you want to meet up with him, let me know and I will set up a meeting if/when ⁴ you don't have time to organize things yourself.
>
> Amy
>
> PS Btw, you wanted some tips for eating out. If/When ⁵ my brother-in-law is in Munich, he always goes here. They have some great regional specialties there (if/when ⁶ you like German food, that is ;-).

Remember:
if = „falls" (Bedingung)
when = „wenn" (Zeit)

Compare the style of the two emails.
Which one is more formal? How do you know?

7 🔊 2.28 Amy gets a voicemail from Tony. What's the problem? Help her write the email.

→ *See page 98 and the Business Correspondence section for help with writing emails.*

108

Part B At a restaurant

▸ What are the local specialities in your region?
What kind of exotic foods have you tried on trips abroad?

1 🔊 2.29 After an afternoon meeting with Kurt, Tony invites him out for a meal. Listen and answer the questions.

1. How do you think the meeting in the afternoon went? Why?
2. What impression do you have of Tony? Is he a friendly, open-minded person or slightly conservative? Why do you say that?
3. How is this German restaurant different from the places Tony knows in the USA?

What did they say? Complete these sentences using the correct form of *get* or an expression with *get*. Then listen again and check your answers.

1. So, you can't .... this type of beer in Cleveland then?
2. We need you to .... the training as soon as possible.
3. We'll make sure that everybody .... each other early on.
4. We try to .... the ideas .... in a light and humorous way.
5. Speaking of which, I .... hungry.
6. I .... Bavarian cuisine.

Changing the subject

Talking of atmosphere, it's very nice here, isn't it.
Speaking of which, let's order.
By the way, have you ever …?
Anyway, what's for lunch?
Well, shall we order now?

2 Match the sentence halves.

1	What main ideas did you manage to get	a	home in the evenings?
2	In what kind of situations do you sometimes get	b	know new colleagues?
3	When are you going to get	c	used to your latest phone?
4	What is the quickest way for you to get	d	impatient or irritated?
5	How long did it take you to get	e	across at your last meeting?
6	How long does it take you to get to	f	started on your next project?

👥 Now ask your partner the questions.

3 Read these two sentences out loud. Do the blue words sound the same or different?

> You can try but it's hard to find.

> That's the heart of the matter, isn't it?

🔊 2.30 Listen and tick the word you hear.

1	☐ heart	☐ hard	5	☐ simple	☐ symbol
2	☐ cap	☐ cab	6	☐ spice	☐ spies
3	☐ piece	☐ peas	7	☐ built	☐ billed
4	☐ life	☐ live	8	☐ safe	☐ save

👥 Now read four of the words out loud. Can your partner tell which words you said?

9 Culture matters — Part B

Explaining a menu

These are cold/hot dishes / starters / main courses / snacks / side dishes / sweets.
It's a sort/kind of … beef/pork/veal/chicken/sausage/vegetable/dumpling/sauce.
It's fried/roasted/boiled/baked (in an oven).
It's salty/sweet/delicious / quite heavy / organically grown / vegetarian.
It's a local speciality.
It's cooked 'house style'.
It's home-made.

4 Can you help Kurt? Use phrases from the box on the left and your dictionary if necessary to help explain the menu to Tony.

SPEZIALITÄTEN

Suppen und Eintöpfe
- Fränkische Brotsuppe •
- Hausgemachter Kalbseintopf •

Hauptspeisen
- Tafelspitz mit Schnittlauchsauce, Apfelkren und Kartoffelbrei (Spezialität des Hauses) •
- Schweinshaxe •
- Allgäuer Kasspatzn mit Röstzwiebeln •
- Ofenfrischer Schweinsbraten mit Semmelknödel •
- Schupfnudeln mit Sauerkraut •
- Wiener Schnitzel mit Pommes frites und gemischtem Salat •

- Knuspriges Brathähnchen •
- Gebackene Kartoffel mit Schmand •

Brotzeit
- Münchner Weißwürste mit Brezn und süßem Senf •

Beilagen
- Sauerkraut • frischer Biospargel •
- Röstkartoffeln • Kartoffelknödel •
- Semmelknödel •

Dessert
- hausgemachtes Apfelkücherl •
- Germknödel mit Vanillesauce •

---

5 You are hosting a dinner for some business partners. You want to serve a nice mix of local specialities and some of your favourite dishes. Write a menu.

> *Asparagus soup*
> ✷ ✷ ✷
> *Grilled chicken breast topped with a creamy garlic and mushroom sauce*
> ✷ ✷ ✷
> *'Rote Grütze' with whipped cream*

Now work with a different partner. Take it in turns as host to explain your menu to your guest.

6 Sutton Associates prints humorous articles on the last page of their newsletter. Read the 'five bad rules' for people doing business abroad. Can you rewrite them so that they make sense?

Five BAD rules for guaranteeing that your corporate relationships with foreign business partners always fail

1. Always expect people to adapt to you. Never adapt to them.
2. Don't do any research into the country beforehand. There's plenty of time for your business partner to show you around when you arrive.
3. Never smile! If you smile too much, people will think you are making fun of them.
4. Speak loudly. When you speak at the top of your voice, it encourages people to understand what you are saying.
5. If your business partner takes you to a local restaurant, complain about the strange meals on the menu. It will show you have special taste.

Part B

9

7 Complete these rules with the missing words. Are the rules 'good' or 'bad'?

to answer · to respect · ~~to share~~ · to speak · not to tell

1 Invite foreign visitors **to share** information about how they do things in their countries.
2 Expect foreigners .... your language if they come to your country.
3 If you want your business partners .... you, make sure you wear a suit and carry a briefcase.
4 Advise visitors .... jokes, as different cultures don't have the same sense of humour.
5 Force people .... questions about their personal life. It's important to know everything about the people you do business with.

Verb + object + infinitive

Do you **want me to help** you?
I'd **like him to arrive** on time.
We **don't expect them to understand** everything at once.
They **warned me not to take** a taxi from the airport.

8 Read these descriptions of how three different companies handle corporate culture, and decide what each company sells: mobile homes, perfume or soft drinks.

A
We have made English our official corporate language because we are fast becoming a global player, and it is easier to communicate in one language. Our motto is 'Think global, act local', so we encourage local staff to keep their national identity. After all, we have to adapt our products to local tastes, and don't expect people in every country to like the same degree of sweetness.

B
We have been expanding and globalizing over the last few years but we still want to keep our national identity, as this is very much a part of our image and important for the marketing of our beauty product. After all, we encourage our foreign staff to adapt to our local culture. It is in their best interests to learn our local language if they are interested in career advancement.

C
We have been downplaying our national origins since we began to globalize in 2008. We stress our unique corporate values such as design, mobility and performance. We want all our staff to understand our culture. To help them do this, we have also set up an internal multinational team to advise our staff across the organization on our company values (e.g. dress code, customer care, etc.).

Which company would you prefer to work in? Why?

9 Work in small groups. Imagine you are relocation specialists who are giving advice to people transfering to your company (or a different company in your country). Make a list of rules they should follow to ensure a smooth transition.

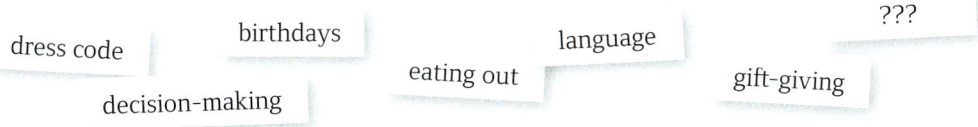

Giving advice

As far as the dress code / … is concerned, it's important to remember …
If you want …, you had better (not) ….
You don't have to …, but you probably should …
Most people here expect …
More and more business people here …
It's hard to generalize, but it's usually better to …

111

9 Culture matters | Business file

I'm very sorry about this

1 🔊 2.31 Megan Taylor works in Sunrise Electronics' customer-service department. It's part of her job to deal with complaints. Listen. Why is her current caller dissatisfied?

Complete the phrases Megan uses. Listen again and check your answers.

1 Yes, Mr Clarke, I .... your call.

2 Oh dear, I'm ....

3 There's been .... for this product.

4 I'm afraid your order .... yet.

5 I .... our shipping department immediately.

6 Should I ask them to .... by express?

7 Thank you so much .... , Mr Clarke.

8 I .... for the delay.

2 Match the phrases Megan uses to the tips a–d below for dealing with complaints.

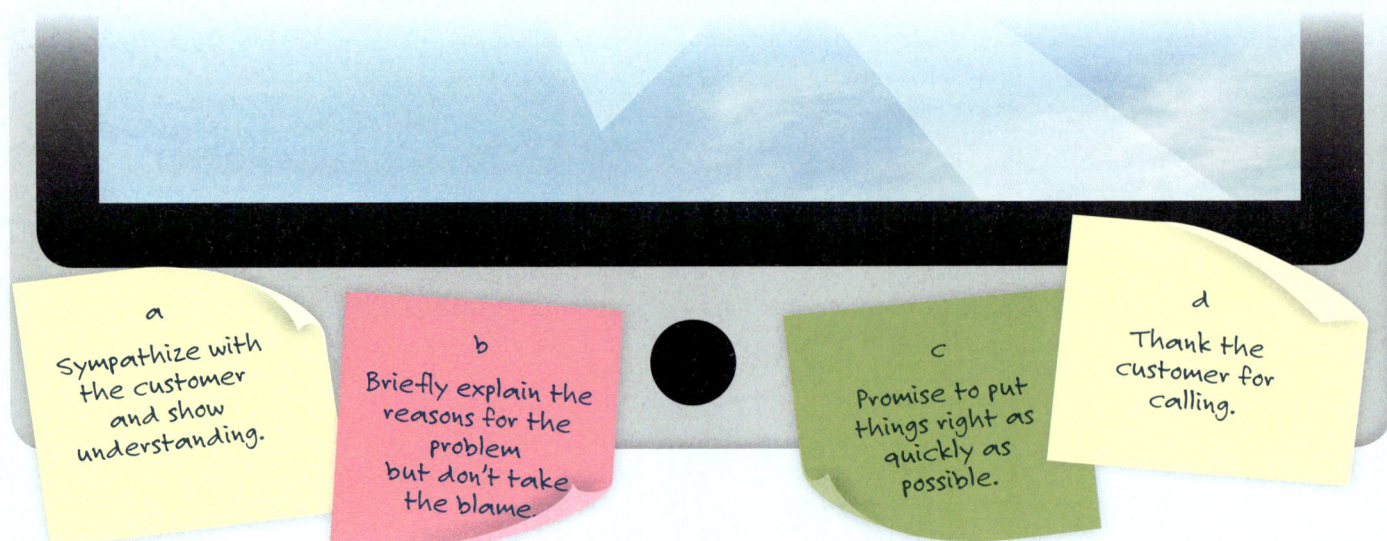

a Sympathize with the customer and show understanding.

b Briefly explain the reasons for the problem but don't take the blame.

c Promise to put things right as quickly as possible.

d Thank the customer for calling.

Business file 9

3 Read the following extract from a business magazine. Whose point of view about handling complaints do you agree or disagree with most? Why?

Ask the experts
This week we asked some customer-care experts for their perspective on customer complaints.

Most customers just want to talk to someone and let off steam. Try to calm the customer down and promise to take care of the matter. Whatever you do, don't take personal responsibility for the problem as this will give the company a bad name. Sometimes it's even OK to tell a few 'white lies' if that's what you need to do to protect your company's reputation. Offer the customers a discount on their next order, a small gift or a cash incentive.

I think companies should set up a hotline, especially for customer complaints. It's important to encourage customers to complain officially, otherwise they will just complain to their family and friends. Your business will get a bad name and you won't understand the reasons why. If you can't help a customer, recommend one of your competitors. The customer will appreciate your honesty and willingness to help.

Write some guidelines for dealing with complaints in your company (or in a company that you know well).

4 Work with a partner to practise making and handling complaints over the phone.

→ *Partner A: file 13, page 135;* → *Partner B: file 27, page 141*

5 Interview your partner.
1 When did he/she last complain to a company?
2 How did he/she complain (by email, in a phone call, in person)?
3 What was the problem? What happened after he/she complained?

Role-play one of the situations and present your dialogue to the class.

Making and handling complaints

Making complaints
I'm calling/ringing about …
There seems to be a slight / a bit of a problem.
I'm afraid we haven't received the shipment yet.
It looks like I was sent the wrong order.
A number of items in the consignment were faulty/damaged/broken.
What do you want me to do with the consignment?
I'm very dissatisfied/unhappy with the service you provided.
What kind of compensation can you offer us?

Handling complaints
How can I help you? / What can I do for you?
What's the problem exactly?
Oh dear, I'm sorry to hear that.
Do you have an order/invoice number for me?
Obviously, something has gone wrong here.
I'm afraid the delivery has been held up a bit.
The order hasn't been processed yet.
I am very sorry about this.
I'll deal with this straight away.
I'll sort this out for you immediately.
I'll look into it now and call you back.
Thank you very much for calling.

> Bei Beschwerden verwenden wir häufig das Passiv um Probleme höflich und indirekt – und ohne Schuldzuweisungen – anzusprechen:
> • I'm afraid the delivery has been held up a bit.

9 Grammar summary

Present perfect continuous

1 I **have been learning** Italian for three years.
She **has been working** here since 1995.
Have you **been sitting** here all evening?
How long **have** they **been living** here?

I	have ('ve) haven't	
he / she / it	has ('s) hasn't	been working
you / we / they	have ('ve) haven't	

Mit dem *present perfect continuous* beschreibt man Ereignisse oder Handlungen, die in der Vergangenheit begonnen haben und bis in die Gegenwart andauern. Dabei wird die Dauer dieser Ereignisse oder Handlungen betont (**1**).

2 I**'ve known** John for three years.
(Nicht: I've been knowing John for three years.)
We**'ve been** here since eight o'clock.
(Nicht: We've been being here since eight o'clock.)

Bei Verben wie *know* und *be* (Zustandsverben) wird keine Verlaufsform, sondern die einfache Form des *present perfect* verwendet (**2**).

Present perfect continuous vs present perfect simple

1 I**'ve been attending** training programmes for years, but this training **has changed** my life!
We**'ve been reading** the newsletter since January, but I **haven't read** the most recent one yet.

2 I**'ve been living** / I**'ve lived** here for three years.
We**'ve been working** / We**'ve worked** for this company since 2001.

Das *present perfect continuous* betont die Dauer, das *present perfect* dagegen das Ergebnis einer Handlung oder eines Geschehens (**1**).

Die Verben *live* und *work* können – meistens ohne Bedeutungsunterschied – sowohl mit der einfachen Form des *present perfect* als auch mit dem *present perfect continuous* verwendet werden (**2**).

Verb + objective + infinitive

1 He **asked me to send** him the email.
I **didn't want my colleagues to ask** any questions.
Would you **like somebody to help** you?

advise	force	teach
ask	invite	tell
cause	like	warn
expect	remind	would like

Auf bestimmte Verben (siehe Auswahl im Kasten) kann ein Objekt und ein *to-infinitive* folgen (**1**).

2 My boss **wants** me to stay longer.
(Nicht: My boss wants that I stay longer.)
I**'d like** you to check this.
(Nicht: I'd like that you check this.)

3 She **didn't ask me to leave**.
= *Sie bat mich nicht, zu gehen.*
She **asked me not to leave**.
= *Sie bat mich, nicht zu gehen.*
They **haven't asked me to call**.
= *Sie haben mich nicht gebeten, anzurufen.*
They**'ve asked me not to call**.
= *Sie haben mich gebeten, nicht anzurufen.*

Vorsicht: Bei *want* und *would like* wird kein *that*-Satz verwendet (**2**).

Bei der Verneinung kann, je nach Bedeutung, entweder das Verb oder der *to-infinitive* verneint werden (**3**).

Extra practice 9

1 Complete the sentences with the present perfect continuous form of the verbs in the box.

feel · not live · produce · sell · wait · work

1. We .... tyres for over 50 years.
2. I'm afraid the customer .... for the delivery for three weeks now.
3. Harry and I .... for our company for 10 years.
4. Since the news was announced, all the employees .... worried.
5. We .... here long. We moved here last June.
6. How long .... you .... insurance?

2 Choose the best verb form: present perfect simple or present perfect continuous.

1. A: Have you written / Have you been writing the report?
   B: Yes, but it isn't finished yet.
2. A: How many reports have you written / have you been writing today?
   B: Three and a half, but I've nearly finished the last one now, luckily.
3. A: Have you seen / Have you been seeing Tim?
   B: No, I haven't. Is he even in the office today?
4. A: How long has Bernd attended / has Bernd been attending English courses?
   B: Well, this is his second one, I'd say.
5. A: Have you ever thought / Have you ever been thinking about moving to a different company?
   B: No, not even once.

3 Complete the message with the correct form of words from the box.

adapt · international · make · mission · range · revolutionize · search

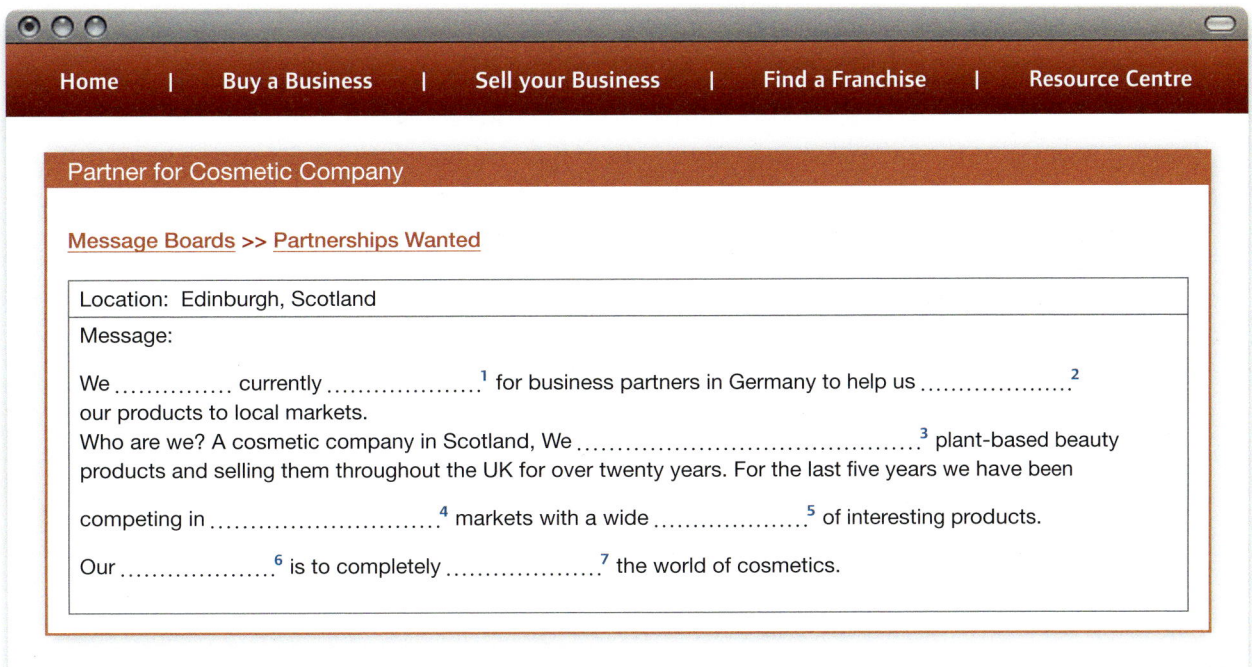

Partner for Cosmetic Company

Message Boards >> Partnerships Wanted

Location: Edinburgh, Scotland
Message:
We .... currently .... ¹ for business partners in Germany to help us .... ² our products to local markets.
Who are we? A cosmetic company in Scotland, We .... ³ plant-based beauty products and selling them throughout the UK for over twenty years. For the last five years we have been competing in .... ⁴ markets with a wide .... ⁵ of interesting products.
Our .... ⁶ is to completely .... ⁷ the world of cosmetics.

9 Extra practice

4 Complete these sentences using expressions with *get*.

1 I didn't really understand the point he was trying to ...., did you?

2 It isn't easy to .... the way people do business over here, but I'm learning a lot every day.

3 It's already ten past nine. Shall we .... then? We have a lot to do today.

4 We first .... each other at university and we've been best friends ever since.

5 It .... late. Shall we stop here and carry on tomorrow?

5 Use the verbs and objects below to complete the sentences. Be careful: you'll need to use two negative forms.

> arrive   hurry   me   him
> smoke   come   them   her
> wait   translate   us   you

1 **A:** Would you like .... the menu for you?
B: No, thanks. I did German at school so I understand most of it.

2 **A:** I didn't expect .... so early.
B: Me neither. I didn't think they'd arrive before seven.

3 **A:** We don't want .... There's still a lot of time left.
B: It's OK. I'll be able to get it to you by Friday.

4 **A:** She warned .... late to the meeting.
B: I know, but he came late anyway.

5 **A:** I wouldn't like .... too long at the railway station.
B: Don't worry. Bill promised to pick her up on time.

6 **A:** They expect .... until after the meeting.
B: That's all right. We're all non-smokers, aren't we?

6 Complete this restaurant dialogue with words and phrases from the box.

> anyway · delicious · I'd like to · It's a sort of · local speciality · speaking of

A: What is this dish here?

B: *Eintopf?* ....¹ soup with meat and vegetables. It's

.................................². You'll like it.

A: Is it a ....³?

B: Yes, and it's very popular in this area. ....⁴ which, would you like to do a bit of sightseeing tomorrow?

A: Well, ...⁵, but I'm not sure if I have time. Can I let you know tomorrow morning?

B: Sure! ....⁶, are you ready to order?

116

Extra practice 9

7 🔊 2.32 Listen and take notes for the customer-care agent.

Customer: ....
Order no.: ....
Reason for call: ....
Action plan: ....

8 Translate into English.
1 Ausländische Besucher zu treffen macht viel Spaß.
2 Seit wann sind Sie schon Geschäftspartner?
3 Letztes Jahr wurde unsere Tochtergesellschaft in Polen von einem kanadischen Unternehmen übernommen.
4 Können Sie mir bitte die Speisekarte bringen?
5 Willst du, dass wir nach einem neuen Trainingsanbieter suchen?
6 Sie sollten Ihren Führungsstil an die lokale Kultur anpassen.
7 Wir arbeiten schon den ganzen Tag an den Beschwerden.

Typical mistakes

1 I think eating local food is **fun**.
   NOT   *I think eating local food is funny.*
2 How long **has** she **been** the HR director?
   NOT   *How long is she the HR director?*
3 Our company will be **taken over** by a Chinese competitor.
   NOT   *Our company will be overtaken by …*
4 Would you like me to translate the **menu** for you?
   NOT   *… to translate the card for you?*
5 Do you **want me to** meet up with the client?
   NOT   *Do you want that I meet up …?*
6 I think we should **adapt** our products **to** the local culture.
   NOT   *… adapt our products on the local culture.*
7 We **have been stressing** our corporate values for years.
   NOT   *We stress our corporate values for years.*

Culture spot

Wining, dining … and paying!

It can be fun to end a business day by going out for a meal or a drink with your business partners, but it can also be awkward, especially when you're with people from another culture who might do things differently. One tricky area is deciding who picks up the tab. If you are officially invited out for a meal by the host, everything is clear. But problems can arise when invitations are given spontaneously.

For example, someone might say to you *We thought we'd go for a drink. Would you like to join us?* If you say yes and end up in a pub in Britain, the usual thing is to take it in turns to buy rounds. When it's your turn, say *It's my round. What's everybody having? Same again, Kim?*

If you're just finishing a meal with your partners, one of them might say *Let's go Dutch!* This means that everyone should pay for their own meal. Or you can offer to treat them, of course, and pay the bill yourself. Remember, don't say 'I invite you', but rather *It's my treat* or *Let me get this*.

On other occasions, you might want to turn down an invitation politely, but leave the way open for a similar invitation in the future. You could say *Well, thanks for the invitation. I appreciate it. But unfortunately I have another engagement. Perhaps another time?* In a less formal situation it might be enough to say *Oh, sorry, I can't on Monday. I'm afraid I'm tied up. But I hope I can take a rain check.*

Hey, let's do lunch sometime…

to pick up the tab	die Rechnung bezahlen
to buy a round	eine Runde ausgeben
to turn sth down	etwas ablehnen
to take a rain check	auf etwas später zurückkommen

10 Smooth operations

In this unit you will ...

- talk about supply chains
- discuss hypothetical situations and consequences
- explore the next steps for learning English

Business file

- pitch a proposal

Part A Supply chains

▶ What's a supply chain? Is it ...

a a special device for locking a factory?
b the series of processes involved in making and selling a product?
c a group of shops that have the same name and are owned by the same company?

👥 With a partner brainstorm five words that can be used to talk about supply chains.

1 Before reading the brochure below, link words from A and B to fit the definitions. What do you think the brochure will be about?

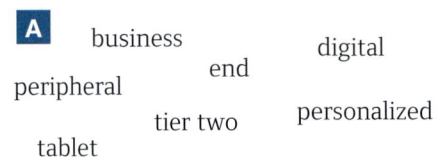
A: business, end, digital, peripheral, tier two, personalized, tablet

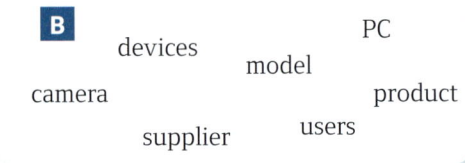
B: devices, PC, camera, model, supplier, product, users

1 a computer which normally only has a small display touch screen
2 a camera without film that uses sensors to take pictures
3 a piece of equipment that is secondary to a main device
4 the way a company plans and does business
5 the customers who actually use the products
6 when a product looks just the way you want it to
7 a company that sells goods to the manufacturer's direct supplier

2 Read the extract from a company brochure and answer the questions.

1 Where is the company based?
2 What do they sell?
3 How do their customers place an order?
4 What makes the firm different to other suppliers?

■ **Did you know?**
USP = Unique Selling Point/Proposition.

Rosco Global – European Supply Chain

The supply chain teams at the European production site of Rosco Global in Shannon, Ireland make sure that everything runs smoothly between our suppliers and their suppliers on the one hand, and our customers on the other.

We have two supply chain planning teams: a long-term and a short-term one. The long-term planning team knows how seasonal order levels rise and fall, and how to plan production weeks or months in advance. The short-term planning team makes sure that the necessary components are at the right place in the production line on a daily and weekly basis according to when and where they are needed.

At Rosco Global we specialize in tablet PCs, but we also make digital cameras, smartphones and peripheral devices like headsets, portable projectors and storage devices. Besides having top of the line products, one of our main USPs is that our customers can customize their order and get a fully personalized product direct from our factory.

Our business model is to sell directly to the end users of our electronic products, which means our customers order from us and not through a wholesaler, retailer or distribution agent. As we need to be able to react very quickly to orders, we have selected our suppliers from the local area. We have suppliers who supply directly to us (our tier one suppliers) and also suppliers who supply them (our tier two suppliers). We all work very closely together so we can react to orders and ordering trends as quickly as possible.

Part A

10

3 🔊 2.33 Declan O'Connor is talking about Rosco Global's logistics centre. Before listening, can you say what these abbreviations stand for? Then listen and check.

JIT	J..................... In T.....................
ERP	E.................... R.................... P....................
RFID	R.................... F.................... Identification
QR codes	Q.................... R.................... codes

A QR code

Are these sentences true or false? Correct the false ones.

		true	false
1	Rosco produces personalized orders in advance so that they are always in stock.	☐	☐
2	Rosco always has a large inventory in their logistics centre.	☐	☐
3	A Kanban system helps you schedule your production so that it is very efficient.	☐	☐
4	Rosco sends people to get components from tier one suppliers when their stock is low.	☐	☐
5	The RFID chips are installed in the lorries during delivery.	☐	☐
6	QR codes allow customers to follow links to information online.	☐	☐

■ **Did you know?**
Kanban ist eine Methode der Produktionsablaufsteuerung, die einen Hersteller informiert was, wann und wie viel produziert wird.

4 Match the parts of these second conditional sentences, and fill in the correct form of the verbs in brackets.

1. **b** If too many customers ordered on the same day,
2. ___ If we didn't have a JIT system in place,
3. ___ Our customers would go to our competitors,
4. ___ If we offered a greater range of products,
5. ___ If more people had smartphones,
6. ___ Our distribution would be faster,
7. ___ If we prepared a report on the European market,

a   if our quality .... (drop).
b   we **wouldn't be able to** (not/be able to) deal with the volume.
c   they .... (not/need) peripheral devices like MP3 players or car navigation systems.
d   we .... (be able to) discuss the benefits of opening a new factory in continental Europe.
e   we .... (get) more customers.
f   we .... (have) too much inventory.
g   if we .... (have) a factory in mainland Europe.

Second conditional

If we **didn't have** the flexibility to deal with orders quickly, we **would go** out of business.
If a customer **wanted** personalized products, we**'d** only **begin** production when we received the order.
It**'d be** no problem **if** they **wanted** their favourite photos on the back of their smartphone.

5 Complete these sentences so they are true for you.

1. I wouldn't have so many … if …
2. If I worked less, …
3. If I got a job offer in another city, …
4. We would … if …

👥 Tell a partner.

119

10 Smooth operations

Part A

6 Read the report. What does it recommend? What would happen if the recommendations weren't followed?

Rosco Global – Current European Market Overview

Executive summary

The report looks at recent research carried out in Rosco Global's main European markets: Germany and France. The research focuses on three main areas: sales statistics, development of country markets and recommendation for the future protection of market share.

Findings

The current European market share is 7.4%, and there are signs of strong competition emerging from Central and Eastern European countries. The fact that Rosco's main production site and distribution centre are in Ireland is increasing delivery times to continental Europe, especially Germany. …

… There are also a number of copycat producers in mainland Europe. They are copying our products and business model, and can offer more variations and faster delivery times. We are maintaining market share largely due to our reputation. Demand for personalized products, such as those produced by Rosco, is growing rapidly.

Conclusion

If action is not taken, Rosco will slowly lose market share at a rate of 1–1.5% per year.

However, if the company purchased fixed assets in mainland Europe, such as buildings or machinery, there would be a net appreciation rather than depreciation over 10–15 years. This is because the property market in Germany is stable and increasing in value.

Recommendation

We recommend that the company opens a secondary production site and distribution centre in Germany. As a result, current market share would be guaranteed and growth of around 3.5–4% would be likely within two years.

I. Braun   H. Malone
Ilke Braun and Henry Malone

Find the words or phrases in the report which mean …

1 the amount of services/products a company sells compared with other companies selling the same thing in the same market.
2 a company which makes products that are not original but instead very similar to products from other companies.
3 items of value that a company owns, normally for a longer period of time.
4 when things increase in value over time.
5 when things lose value over time.
6 the buying, selling and renting of land or buildings.

7 Make some notes and then summarize the report. Compare your summary with a partner's.

8 What do you know about these aspects of your company or a company you know well? Tell your partner.

- market share
- business model
- company software
- USPs
- production strategy
- distribution channels

Part B

Part B Budget talk

> Are you responsible for your own budget? If not, who do you talk to if you need it increased?

1 Look at the words that collocate with budget. Can you add any more to the diagram?

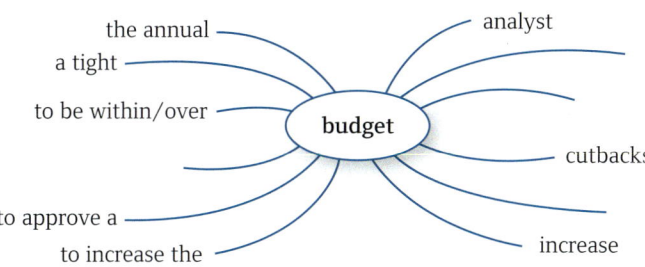

- the annual
- a tight
- to be within/over
- to approve a
- to increase the
- analyst
- cutbacks
- increase

Das englische Wort *budget* kann als Verb (to budget), Nomen (a budget) oder Adjektiv (a budget hotel) verwendet werden.

Vorsicht:
Auf Englisch wird das „t" am Ende des Wortes ausgesprochen.

budget ['bʌdʒɪt]

2 🔊 2.34 Henry Malone and Ilke Braun are talking to Declan O'Connor about the findings in their report. Listen for budget collocations from exercise 1 and tick the ones you hear.

Listen again and answer the questions.

1. What changes were made to the budget last year?
2. How much of an increase are Henry and Ilke proposing?
3. What will happen if Declan doesn't increase the budget?
4. What major investment do Henry and Ilke suggest?
5. What does a SWOT analysis look at?
6. What is Declan going to do by the end of the month?

3 What did they say? Select the right words to complete the sentences. Then listen again and check.

1. The best and most-efficient way to achieve this is to open another production site   in mainland Europe / in Ireland .
2. If you want long-term   awareness / sustainability   of the brand and company, you need to increase the annual   budget / turnover   of the company.
3. You should also look at the long-term   benefits / advantages   of this budget increase and change in   strategy / policy .
4. Sales and market   share / appreciation   will both rise, and   distribution / transport   costs will be reduced.
5. If I   approve / OK   this, we'll also need to have a back-up plan to   reduce / minimize   our risk, just in case.
6. That's why we recommend   purchasing / leasing   the new   site / factory   in Germany rather than in another country.

10 Smooth operations — Part B

Unless and in case

Unless we can speed up our delivery times, we're going to lose customers.
Unless we do this, we'll see a steady decrease in revenue.
We need to protect our brand **in case** our competitors launch an attack.
We need to aim high **in case** we have delays.

unless = „wenn ... nicht" oder „es sei denn"
in case = „für den Fall, dass"

4 Complete the sentence with *unless* or *in case*.

1. The standard delivery time has been calculated longer than necessary .... you want a personalized design.
2. .... I get the order today, I won't be able to process it before the end of the week.
3. We're going to miss our deadline .... we all work overtime.
4. We need a back-up plan .... the supplier doesn't agree to the new terms.
5. We always overestimate our development times .... there are delays.
6. We'll need to increase the budget .... we can extend the deadline.
7. We should prepare a detailed analysis .... he asks for one.

5 Make sentences relating to you and your job using *unless* and *in case*.

meet the project deadline   go over budget   ???
   work overtime   finish on time

6 First agree a topic with your partner. Then use the flow chart to practise asking for and giving approval.

Asking for and giving approval

Asking for approval
We need to increase the budget.
It's as simple as that, really.
You should also look at the long-term benefits of this.
We should see it as an investment.
That's why we recommend / need to / propose …

Giving (or denying) approval
I understand, but we're already operating under a tight budget.
Yes, I see your point. And you think this is really necessary, do you?
That's just not possible. I can't approve such a high budget increase.
If I approve this, we also need to have a back-up plan to minimize our risk, just in case.

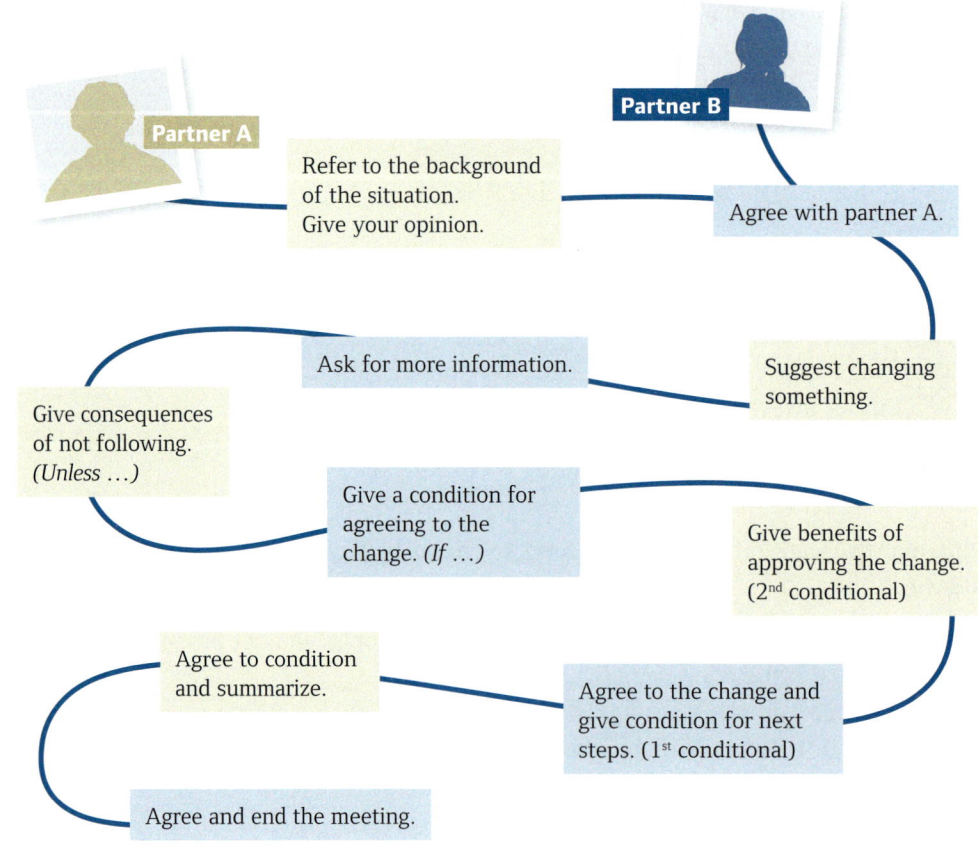

Partner A / Partner B

Refer to the background of the situation. Give your opinion. → Agree with partner A. → Suggest changing something. → Ask for more information. → Give consequences of not following. (Unless …) → Give a condition for agreeing to the change. (If …) → Give benefits of approving the change. (2nd conditional) → Agree to condition and summarize. → Agree to the change and give condition for next steps. (1st conditional) → Agree and end the meeting.

7 Work with a partner to practise asking for and giving (or denying) approval.

→ Partner A: file 14, page 135; → Partner B: file 28, page 141

Part B   10

8 **What's most important to you in a project?**

- Finishing on time.
- Finishing within budget.
- Having a solution that works 100%.
- Having a solution that works but isn't perfect; the rest can be fixed later.

List the reasons for your choice. Then find a partner who thinks differently and argue your point.

9 🔊 2.35 **Declan has been learning German for a number of years now. Listen and tick the learning strategies he mentions.**

1. ☐ listening to coursebook CDs
2. ☐ listening to German podcasts
3. ☐ chatting with native speakers over the Internet
4. ☐ playing online scrabble
5. ☐ reading German newspapers
6. ☐ taking pictures and discussing them
7. ☐ watching German TV programmes
8. ☐ doing a treasure hunt

How has he used technology for language learning over the years? Complete the sentences in your own words.

1. Declan used to drive to work. During the commute he …
2. After he started to commute by train, he …
3. Ever since he has owned a smartphone, …
4. At a recent lesson, he and the other students …
5. He is currently …
6. He's also just started to …
7. He's going to visit Germany soon and …

Which strategies above have you already tried for learning English? If you had time or the right equipment, what else would you try? Tell your partner.

10 **Brainstorm ways to practise English in your spare time, either using a smartphone or not.**

Watching videos

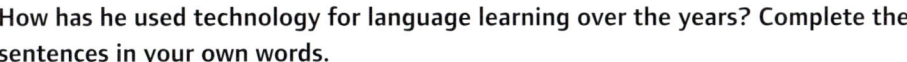

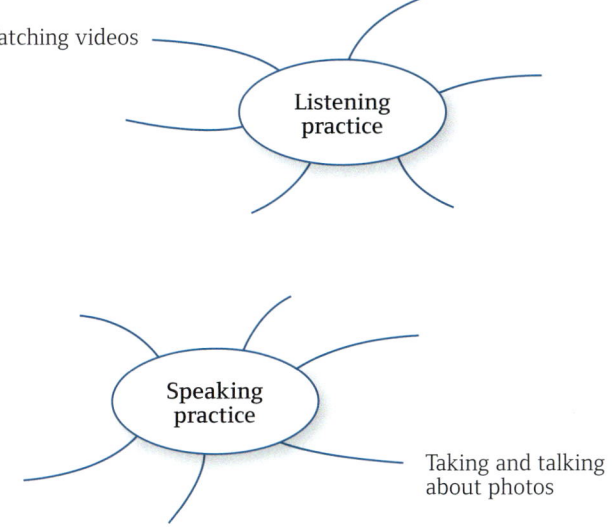

Taking and talking about photos

Which group has an idea that nobody else has?

10 Smooth operations

Business file

📁 Here's my idea

1 🔊 2.36-38 Listen to three project leaders trying to get the finance department to increase their budget, and take notes in the table.

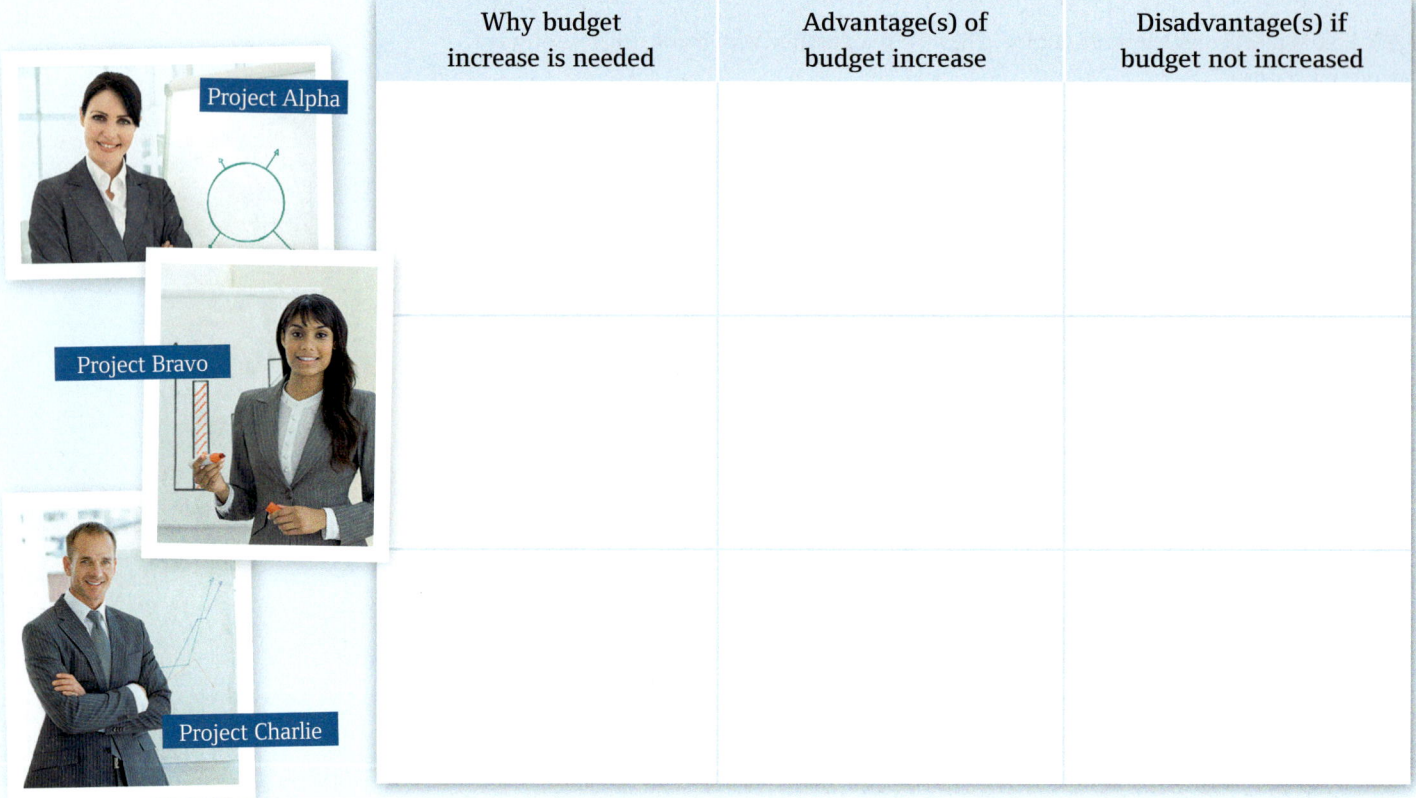

	Why budget increase is needed	Advantage(s) of budget increase	Disadvantage(s) if budget not increased
Project Alpha			
Project Bravo			
Project Charlie			

2 What did they say? Listen again and complete the sentences from the beginning, middle and end of the three pitches.

Beginning

The reason I want to talk to you today is because …

1 we have .... with the budget for the Alpha project.

2 we've identified a .... to reduce costs in the department by 30 %.

3 we're .... with the Charlie project.

Middle (positive focus)

4 I know that's high, but we would definitely double the .... with this increase.

5 If we do this properly, then we .... we're aiming for.

6 If we do this, we'll be able to .... and finish the project on time.

End (consequences of no action)

7 Unless we increase the budget, we .... finish the project.

8 Unfortunately, if we don't update, we .... more data.

3 🔊 2.39 Now listen to the rest of the meeting. Which project got the budget increase?

Business file 10

Pitching a proposal

The reason I want to talk to you today is because …
We've identified a great opportunity to …
The advantages (of doing it like this) are …
We would definitely double the return on our overall investment.
In that sense we should look at the long-term benefits rather than the immediate cost.
If we do this properly, then we'll achieve what we're aiming for. If we don't, well, then …
Productivity and efficiency will both rise and the problems we've been having will disappear.
This is a great opportunity to make some large savings for the whole department.
It's been quite successful so far and we want to build on that success.
Increasing the budget will mean that the project can continue the success it's had so far.

4 You are going to try to get funding for a project. First, as a class decide how much money for funding is available. Then follow the steps below.

1 Work with a partner and think of a project or an idea. Prepare a two-minute pitch to ask for funding.

Think of …
- a project you are currently working on or an idea for a new one (whether work-related or not).
- a reason or reasons why it needs (more) funding.
- both the benefits of your idea and the downside of not doing it.

→ *See phrases above and on page 89 for help with your pitch.*

2 Now get into groups of six or eight. Take turns pitching your ideas in two minutes or less. When you are not making a pitch, take notes and ask questions.

3 As a whole group, decide which proposal should get the funding and why.

10 Grammar summary

Second conditional

1. If customers **ordered** more RFID chips, we **would increase** production.
   (Nicht: If customers ~~would order~~ more RFID chips, …)
   We**'d lose** customers if we **didn't have** the flexibility.
2. If the producer **delivered** faster, we **could place** a bigger order.
   If prices **went down**, we **might open** a second factory.
3. We **would be** out of business if we **didn't have** a JIT system.
4. If I **were** you, I **would increase** the budget.
   (Besser als: If I ~~was~~ you, …)

Kein „would" im if-Satz!

Mit dem *second conditional* drückt man aus, was unter bestimmten Voraussetzungen geschehen könnte, aber unwahrscheinlich ist. Dann steht im if-Satz das *simple past* und im Hauptsatz *would + infinitive* (**1**).

Um darüber zu spekulieren, was unter bestimmten Voraussetzungen geschehen könnte, aber für unwahrscheinlich gehalten wird, können im Hauptsatz auch Modalverben wie *could* und *might* verwendet werden (**2**).

Wie beim *first conditional* gilt auch hier: Beginnt der Bedingungssatz mit dem Hauptsatz, folgt kein Komma (**3**).

Achtung: *If I were you, …* entspricht „Wenn ich du/Sie wäre, …" (**4**).

First conditional vs second conditional

1. If we **make** our USPs clearer, we **will increase** our chances.
2. If we **made** our USPs clearer, we **would attract** many more customers.

Remember:

	If-clause	Main clause
1st	if + simple present	will + infinitive (or can/may/might)
2nd	if + simple past	would + infinitive (or could/might)

Welche Form des *conditionals* gewählt wird, hängt auch von der Einstellung des Sprechers ab.

Mit dem *first conditional* beschreibt der Sprecher eine Situation, die sehr wahrscheinlich und durchaus möglich ist (**1**). Im Beispielsatz ist der Sprecher durchaus bereit, die Alleinstellungsmerkmale zu überarbeiten, weil er sicher ist, damit die Chancen am Markt zu erhöhen.

Mit dem *second conditional* dagegen werden spekulative Aussagen getroffen über eine Situation, die eher unwahrscheinlich oder sogar unmöglich ist (**2**). Im Beispielsatz ist die Überarbeitung der Alleinstellungmerkmale nur eine eventuelle Option, die nicht unbedingt umgesetzt werden wird.

Unless and *in case*

1. They will lose customers **unless** they reduce their prices.
   (= They will lose customers **if** they do**n't** reduce their prices.)
   Unless we can guarantee faster delivery, we're not going to get the contract.
2. We need to protect our brand **in case** our competitors launch another attack.
   Let's go ahead and prepare a SWOT analysis **in case** they ask for it at the meeting.
3. I'll take my mobile **in case** there's an emergency.
   (= I'll take it because the emergency might happen later.)
   I'll use my mobile **if** there's an emergency.
   (= I'll use it if the emergency has already happened.)

Unless und *in case* können anstatt *if* in Bedingungssätzen verwendet werden.

Unless entspricht „wenn nicht", „außer wenn" oder „es sei denn" und kann anstatt *if … not* verwendet werden. (**1**).

In case entspricht „im Falle" oder „für den Fall, dass" (**2**).

Achtung! *In case* entspricht nicht *if*! *In case* wird benutzt, um Handlungen zu beschreiben, die für eine zukünftige Situation Vorsorge treffen. Mit *if* werden Handlungen oder Situationen beschrieben, die eine mögliche Bedingung darstellen (**3**).

Extra practice 10

1 Complete these second conditional sentences with the correct form of the verbs in brackets.

1 If we .... (have) a larger budget, we .... (can/open) a new centre in Wales.
2 What .... (happen) if they .... (not/deliver) the goods by Friday?
3 What .... (you/do) if the order .... (be) late?
4 If I .... (know) more about the European market, I .... (can/help) you.
5 Where .... (your company/open) new offices if it .... (want) to expand?
6 If they .... (not/spend) so much time in meetings, they .... (get) better results.

2 Match these sentence halves to make first or second conditional sentences.

1 If I were you,
2 If we spent more money on logistics,
3 If you don't agree,
4 If the customer called to complain,
5 If Ilke doesn't get here by ten,
6 If our supplier delivers the goods today,
7 If you were the CEO,

a we'll have to think of something else.
b what would you tell him?
c the meeting will have to start without her.
d would you change the company structure?
e I'd write a more detailed report.
f we won't have to stop production.
g we could distribute more products.

3 Complete the sentences using *unless* or *in case*.

1 We have QR codes on our packaging .... we need to identify them.
2 .... we change our systems, we won't remain competitive.
3 We're going to lose customers .... we speed up our delivery times.
4 We should increase the budget plan by 10% .... we need more money during the project.
5 .... we do this, we'll see our market share slowly decrease.
6 Please take this report with you .... you see John and can give it to him in person.

4 Each sentence has one mistake. Write the corrected sentences.

1 He would buy a new laptop if he would have more money.
....
2 We won't be competitive in Europe unless we don't open a new logistics centre.
....
3 In case we want to opened more factories, we need to increase the budget.
....
4 Unless we finish now, we wouldn't finish in time for lunch.
....
5 If the delivery date will be OK, we'll sign the contract.
....
6 Let's exchange phone numbers if we have to call each other later.
....
7 If he would go to the meeting, he could discuss the ideas in the report.
....

10 Extra practice

5 Complete the sentences with the words from the box.

> business model · e-book readers · end users · peripheral devices · tablet PCs · tier-one suppliers

1 The introduction of .... has led to the death of netbooks.
2 Many .... don't know the real production costs of their hardware.
3 There is no perfect .... Companies have to find out what works best for them and their market.
4 .... supply goods directly to the manufacturer.
5 Many smartphones are also ....
6 Most people have two or three .... in addition to their PC or laptop.

6 Choose the correct words to complete the sentences.

1 We need to increase our `market share / business model` so that we are stronger than our competitors.
2 The law can't always protect a company from `copycat producers / depreciation` .
3 A strong `company reputation / production site` can help new products gain market share.
4 `Fixed assets / A budget increase` can be a good investment over time.
5 It's not good for the company balance when the assets `appreciate / depreciate` .

7 Which word or phrase doesn't collocate with the word in the circle? Cross it out.

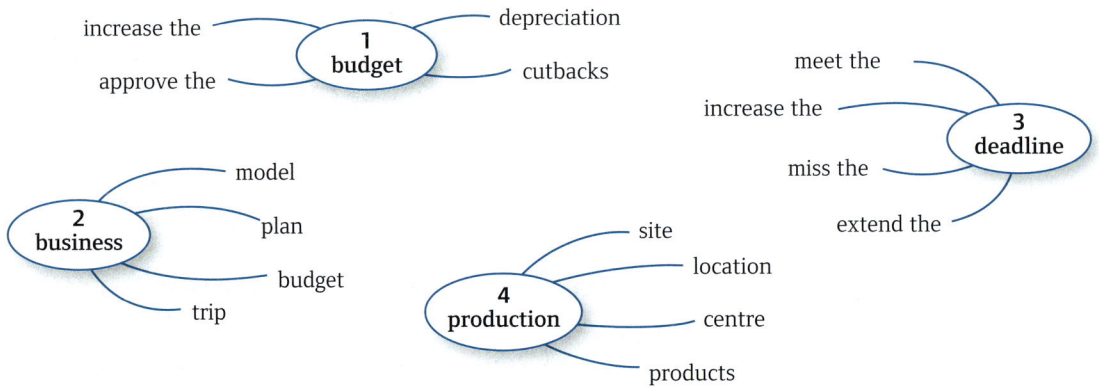

8 Complete the pitch with the phrases from the box.

> budget increase · competitive · financing · great opportunity ·
> market share · operating budget · the reason

Well, ...¹ I want to talk to you today is because we've identified a way to increase our market share by 10%. This is a ....² for us, but it does need some ....³. We need to increase the department's marketing budget by just 15% for this year. We need this ....⁴ to implement a marketing campaign and communicate it to the whole company. If we do this properly, then we'll gain the increase in ....⁵ we're aiming for. If we don't, well, then we might lose some of it. Actually, we'll probably need to increase our ....⁶ then by about 5% to stay ....⁷. So, what do you think?

Extra practice

10

9 Translate into English.

1. Unser Werk ist im Besitz eines spanischen Unternehmens.
2. Ein guter Zulieferer sollte immer ausreichend Ersatzteile am Lager haben.
3. Außer Beamern liefern wir auch Tablet PCs.
4. Sie hat sich auf das Projektmanagement spezialisiert.
5. Wenn wir das Budget erhöhen würden, würden wir das Risiko verringern.
6. Wir werden Kunden verlieren, es sei denn wir reagieren schnell.
7. Ich benötige mehr Daten für den Bericht.
8. Am Ende des Trainings haben wir von allen Fotos gemacht.

Typical mistakes

1. They are **owned by** a holding company.
   NOT *They are owned from* ….
2. We have sufficient components **in stock**.
   NOT *… sufficient components on stock*.
3. **Besides** having more products, we deliver faster.
   NOT *Beside having more products, we* …
4. We **specialize in** personalized products.
   NOT *We specialize on personalized products*.
5. If we **had** more inventory, we would be more flexible.
   NOT *If we would have more inventory, …*
6. Most goods **lose** value over time.
   NOT *Most goods loose value* …
7. We need more **data** to update the plan.
   NOT *We need more datas* …
8. I've **taken** new photos for my Italian lesson.
   NOT *I've made new photos* …

Culture spot

Time to say goodbye

There are many ways of saying goodbye in English, just as there are many ways of saying hello, and it is important to use an expression that's appropriate to the situation. In the end, it's all up to your judgement but remember that what's normal in your culture may not be in your business partner's culture.

Let's get physical

In Germany, the standard gesture for saying goodbye is to shake hands and simultaneously make eye contact. In your business partner's country there may be a different norm. In some cultures, people may move closer than you're used to, or touch you on the arm or shoulder. For example, don't be surprised if you get a hug from your partners in England or just a wave of the hand in America. You might feel uncomfortable if you extend your hand and your partner gives you a hug!

If you're not sure, prepare by asking a colleague who has already done business with people from the same country about the best way to say goodbye. If that's not possible, then try to let the other person make the first move and do your best to react spontaneously.

A way with words

When saying goodbye, it's quite usual to: make reference to the reason you came together (*I think we had a very productive meeting. It was good to discuss things face-to-face*); show that you enjoyed the meeting (*It was nice to finally meet you* or *It was great seeing you again*); or refer to the next steps (*OK, if you send me the data, I'll finish the report*) or the next time you will meet (*I look forward to seeing you again next month*).

Above all, it's important to be natural and sincere when saying goodbye. This is yet another opportunity to build on the rapport you have with your business partners and help strengthen your business relationship.

Take care! Bye! See you soon!
Goodbye! Bye for now!

Partner files

→ File 1

Partner A

Read out the text below while your partner fills in the missing information in his/her file.

Anthony works in H&S (Health and Safety). He is a junior manager and a member of a small team. He reports to his team leader Sebastian Ehlers. He has two direct reports: Monika Schürmann, a data input clerk, and Frank Taylor, a safety engineer. When he can, Anthony has lunch with a friend of his, Janice Schalk, who is a sales representative at the same company.

Now listen to your partner. Fill in the missing information (A–D) in the diagram and complete the sentences 1–4. Then summarize Christina's main relationships in the company.

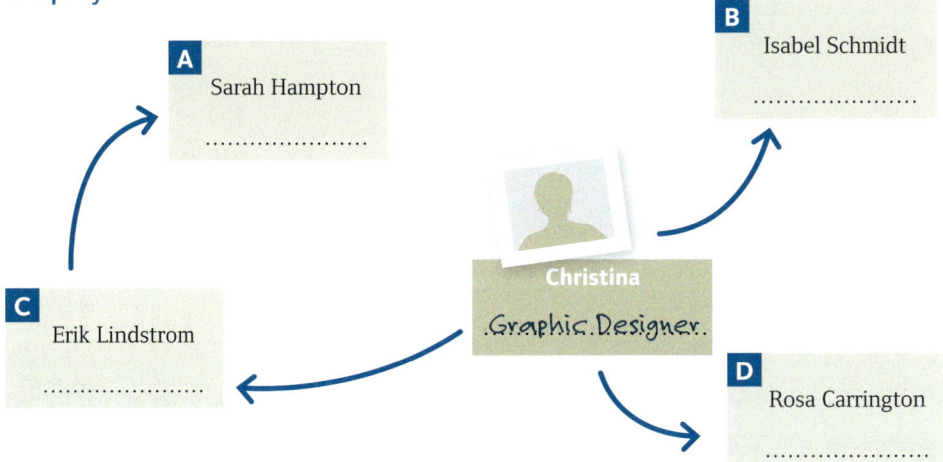

1 .... is Erik's boss.

2 Christina reports to ....

3 Christina is supervising ....

4 .... is one of Christina's colleagues.

→ File 2

Partner A

Before working with your partner, look at the two products below. They are both trusted brand names in Germany (and beyond). Think of another product that is also well known in your country and write it in the space below.

1 Haribo gummi bears

2 Nivea hand cream

3 ....

Now work with your partner, who also has three well-known products. Take turns asking each other 'yes' and 'no' questions about them. Can you guess each of your partner's products in 10 questions or less?

Is it designed for children?   Yes, it is. / No, it isn't.
Are they sold in supermarkets?   Yes, they are. / No, they aren't.

Partner A

→ File 3

Exchange contact information with your partner.

Partner A

→ File 4

Make a phone call. (Use your real name.)

- You work for the IT department of your company.
- You want to check an order for new software that was placed two weeks ago.
- The new software should manage the purchasing department's orders.
- Call Paul/Paula Brown at Management Software GmbH for information.

Now answer the phone and use the information below during the call.

- Make sure that the software can be used with all SAP systems.
- You're a good customer! Can you get a better price on the software? Try to get a 5% discount.

Partner A

→ File 5

You work in the sales department of a medium-sized company. Decide with your partner what products you sell. First describe the line graph on the left to your partner while he/she draws it. Then listen and draw the line graph that your partner describes.

Sales Figures (in 000s)

Past

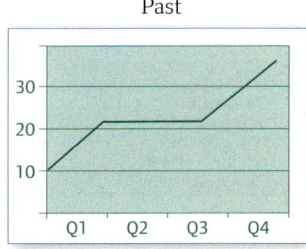

Forecast

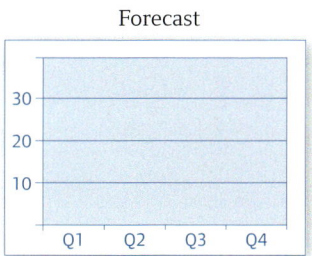

Now compare the graphs. How similar are they?

Partner files

→ **File 6**

Partner A

Here is an excerpt from the GIVE-IT price list. Answer your partner's questions about the prices, order numbers and minimum order quantities for the items on the list. Then ask questions and find out the missing information below. If you have a problem understanding, use the phrases in the box on the left.

Checking information

Sorry, I didn't catch that.
Could you say it again / repeat it, please?
Was that seventy or seventeen?
– Seventeen, one-seven.
How much does it cost?
If I understand correctly, that means …
Let me read that back to you:
P for Papa, W-4-8 …

GIVE-IT CORPORATE GIFTS

Item	Order no.	Price €	Minimum order
men's T-shirt	JGTM9090	2.22	..................¹
women's T-shirt	JGTW9091		
USB memory stick	..................²	3.88	..................³
umbrella	IYYI0007	4.50	..................⁴
travel bag	DTPL7561	5.30	..................⁵
beach towel	..................⁶	7.50	40
key ring	..................⁷	0.62	4,000
mug	UHOH9752	..................⁸	..................⁹
plastic spoon	..................¹⁰	..................¹¹	500
quality pen	..................¹²	0.22	2,000

→ **File 7**

Partner A

You represent the marketing department on the project team. Look at the pages from your diary and the email from a British colleague to find a good time for the meeting.

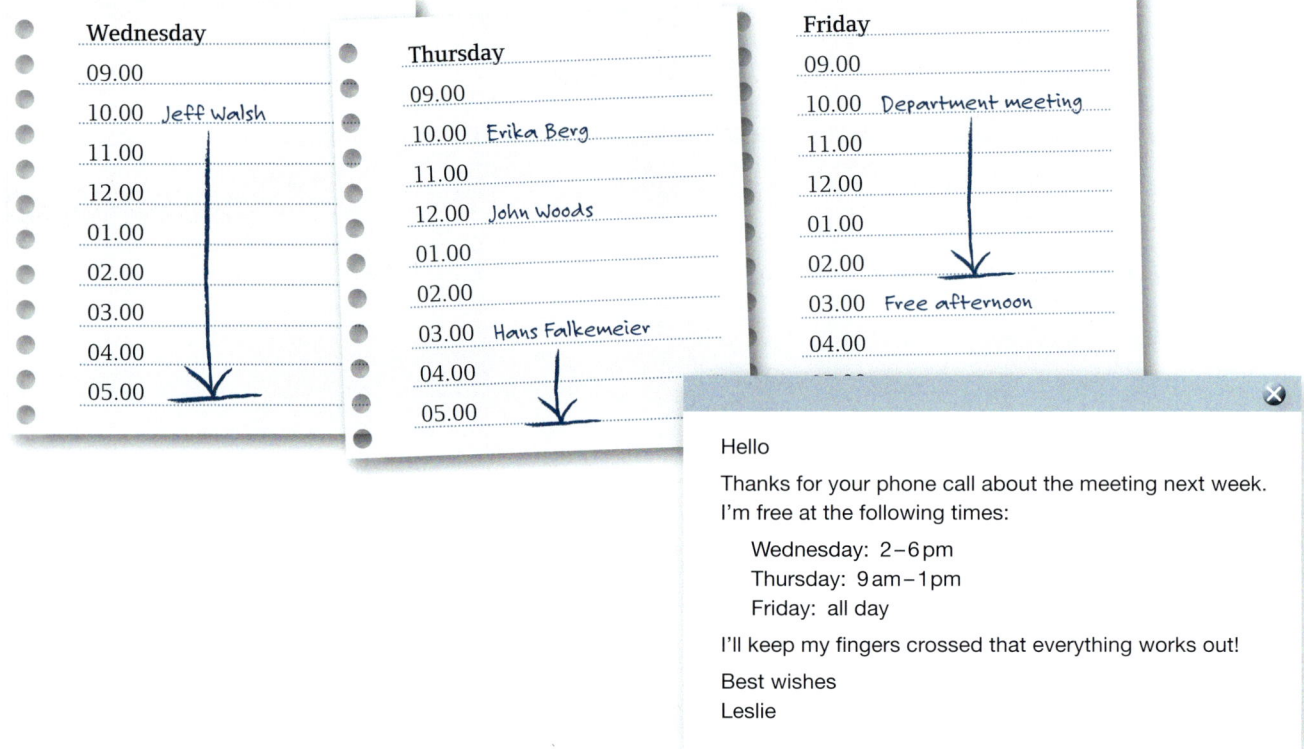

Wednesday
09.00
10.00 Jeff Walsh
11.00
12.00
01.00
02.00
03.00
04.00
05.00

Thursday
09.00
10.00 Erika Berg
11.00
12.00 John Woods
01.00
02.00
03.00 Hans Falkemeier
04.00
05.00

Friday
09.00
10.00 Department meeting
11.00
12.00
01.00
02.00
03.00 Free afternoon
04.00

Hello

Thanks for your phone call about the meeting next week. I'm free at the following times:

Wednesday: 2–6 pm
Thursday: 9 am–1 pm
Friday: all day

I'll keep my fingers crossed that everything works out!

Best wishes
Leslie

Partner A

Tell your partner about the company below.

ZEB makes clothing and equipment for winter sports. You employ around 800 people and produce around 80,000 skis and snowboards a year. You're one of the global market leaders in your sector.

Company turnover (€ million)

3 years ago	2 years ago	1 year ago	so far this year	In 2 years (forecast)
28	30.5	32	17.4	37

Relevant recent activities:
Two years ago: Competitor released a new product line. Our sales didn't grow as we wanted.
One year ago: Introduced new line of skis and snowboards.
So far this year: Had unique innovations in winter clothing.

Now listen to your partner talk about a company, and take notes. Then check with your partner to make sure you wrote down the correct information.

→ File 8

Partner A

Use the information below to make conversations with your partner.

Situation 1: You work at the hotel bar.
It's evening and your guest has just walked into the bar. You don't have the drink they want at the moment, so recommend something else as an alternative. You also have the following snacks (and only these) in case they ask: crisps, salted peanuts, olives.

Situation 2: You are the guest.
You're in the restaurant and you've just waited a long time for your food to come and now the order is wrong.

Situation 3: You are the waiter/waitress in the restaurant.
The computer in the restaurant has just crashed. You can manually calculate the cost of the bill, but you can't do a computer printout.

→ File 9

Partner A

Use the information below to present a new product to your partner. Use four of the techniques from page 88.

New Product	
Name:	Oscar33
Function:	Small loan for 18 to 25-year-olds
Benefit:	Low interest rates; easy approval
Length of loan:	5–7 years
Good for:	Holidays, first car, computers, furniture (e.g. first apartment)

Now listen to your partner's presentation and note the techniques he/she uses.

→ File 10

Partner files

→ **File 11**

Partner A

Look at Pauline's email attachment with her comments. Check the invoice against HTR's price list and Paulines's last invoice (which Partner B has). Then work with your partner to finish Tracy's email on page 98.

Do you have two types of Ecoclean Extra? The detergent I received this time is in tablet form and not a powder.

Cat. No.	Qty	Description	Unit price per Drum/Set (EUR)	Amount (EUR)
3038	10	Ecoclean Standard	3.10	31.00
3527	10	Ecoclean Extra-Tablet	3.90	39.00
3157	5	Ecoclean Superconcentrate	6.00	30.00
3819	30	Ecoclean Elite	7.50	225.00
3063	10	Ecoclean Family Elite	7.00	70.00
9338	10	Ecoclean assortment 5-piece set	32.00	320.00
				715.00
		SUBTOTAL WITH 5% DISCOUNT		-35.75
		SHIPPING		+20.00
		Please pay this amount:		**€679.25**

Don't want to pay extra (!) but I'm sure the list price was 7.50.

On my last order I got 10%

→ **File 12**

Partner A

Work with your partner to find the missing information in your sales performance chart.

- How many did we sell last year?
- How many have we sold so far this year?
- What was the customer rating last year?
- What's the customer rating this year?

Model	Units sold last year (000s)	Customer rating last year	Units sold this year (000s)	Customer rating this year
PW1710			12	●●●●●
PW2340	9	●●●●		
PW3500	18		22	
PW4500		●●		●
PW5340	11	●●●		
PW6240			9	●●

Customer rating key*

- very poor ●
- poor ●●
- average ●●●
- good ●●●●
- very good ●●●●●

* in terms of reliability and price

Partner A → File 13

Call 1

Use the notes below to make a phone call.

- You are the manager of a computer shop. You have been buying computer goods from Central Computers Ltd for five years and have always had good service. But the consignment of tablet PCs that you received this morning contained four damaged items (out of a total of ten).
- Call your partner who works in customer care at the company. Find out why this happened and whether it will happen again, and what should you do with the damaged PCs.

Call 2

Now use the notes below to take your partner's call.

- You deal with customer care at the Vista Conference Centre, which offers full conference facilities (meetings rooms, data projectors, etc.) to companies for meetings and seminars.
- You are about to handle a complaint from your partner, who used your conference facilities last weekend. Decide on your strategy. Should you apologize, offer a discount on the next seminar, downplay any problems, take personal responsibility?

Partner A → File 14

Call your partner. He/She is your manager.

- You want to get approval to purchase a high-end espresso machine for the team.
- You think this will improve the team's motivation, which has been low recently.
- Remember to give advantages of making the purchase and consequences of not making it.

Take your partner's call. Now he/she is a member of the team you lead.

- Note that the department is currently within its budget and you don't want to waste money. However, you also know that the Christmas party was cancelled last year and many team members were disappointed.
- Listen to your partner's request and decide how to respond. Are there any conditions you'd like to give?

Partner A → File 15

Use the information below and negotiate with your partner.

You have a new job in Berlin and need to sell your house in Stuttgart. The current market value is €320,000. You have placed an advert online with the asking price of €330,000. You want to get as much as you can for it, but are willing to accept €300,000 because you need the money for your new flat in Berlin. As an extra, you will add furniture (value €10,000) to the deal if necessary. It was specially made for the house.

→ File 16

Partner B

Listen to your partner. Fill in the missing information (A–D) in the diagram and complete the sentences 1–4. Then summarize Anthony's main relationships in the company.

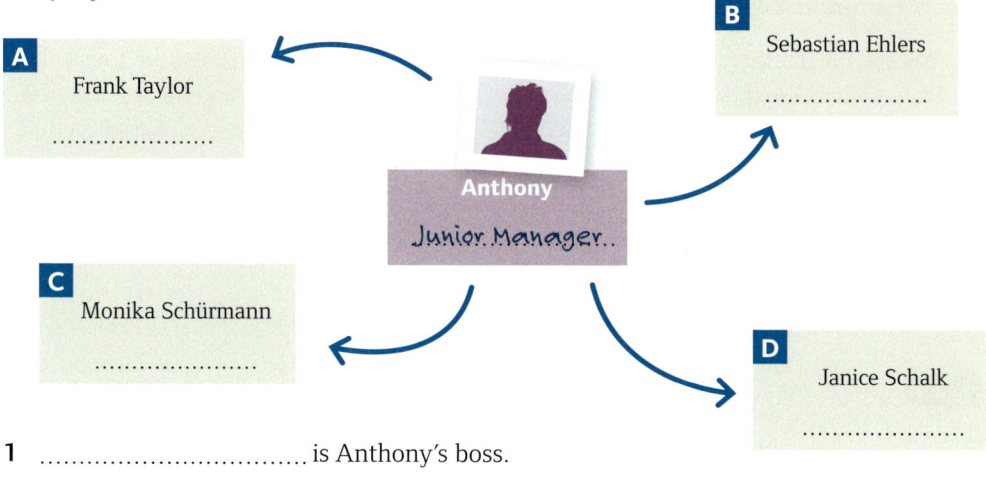

A Frank Taylor ....

B Sebastian Ehlers ....

C Monika Schürmann ....

D Janice Schalk ....

Anthony
Junior Manager

1 .... is Anthony's boss.

2 .... and .... report to Anthony.

3 Anthony and .... are friends.

4 .... is not a member of Anthony's team.

Now read out the text below while your partner fills in the missing information in his/her file.

Christina is a graphic designer in the marketing department. Her immediate boss is Erik Lindstrom, who's a senior graphic designer. Erik reports directly to Sarah Hampton, who is the head of the marketing department. Christina works closely with Isabel Schmidt from the advertising department. At the moment Christina is supervising a new trainee, Rosa Carrington.

→ File 17

Partner B

Before working with your partner, look at the two products below. They are both trusted brand names in Germany (and beyond). Think of another product that is also well known in your country and write it in the space below.

1 Birkenstock sandals

2 Playmobil figures

3 ....

Now work with your partner, who also has three well-known products. Take turns asking each other 'yes' and 'no' questions about them. Can you guess each of your partner's products in 10 questions or less?

Is it designed for children?   Yes, it is. / No, it isn't.
Are they sold in supermarkets?   Yes, they are. / No, they aren't.

136

Partner B

→ File 18

Exchange contact information with your partner.

Partner B

→ File 19

Answer the phone (using your real name) and take a message.

- You are an employee in the sales department at Management Software GmbH.
- Paul/Paula Brown's not in today. (Think of a reason why, if you want.)

Message for:	Date/Time: ....
Caller:	
Message:	

Now call back (this time you're Paul/Paula Brown) and use the information below to confirm the order.

- The software has changed. You used to only have version 2.2 but now you also have version 3.0. Which version does the customer want?
- Version 3.0 is 10 % more expensive, but it can be used with *all* SAP systems.

Partner B

→ File 20

You work in the sales department of a medium-sized company. Decide with your partner what products you sell. First listen to your partner and draw the line graph that he/she describes. Then describe the line graph on the right to your partner.

Sales Figures (in 000s)

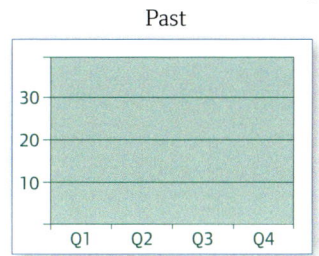
Past

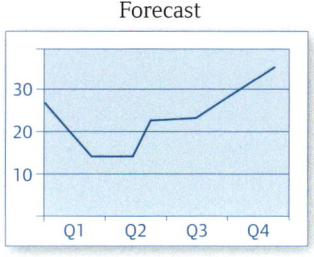
Forecast

Now compare the graphs. How similar are they?

Partner files

→ **File 21**

Partner B

Work with your partner to compare this invoice with the one on page 53.

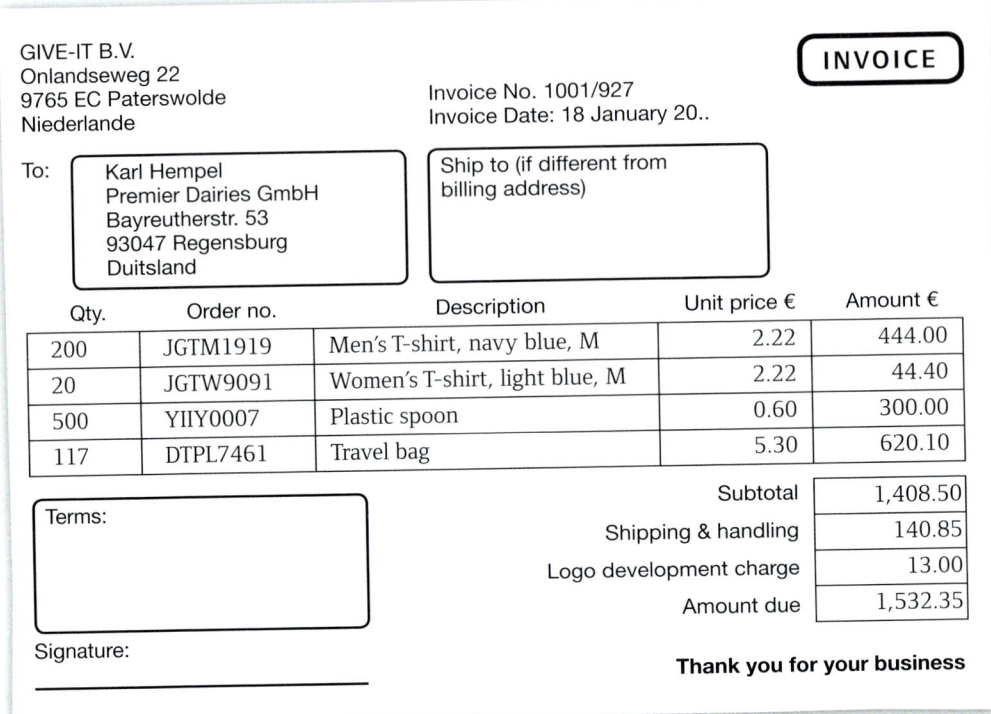

→ **File 22**

Partner B

You represent the finance department on the project team. Look at the pages from your diary and the email from a British colleague to find a good time for the meeting.

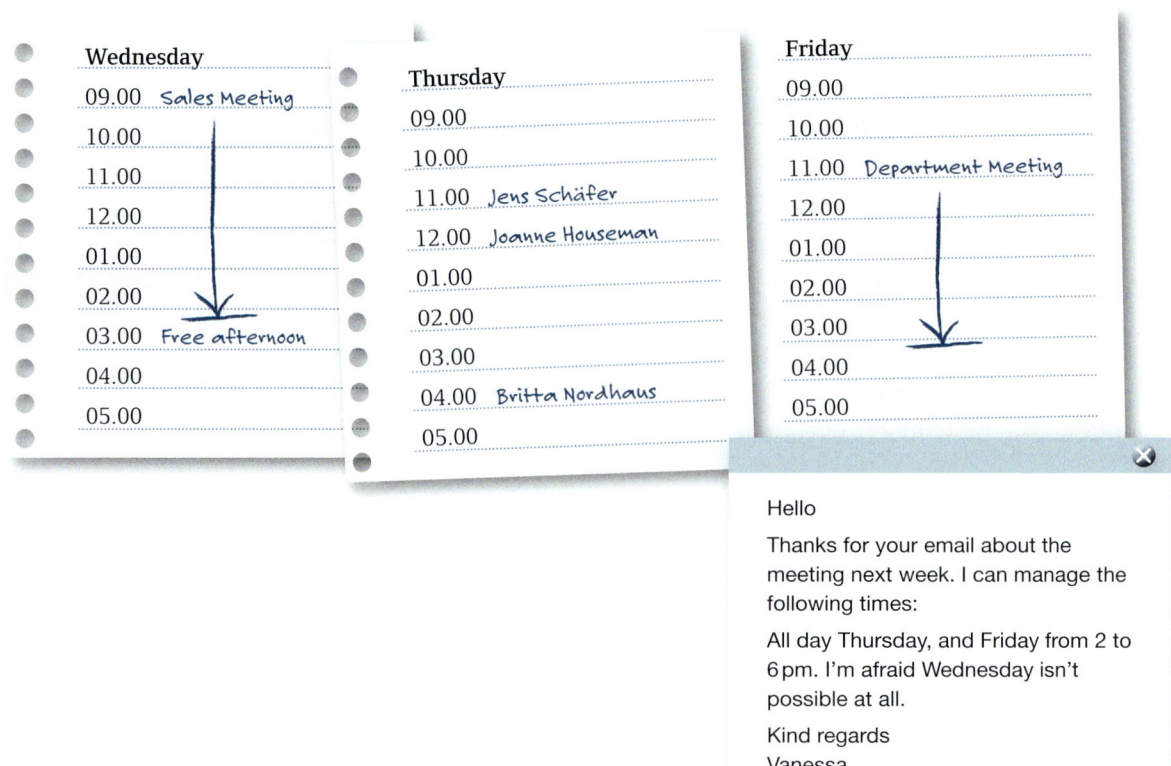

Partner B → File 23

Listen to your partner talk about a company, and take notes. Then check with your partner to make sure you wrote down the correct information.

Now tell your partner about the company below.

Gonz Apps began only six years ago with two friends and € 20,000 capital. Today it is one of the world's top producers of apps (applications) for mobile phones.

Company turnover (€)

6 years ago	4 years ago	1 year ago	so far this year	next 12 months (forecast)
40,000	470,000	6.75 m	17 m	35 m

Relevant recent activities:

Two years ago: Had an early market entry. Good for sales.
One year ago: Reputation established. Had very strong sales.
So far this year: There have been no new products from competitors.

Partner B → File 24

Use the information below to make conversations with your partner.

Situation 1: You are the guest.
You've just arrived in the bar at your hotel after a long day of meetings, and are quite thirsty. You can see the logo of your favourite drink at the bar. Order it and also something to snack on, like dry roasted peanuts or salt sticks.

Situation 2: You are the waiter/waitress in the restaurant.
Check with your guests if everything is OK. Offer to solve any problems they might have. You can also give them something free, like their coffees or dessert if they're really unhappy about anything.

Situation 3: You are the guest.
You're in the hotel restaurant after a nice meal. Ask for the bill, and remember to get a printout as you need it for your travel expenses when you get back to the office.

Partner B → File 25

Listen to your partner's presentation and note the techniques he/she uses.

Now look at the information below and present it to your partner. Use four of the techniques from page 88.

New Product	
Name:	Bam2
Function:	Medium-sized loan for young couples
Benefit:	Long loan term; fast approval
Length of loan:	8–10 years
Good for:	Renovations, family car, honeymoon, furniture (e.g. moving to a larger house/apartment)

Partner files

→ *File 26*

Partner B

Use HTR's price list and Pauline's last invoice below to help Partner A find out what went wrong with Pauline's new invoice. Then work with your partner to finish Tracy's email on page 98.

Price List – Ecoclean Detergents

Catalogue Number	Description	Unit price per Drum/Set (EUR)
Drums (detergents sold in bulk)		
3038	Ecoclean Standard	3.10
3063	Ecoclean Family Elite	7.50
3157	Ecoclean Superconcentrate	6.00
3259	Ecoclean Extra-Powder	3.00
3527	Ecoclean Extra-Tablet NEW	3.90
3819	Ecoclean Elite	7.50
Sets (assortments of different Ecoclean pre-packaged products)		
9338	Ecoclean Assortment: 5-piece set	32.00
9448	Ecoclean Assortment: 6-piece set	35.00
9558	Ecoclean Assortment: 7-piece set	40.00
9668	Ecoclean Assortment: 9-piece set	45.00
9778	Ecoclean Assortment: 12-piece set	72.00

Notes:

There is a special deal on the Ecoclean Family Elite until the end of June. Normal list price €7.50 Special offer price €7.00 A new version of Ecoclean Extra in tablet form is now available.

Discount on orders:

- €500-1000 = 5%
- €1001-2000 = 10% + Free Shipping
- over €2000 = 15% + Free Shipping

Cat. No.	Qty	Description	Unit price per Drum/Set (EUR)	Amount (EUR)
3038	5	Ecoclean Standard	3.10	15.50
3527	5	Ecoclean Extra	3.00	15.00
3157	10	Ecoclean Superconcentrate	6.00	60.00
3819	20	Ecoclean Elite	7.50	150.00
9338	10	Ecoclean assortment 5-piece set	32.00	320.00
9558	10	Ecoclean assortment 7-piece set	40.00	400.00
9668	10	Ecoclean assortment 9-piece set	45.00	450.00
				1410.50
		SUBTOTAL WITH 10% DISCOUNT		-141.05
		SHIPPING		0.00
		Please pay this amount:		**€1269.45**

Partner B

→ File 27

Call 1

Use the notes below to take your partner's call.

- You work as a customer-care clerk at Central Computers Ltd. You sell tablet PCs and you are very keen on promoting the product.
- You are about to handle a complaint from your partner, who is the manager of a computer shop. Decide on your strategy. Should you apologize, offer a discount on the next seminar, downplay any problems, take personal responsibility?

Call 2

Now use the notes below to make a phone call.

- Last weekend you used the Vista Conference Centre for a weekend seminar on intercultural training. It was terrible. The data projector didn't work and there weren't enough chairs for all the participants. On Saturday morning the dirty coffee cups from the previous seminar were still on the tables. Things were better on Sunday, but it was embarrassing because you had invited some important customers.
- Call the centre and complain. Find out why this happened and whether it will happen again, and try to get a refund for at least part of the cost of the seminar.

Partner B

→ File 28

Take your partner's call. He/She is a member of the team you lead.

- Note that your department is currently over budget and doesn't have any money to spare. However, you also know that motivation is low and you want to do something for your partner's team.
- Listen to your partner's request and decide how to respond. Are there any conditions you'd like to give?

Call your partner. Now he/she is your manager.

- You want to get approval for a team day out at the beach including a picnic, drinks and transport.
- You think this will improve the team's motivation, especially as the Christmas party was cancelled last year.
- Remember to give advantages of having the picnic and consequences of not having it.

Partner B

→ File 29

Use the information below to negotiate with your partner.

You live in London and have a new permanent job starting next month in Stuttgart. Your partner's house is advertised at € 330,000. You would like to buy a house and have a budget of € 320,000, but obviously it'll be better if you can get one cheaper. However, you will also need furniture for the house and will be happy if it's included in the price.

Partner files

→ File 30

Information file

Germany
Flexitime arrangement in 51% of companies.
Overtime work in 87% of companies.
Male employees are able to take parental leave in 14% of companies.
Phased retirement available in 49% of companies.

Austria
Flexitime arrangement in 52% of companies.
Overtime work in 84% of companies.
Male employees are able to take parental leave in 12% of companies.
Phased retirement available in 48% of companies.

Switzerland
The statistics are from an EU study. See if you can find out similar statistics for Switzerland.

→ File 31

Information file

The trade fair is a leisure show. All the companies below are based in your country (they can be as big or small as you like). Choose one of the companies and fill in the form on page 65. Decide your prices and terms with your partner.

Albatross Engineering
You build and sell small motor boats for water sport enthusiasts. You have a range of boats from relatively cheap to one luxury model.

Pro-Tennis
You manufacture and sell tennis equipment: racquets, balls, clothing, tennis shoes. Your products are 'top of the range', and many professionals buy them.

AVC Electronics
You make and sell consumer electronic equipment. At the trade fair you're showing your latest Home Movie Theatre – a complete package of widescreen TV, DVD player and sound system.

Fitness Unlimited
You manufacture and sell fitness equipment (home gyms, weights machines, etc.).

Galaxy Guides
You write and sell travel guides and illustrated books in a country by country series. You began only two years ago, but already your guides are in every good bookshop.

Partner C

→ *File 32*

You represent the production department on your project team. Look at the pages from your diary and the email from a British colleague to find a good time for the meeting.

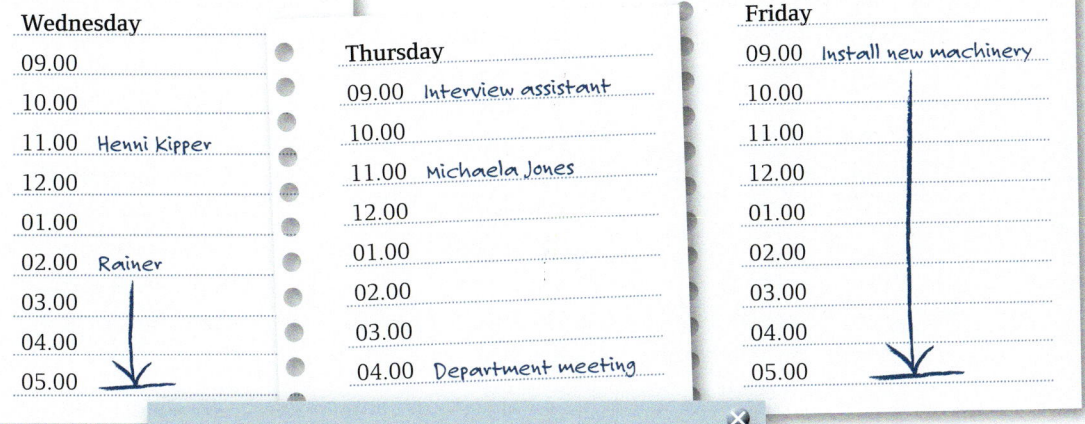

Wednesday	Thursday	Friday
09.00	09.00 Interview assistant	09.00 Install new machinery
10.00	10.00	10.00
11.00 Henni Kipper	11.00 Michaela Jones	11.00
12.00	12.00	12.00
01.00	01.00	01.00
02.00 Rainer	02.00	02.00
03.00	03.00	03.00
04.00	04.00 Department meeting	04.00
05.00		05.00

Hi,

Thanks for your email. I can attend the meeting at the following times:

- Wednesday from 9 am to 1 pm
- Thursday all day
- Friday from midday until about 6 pm

Hope this helps!
Steven

Numbers, dates, years and times

Numbers

Cardinal numbers		Ordinal numbers		Cardinal numbers		Ordinal numbers	
1	one	1st	first	21	twenty-one	21st	twenty-first
2	two	2nd	second	22	twenty-two	22nd	twenty-second
3	three	3rd	third	23	twenty-three	23rd	twenty-third
4	four	4th	fourth	30	thirty	30th	thirtieth
5	five	5th	fifth	31	thirty-one	31st	thirty-first
6	six	6th	sixth	40	forty	40th	fortieth
7	seven	7th	seventh	50	fifty	50th	fiftieth
8	eight	8th	eighth	60	sixty	60th	sixtieth
9	nine	9th	ninth	70	seventy	70th	seventieth
10	ten	10th	tenth	80	eighty	80th	eightieth
11	eleven	11th	eleventh	90	ninety	90th	ninetieth
12	twelve	12th	twelfth	100	one/a hundred	100th	hundredth
13	thirteen	13th	thirteenth				
14	fourteen	14th	fourteenth				
15	fifteen	15th	fifteenth				
16	sixteen	16th	sixteenth				
17	seventeen	17th	seventeenth				
18	eighteen	18th	eighteenth				
19	nineteen	19th	nineteenth				
20	twenty	20th	twentieth				

110	one hundred **and** ten
1000	one/a thousand
6,496	six thousand four hundred **and** ninety-six
100,000	one/a hundred thousand
1,000,000	one/a million (1m)
5,000,000,000	five billion (1bn)

■ Did you know?
Sowohl im Deutschen als auch im Englischen gibt es das Wort „Billion". Eine US-amerikanischen *billion* entspricht im Deutschen einer „Milliarde". Für die deutsche „Billion" sagt man im Englischen *trillion*. Im britischen Englisch wird *billion* meist für „Milliarde", manchmal aber auch (leicht veraltet) für „Billion" gebraucht. Hier ist also Vorsicht geboten.

> Im amerikanischen Englisch entfällt „and" normalerweise (zwischen Hunderter und Zehner):
> • one hundred ten

Dates

Britain 🇬🇧
Dates are normally written with a cardinal number followed by the month:
23 March

When only numbers are used, the order is day, month, year:
12/09/14   12 September 2014

USA 🇺🇸
In the USA, the day is usually written after the month:
March 23

When only numbers are used, the order is month, day, year:
09/12/13   September 12, 2014

Years

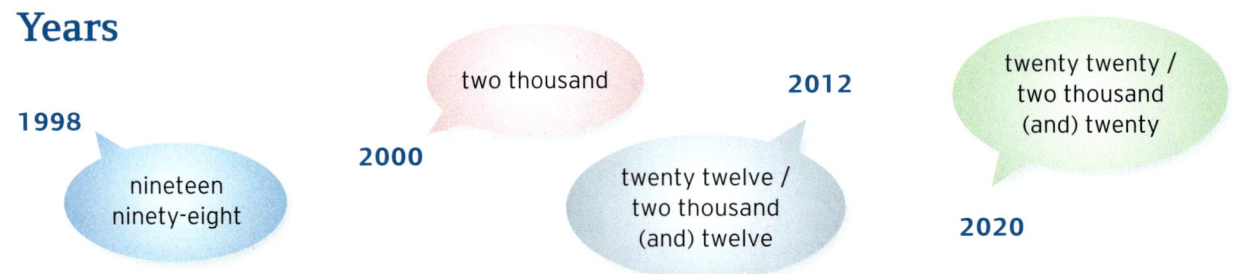

1998 — nineteen ninety-eight
2000 — two thousand
2012 — twenty twelve / two thousand (and) twelve
2020 — twenty twenty / two thousand (and) twenty

Times

The 12-hour clock
The 12-hour clock is used in everyday conversation.

Achtung: half past ten bedeutet 10.30 nicht 9.30!

| ten o'clock | five past ten | (a) quarter past ten | twenty past ten | half past ten |

| twenty-five to eleven | (a) quarter to eleven | ten to eleven | twelve minutes to eleven | midnight or noon/midday |

🇺🇸 In American English *after* is sometimes used instead of *past*, and *of* instead of *to*:

10.15 — a quarter after ten

10.40 — twenty of eleven

The 24-hour clock

Travel times
In everyday situations, the 24-hour clock is used in Britain only when talking about travel timetables (flight times for example). It is almost never used in the USA (except in the military).

0000	zero hundred
0015	zero zero (oh oh) fifteen
0950	zero (oh) nine fifty
0955	zero (oh) nine fifty-five

1100	eleven hundred
1103	eleven oh three
1430	fourteen thirty
2250	twenty-two fifty

Appoinments, etc.
In many everyday business situations in Britain, the 24-hour clock is used to write times (for example in a diary or to confirm the time of a meeting in an email), but when speaking we use the 12-hour clock. It is not normal in Britain – as it is in German-speaking countries – to talk of a meeting beginning at sixteen hundred (*sechzehn Uhr*). Instead, we can use the 12-hour clock (above), but very often we just say figures (five, six, etc.) and am or pm (or a.m. and p.m.) for morning or afternoon/evening.

Sometimes we write these times with a colon:

06:00	six am	13:00	one pm
08:05	eight oh five	14:47	two forty-seven pm
09:15	nine fifteen	00:05	twelve oh five am (five minutes past midnight)
10:30	ten thirty	12:05	twelve oh five pm (five minutes past midday)

Prepositions in time expressions

in + years, seasons, months, parts of the day	*on* + days, dates	*at* + times, parts of the day
in 2013	on Monday (at ten o'clock)	at ten o'clock
in spring/winter	on Fridays	at 3.25 pm
in February/August	on 23 June	at noon/midday/midnight
in the morning/afternoon	on September 18th, 2012	at night

at the weekend 🇬🇧
on the weekend 🇺🇸

Telephone numbers and addresses

Telephone numbers

The important thing to remember is that in English we say the individual numbers of telephone numbers one after the other. If you give your telephone number as some people do in German (e.g. if you say the number 416723 as 'forty-one sixty-seven twenty-three'), people probably won't understand you. When saying a phone number, make a pause after the code (*Vorwahl*) and also in the middle of longer numbers. You can also say 'That's' plus the number, e.g. 'That's four one six, seven two three.'

- In the USA, all phone numbers are made up of seven digits plus the three-digit area code. Americans often give their phone numbers like this:
  (313) 845-3912   Area code three one three, eight four five, three nine one two

- '0' is usually said as the letter 'o' (also sometimes as zero in the USA):
  (01206) 451879   oh one two oh six, four five one, eight seven nine

- In British English, double numbers (eg 22, 33) are said as double-two, double-three, etc.
  744311 seven double-four, three double-one
  (US: seven four four, three one one)

- Three identical numbers (eg 555) can be said as treble five, five double-five or double five five. (US: five five five).

- A few numbers, usually of larger companies, can end in 000. These are usually said as thousand:
  020 785 8000 oh two oh, seven eight five, eight thousand

- The number you give to people so they can reach you directly is called your 'direct line'. If someone first calls the reception, they might need your 'extension' number. This is the internal version of your direct line.

Postal addresses

British and American postal addresses each follow a standard format: (company) name, street, town or city and in the UK a 'postcode', in the USA a five (or sometimes a nine) digit 'zip code'. Remember that in the UK and the USA the street number is placed before the street name.

Britain 🇬🇧

Sigma Consulting Ltd.
Attn: Jane Goldsmith
4 Mosspark Road
Glasgow
G62 8NL UK

USA 🇺🇸

DataCorp, Inc.
1037 Richmond Avenue
Houston, TX 77042-1810
USA

Email and website addresses (URLs)

Email addresses & websites

.	dot	-	dash/hyphen
@	at	_	underscore
:	colon	/	(forward) slash

peter.morris@aol.com	Peter dot Morris at A-O-L dot com
d_klein@t-online.de	D underscore Klein at T dash online dot D-E
john.smith@citybank.co.uk	John dot Smith at City Bank dot co dot U-K
http://www.kulinar.at/sales	H-T-T-P colon forward slash forward slash W-W-W- dot Kulinar dot A-T slash sales

Wenn wir E-Mail- oder Webadressen buchstabieren, verwenden wir nicht „minus", sondern <u>dash</u> oder <u>hyphen</u> für den Bindestrich.

Business correspondence

Letters

1 The layout of a business letter — 148

Emails

2 Formal and informal emails — 150
3 A first contact with a company — 152
4 A reply to a first contact — 154
5 Asking for a quotation — 156
   Incoterms
6 An offer — 158
7 An invitation — 160
8 A job application — 162

Faxes

9 A confirmation — 164

Text messages

10 Communicating with mobile devices — 166

1 The layout of a business letter

The standard style for business letters is block style although other variations are also possible. Note that many companies have a specific corporate style of writing which may include using a specific font, greeting and closing statement when corresponding with business partners and colleagues. Make sure to check whether this is the case in your company.

Although these days emails fulfill many of the business functions that letters did in the past, letters are still often used for invoices, contracts and also to accompany promotional material, as you will see in the example below.

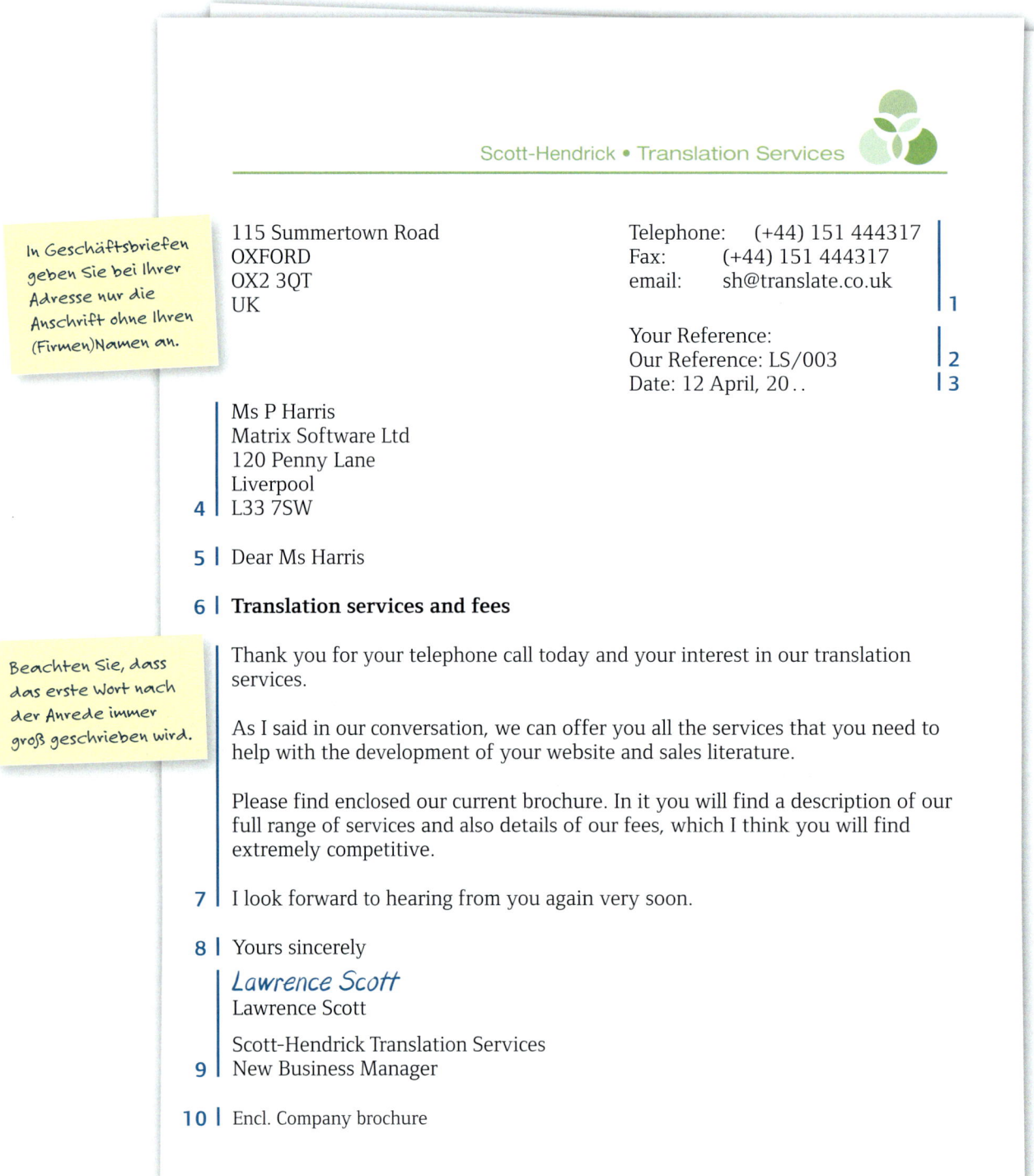

■ **The parts of a business letter**
1 **The letterhead or the sender's address** (Briefkopf)
2 **The reference** (Betreffzeile) Oft abgekürzt: *Your Ref./Our Ref.*
3 **The date** (Datum) Beachten Sie, dass die Reihenfolge in Großbritannien Tag/Monat, aber in den USA Monat/Tag ist. Um Verwirrungen zu vermeiden, empfiehlt es sich, den Monat auszuschreiben.
4 **The inside address or recipient's address** (Empfängeranschrift) Wenn Ihnen der Name des Empfängers bekannt ist, sollte er über dem Firmennamen stehen.
5 **The greeting or salutation** (Anrede):

Dear Sir or Madam	Diese Anrede wird verwendet, wenn Ihnen der Name des Empfängers nicht bekannt ist. Sie kommt der deutschen Form „Sehr geehrte Damen und Herren" am nächsten.
Dear Mr Jones	Diese Anrede wird verwendet, wenn Ihnen die Person namentlich bekannt ist. Wenn Sie an eine Frau schreiben, sollten Sie Ms als neutrale Form der Anrede verwenden (sofern nicht ausdrücklich eine andere Form der Anrede gewünscht ist).
Dear Sarah	So beginnen Sie den Brief, wenn Sie sich mit dem Empfänger mit Vornamen ansprechen.

In den USA wird auch folgende Formel benutzt:

To whom it may concern	Wenn dem Absender die zuständige Person oder Abteilung nicht bekannt ist. (entspricht etwa: „an die zuständige Abteilung" und ist auch bei Schreiben an Firmen üblich)

Beachten Sie, dass auf Mr/Mrs/Ms/Dr in den USA ein Punkt folgt (Mr./Mrs./Ms./Dr.). Darüber hinaus wird in amerikanischen Geschäftsbriefen ein Doppelpunkt hinter die Anrede gesetzt (Dear Mr. Jones:).

6 **The subject line** (Betreffzeile) Nur in britischen (nicht in amerikanischen) Briefen steht die Betreffzeile hinter (!) der Anrede.
7 **The body of the letter** (Brieftext) Dies ist der eigentliche Text des Briefes. In Großbritannien wie auch in den USA beginnt der erste Satz mit einem Großbuchstaben.
8 **The complimentary close** (Schlussformel)
In Großbritannien ist die Schlussformel abhängig von der zu Beginn des Briefes gewählten Anrede.

🇬🇧	Dear Sir or Madam	Yours faithfully
	Dear Mr Jones	Yours sincerely
	Dear John	

In den USA werden alle Geschäftsbriefe bevorzugt mit *Sincerely* geschlossen, aber *Yours truly* oder *Sincerely yours* werden auch verwendet.

🇺🇸	Dear Sir or Madam	Sincerely
	Dear Mr Jones	Yours truly
	Dear John	Yours sincerely

9 **The signature block** (Unterschriften)
10 **Enclosure(s)** (Anlage(n)) Die Abkürzung *Enc.* (manchmal *Encl.*) weist darauf hin, dass dem Brief etwas beigefügt (*enclosed*) wurde – in diesem Fall eine Broschüre.

Now you …

❶ **Look at the letter on page 148 (but don't look above) and find:**

   a the greeting/salutation   **b** the reference   **c** the subject line

❷ **How is the position of the subject line different in English and German letters?**

❸ **What is the English for 'Anlage'?**

❹ **What are the best complimentary closes for the following greetings/salutations?**

   a Dear Sir or Madam   **c** Dear Ms. Morgan (USA)
   b Dear Mr Williams (UK)   **d** Dear Jack

Business correspondence – Emails

2 Formal and informal emails

There aren't many clear rules for writing emails. Emails (sometimes written 'e-mails') vary from formal (like a business letter) to very informal (similar to a telephone conversation in writing). See page 99 in Unit 8 for more details on the differences between formal and informal emails.

1 Look at the two emails below. Which is formal and which is informal? What differences can you find between the two emails that indicate whether the style is formal or informal?

To: Dr. Eva Bernstein <eva.bernstein@aquariusmarketing.com> | 1
From: Anna Pariola <anna.pariola@nama.org>
CC: | 2
Subject: Invitation to speak at this year's NAMA conference November 16-19 | 3
1 Attachment: venue_details.pdf | 4

Beachten Sie, dass sich die Rechtschreibung und Interpunktion hier an den amerikanischen Konventionen orientieren.

Dear Dr. Bernstein: | 5

I am the organizer of this year's North American Marketing Association conference which will take place from November 16-19 in Chicago, Illinois. The theme this year is 'Multi-cultural Marketing in the Global Economy'. I am attaching details of the venue, etc.

As you are one of the USA's leading experts in international marketing, we would be delighted if you could speak at the conference. We can offer you a speakers' fee and reimburse you for your expenses.

Please let me know if you would be interested. I look forward to hearing from you in due course.

Sincerely

Anna Pariola

Conference Organizer, NAMA
Tel. (939) 104 2510
Fax (939) 104 2512
www.nama-marketing.org | 6

To: James Ritchie <j.ritchie@packer-engineering.net>
From: George Edwards <g.edwards@packer-engineering.net>
CC: Tessa Smith <t.smith@packer-engineering.net>
Subject: RE: ideas about project | 7

Beachten Sie, dass das erste Wort nach der Anrede groß geschrieben wird.

Jim

8 ▶ Thnx for your email – sorry for the delay in replying. All a bit hectic here ;-) ◀ 9

> and do you agree with me that Sue Macfarlane is actually the best person to
> lead the project | 10

Yes. But does she have time?

Best
George

150

The parts of an email

1 **The recipient** (Empfänger)
2 **Copies** (Kopien, weitere Empfänger) (Cc = *carbon copy*: Durchschlag)
3 **The subject line** (Betreffzeile) Die Betreffzeile sollte möglichst immer ausgefüllt werden und dem Empfänger eine Vorstellung vom Inhalt der E-Mail geben. Der Empfänger kann die E-Mail später anhand des Betreffs leichter wiederfinden.
4 **Attachment(s)** (Anhang) Entspricht der Anlage eines Briefes.
5 **The salutation** (Anrede) In förmlichen E-Mails entsprechen Anrede und Schlussformel denen eines Geschäftsbriefes (siehe Seite 149). In informellen E-Mails werden die folgenden Gruß- und Schlussformeln verwendet:

Salutation and complimentary close

Informal

| Dear Jim | Kind regards / Regards / Best wishes |

Very informal

| Hi/Hello Jim | All the best / Very best / Best |
| Jim (nur Vorname) | |

> Wenn Sie nicht wissen, ob der Empfänger ein Mann oder eine Frau ist, verwenden Sie am besten Vor- und Nachnamen.
> • Dear Chris Evans
> • Dear T.K. Spinazola
>
> Wenn Sie den Ansprechpartner nicht namentlich kennen, empfiehlt es sich, eine allgemeine Begrüßungsformel zu verwenden:
> • Dear Sir or Madam

6 **The signature** (Signatur) E-Mail-Programme erlauben es dem Verfasser, automatisch eine elektronische Signatur hinzuzufügen. Auf diese Weise kann der Verfasser dem Empfänger seine Kontaktdaten mitschicken.
7 **Re** (*With reference to*) (Betreff) Meistens beantwortet man eine E-Mail, indem man auf *Reply* (Antworten) klickt. Eine Folge von E-Mails, bei der zwei Personen immer wieder auf die eine eingehende E-Mail geantwortet haben, heißt *a thread*.
8 **Abbreviations** (Abkürzungen) Abkürzungen wie *thnx* für *thanks* sowie unvollständige Sätze sind üblich in informellen E-Mails zwischen Muttersprachlern.
9 **An emoticon** or **smiley** Siehe unten.
10 **A quotation/quote** (Zitat) Der Verfasser hat einen Abschnitt aus der E-Mail des Senders in seine eigene E-Mail eingefügt: So lässt sich schnell und eindeutig darstellen, worauf man sich bezieht.

Abbreviations and emoticons

Täglich werden neue Abkürzungen und Smileys erfunden. Hier sind nur einige Beispiele aufgeführt. Aber Vorsicht! Ihr Sinn muss vollkommen klar sein – Abkürzungen können sonst verwirren. Am besten bleibt man bei den bekanntesten wie ASAP, BTW und FYI.

Some abbreviations in emails

ASAP	as soon as possible	BTW	by the way	IMHO	in my humble/honest opinion
ATB	all the best	BW	best wishes	Pls	please
B4	before	FYI	for your information	Thnx/Thx	thanks

Some common emoticons

| :-) | glücklich oder freundlich | ;-) | ironisch oder mit einem Augenzwinkern | :-/ | perplex |
| :D | sehr glücklich | :-o | überrascht | :-(| enttäuscht oder unglücklich |

Now you …

2 Find suitable closes for these greetings/salutations:

a (US) Dear Mr. Friedman b (UK) Dear Ms Walters c Hi Lucy d Mike

3 Write in more formal language:

a Pls send me the info asap. Thx.
b FYI: The payment is in the post. Will be with you asap.
c Btw, sorry for the delay. Was on holiday. :-)

Business correspondence – Emails

3 A first contact with a company

Companies can find new business partners from:
- advertisements in magazines and trade journals
- trade fairs
- the Internet
- chambers of commerce
- mutual customers

1 Look at the email below. How did Dennis Sandford learn about the German company? What does he request?

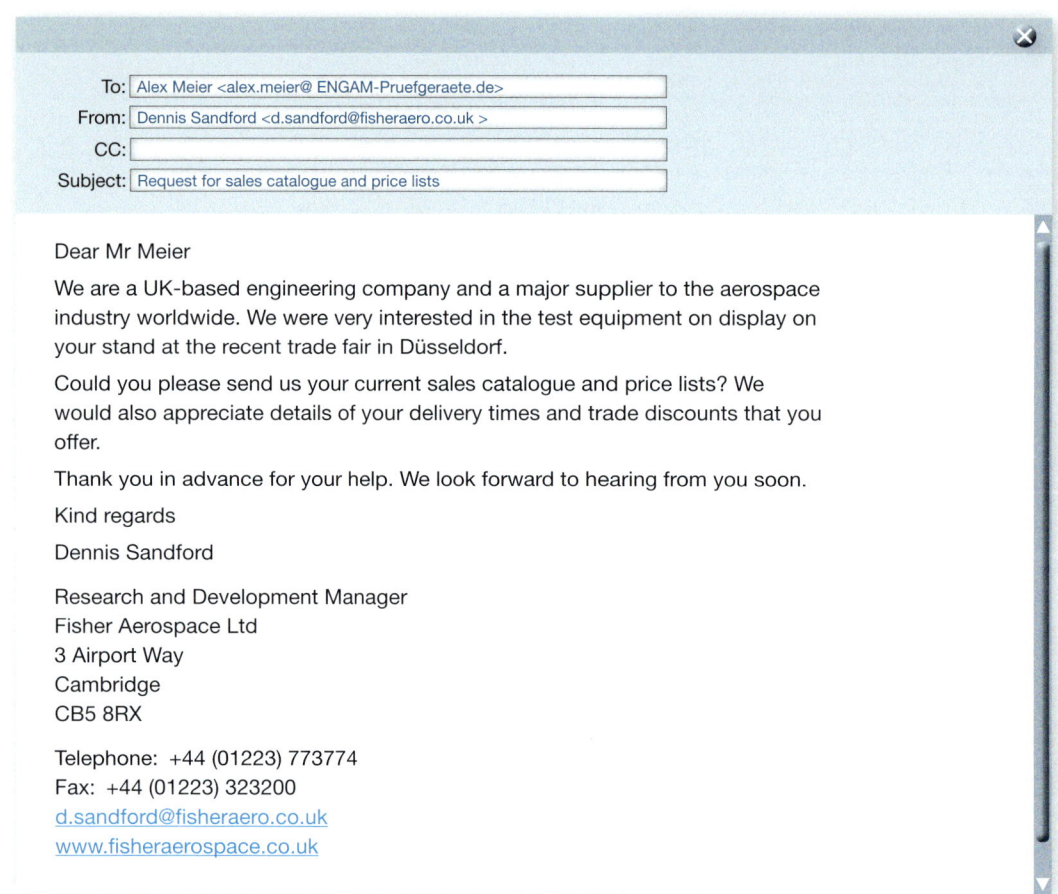

To: Alex Meier <alex.meier@ ENGAM-Pruefgeraete.de>
From: Dennis Sandford <d.sandford@fisheraero.co.uk >
CC:
Subject: Request for sales catalogue and price lists

Dear Mr Meier

We are a UK-based engineering company and a major supplier to the aerospace industry worldwide. We were very interested in the test equipment on display on your stand at the recent trade fair in Düsseldorf.

Could you please send us your current sales catalogue and price lists? We would also appreciate details of your delivery times and trade discounts that you offer.

Thank you in advance for your help. We look forward to hearing from you soon.

Kind regards

Dennis Sandford

Research and Development Manager
Fisher Aerospace Ltd
3 Airport Way
Cambridge
CB5 8RX

Telephone: +44 (01223) 773774
Fax: +44 (01223) 323200
d.sandford@fisheraero.co.uk
www.fisheraerospace.co.uk

Now you …

2 Here are some useful phrases for contacting a company. Use the phrases to write the emails below.

We understand from	your	advertisement		in this month's …
				in the May edition of …
	your	website …		
We obtained	your	name	from	the chamber of commerce in …
		address		a mutual customer.
				an online trade directory.

We were interested in the products on display on your stand at the recent trade fair in …

| We are | a | German/Swiss | company/importer/manufacturer … |
| | an | Austrian | retailer/wholesaler … |

Please	send us your current catalogue and price lists./?
Could you please	arrange a visit by your sales representative./?
	arrange a product presentation for us./?

We would also	like	details of	delivery times.
	be grateful for	information about	trade discounts.
	appreciate	samples of your products.	

Thank you in advance for your help.

We look forward to hearing from you soon/shortly.

Email 1
Sie sind als Einkäufer/in für eine Hotelkette in Ihrem Land tätig. Sie sehen in der aktuellen Ausgabe des International Hotel Trade Magazine die Anzeige eines englischen Unternehmens, das Seifen (*soaps*) vertreibt. Verfassen Sie eine E-Mail an Wildflower Soaps Ltd (info@wildflower.co.uk), in der Sie um einen Katalog, Preislisten und Muster der Produkte des Unternehmens bitten. Denken Sie sich relevante Einzelheiten wie z. B. den Namen Ihres Unternehmens usw. selbst aus.

Email 2
Sie sind Fabrikleiter/in einer Herstellerfirma in Ihrem Land. Sie müssen Luftfilter (*air filters*) für Ihre Fabrik kaufen und ein gemeinsamer Kunde empfiehlt Ihnen ein französisches Unternehmen: Mécanélec, 43 rue du Chemin des Vignes, 93012 Bobigny, Frankreich. Verfassen Sie eine E-Mail an Dominic Lautrec (dominic.lautrec@mecenelec.fr), in der Sie um einen Katalog und eine Produktpräsentation bitten. Denken Sie sich relevante Einzelheiten wie z. B. den Namen Ihres Unternehmens usw. selbst aus.

> ■ **Writing tip**
> Die goldene Regel für das Verfassen von Geschäftsbriefen und Emails lautet: **KISS**
> **K**eep **I**t **S**hort and **S**imple
> Versuchen Sie nicht, den Leser mit langen Sätzen und wichtig klingenden Wörtern zu beeindrucken – es erhöht die Wahrscheinlichkeit, dass Sie Fehler machen.

Business correspondence – Emails

4 A reply to a first contact

Susanne Klein's German electronics company is looking for a new storage system (*Lagerungssystem*) for its warehouse. Susanne works in her company's purchasing department. A customer recommends Alite, a British manufacturer. Susanne visits their website, fills in a contact form and requests a catalogue. This is Alite's reply.

1 Look at the email. In what four ways could you contact the English company below?

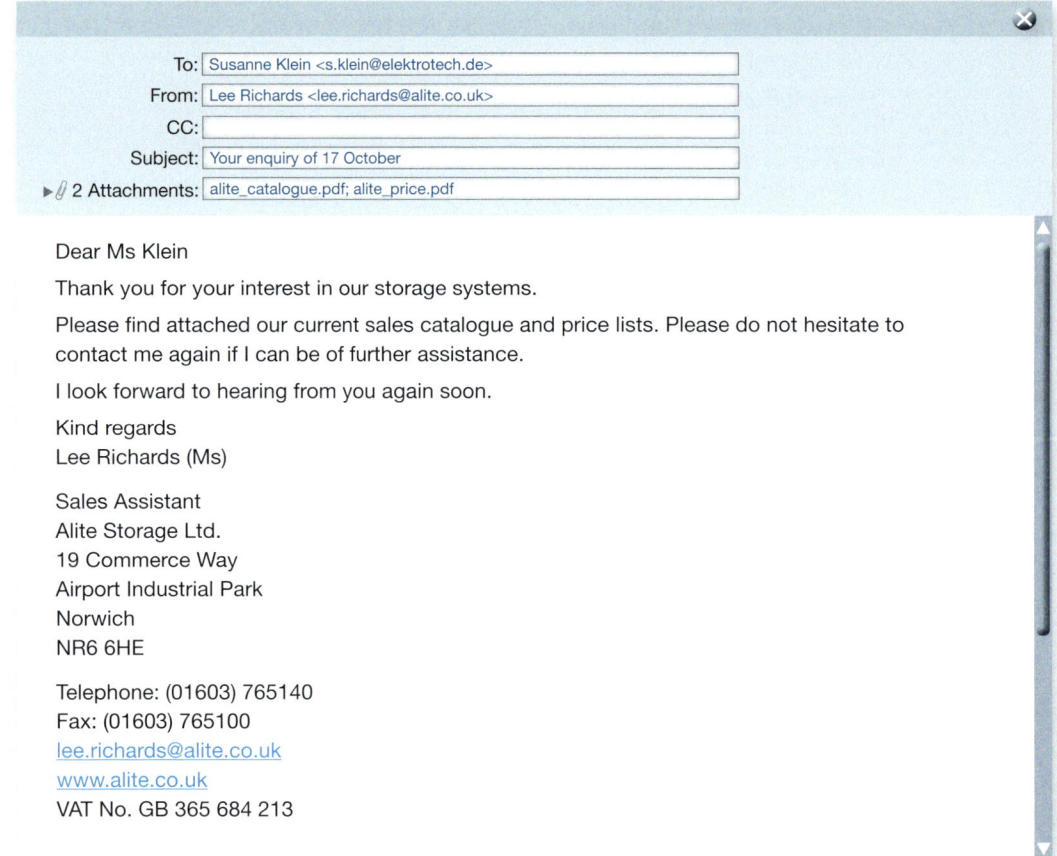

To: Susanne Klein <s.klein@elektrotech.de>
From: Lee Richards <lee.richards@alite.co.uk>
CC:
Subject: Your enquiry of 17 October
2 Attachments: alite_catalogue.pdf; alite_price.pdf

Dear Ms Klein

Thank you for your interest in our storage systems.

Please find attached our current sales catalogue and price lists. Please do not hesitate to contact me again if I can be of further assistance.

I look forward to hearing from you again soon.

Kind regards
Lee Richards (Ms)

Sales Assistant
Alite Storage Ltd.
19 Commerce Way
Airport Industrial Park
Norwich
NR6 6HE

Telephone: (01603) 765140
Fax: (01603) 765100
lee.richards@alite.co.uk
www.alite.co.uk
VAT No. GB 365 684 213

Now you …

2 Here are some useful phrases for replying to a first contact. Use the phrases to write the emails below.

Thank you for	your letter email your telephone call	of 13 May dated 13 May today	in which you enquired about … in which you requested …
Thank you for	your request for your enquiry about		our latest sales catalogue. our products and prices. our services and fees.
Thank you for	your interest in		our products/services.
Please find	our latest brochure attached / enclosed.		
I am attaching I am happy to send you	our sales catalogue and current price lists. samples of our products.		
Our representative Ms Webster will contact you in the next few days to arrange an appointment.			
I am sure that you will find	our products/services of the highest standard. our prices extremely competitive.		
Please do not hesitate	to contact us again to phone me	if I can help further. if I can be of further help/assistance. if you have any questions.	
I look forward to	hearing from you receiving your order calling you	very soon. in due course. in the next few days.	

Emails

Sie arbeiten in Ihrem Land für ein Unternehmen, dass Ferngläser (*binoculars*) und andere optische Geräte herstellt. Sie haben heute auf Ihrer Website zwei Anfragen bekommen. Die Erste ist von Herrn Kees Heijn von Calmar BV (k.heijn@calmar.nl), der um einen Produktkatalog bittet. Die Zweite ist von Ms Judy Lake (judy@outdoorsports.co.uk), die um einen Besuch Ihres Außendienstmitarbeiters bittet. Schreiben Sie entsprechende Antworten auf beide Anfragen. Denken Sie sich relevante Einzelheiten wie z. B. den Namen Ihres Unternehmens etc. selbst aus.

■ **Writing tip**

In förmlichen Briefen sollten Kurzformen wie *I'm*, *we're*, *they don't*, *it hasn't*, *I'd* usw. vermieden werden, die Wörter werden ausgeschrieben.

Business correspondence – Emails

5 Asking for a quotation

Wolfgang Müller is one of the buyers at Maximilian Scheling Weinimport, a wine wholesaler in Cologne. Last week Wolfgang was at a trade fair and became interested in the products of Golden Valley Vineyards, a Californian wine producer in the Napa Valley. Now he is writing for a quotation for a number of cases of wine.

1 Read the email and decide what the functions of Wolfgang's sentences 1–5 are.

To: Nina Bartlett <n.bartlett@goldenvalley.com>
From: Wolfgang Müller <w_mueller@maxwein.de>
CC: Tessa Smith <t.smith@packer-engineering.net>
Subject: Quotation

Dear Ms Bartlett

1 | I very much enjoyed meeting you at the trade fair last week here in Cologne and was impressed with your wines.

2 | If your prices and terms are right, we may want to place a substantial order with you.

3 | Would you please send us a quotation DDP Hamburg for the following?

    15 cases of Golden Valley Chardonnay 2011
    10 cases of Golden Valley Cabernet Sauvignon 2010
    20 cases of Golden Valley Merlot 2010
    10 cases of Golden Valley Zinfandel Reserve 2009

4 | We would also be grateful for details of discounts that you can offer us, delivery times and your terms of payment.

5 | We look forward to receiving your quotation shortly.

Best regards

Wolfgang Müller
Buyer

Maximilian Scheling Weinimport GmbH
Hansaring 20
D-50670 Köln
Germany
Telefon: (+49) (0) 221 139 72 58
Fax: (+49) (0) 221 139 72 59
www.maxwein.de

shortly = „bald" (formell)

Incoterms

Wolfgang asks for a price for the wines 'DDP Hamburg'. In international commerce, companies often use Incoterms (International Commercial Terms) to show what a price includes. Here are six common Incoterms.

EXW Ex works (*ab Werk*) The basic price.

FAS (San Francisco) Free alongside ship (*frei Längsseite Schiff*). The seller pays the costs until the goods are at the port (e.g. San Francisco).

FOB (San Francisco) Free on board (*frei an Bord*). The seller pays the costs until the goods are on the ship.

CIF (Hamburg) Cost, insurance and freight (*Kosten, Versicherung, Fracht*). The seller pays the costs (including insurance) until the goods are at the port in the buyer's country.

DAT (Hamburg) Delivered At terminal (*geliefert zum Terminal*). The seller pays the costs until the goods have been unloaded at the terminal/port of destination.

DDP (Buyer's works) Delivered duty paid (*geliefert verzollt*). The seller pays all the costs until the goods are at the buyer's works.

Now you …

2 Use these phrases and Wolfgang's email to write the email below.

Thank you for	your sales catalogue.
	the samples.
	the information that you sent us.
We find your products	(very) satisfactory.
We are impressed by	your products.
We are particularly interested in	
Could you please	send us a quotation for the following …?
Would you please	quote us for …?

We would also	like	details of	discounts.
	be grateful for	information about	delivery times.
	appreciate		your terms of payment.

If your prices and terms are right, we may want to place substantial orders with you.
We look forward to receiving your quotation shortly.

Email

Sie arbeiten für ein Bauunternehmen (*construction company*) in Ihrem Land. Sie haben Interesse am Kauf von schwedischem Bauholz (*timber*) von Scanwood Timber. Ihre Kontaktperson ist Axel Enströms (a.enstroems@scanwood.se). Sie haben Muster des Produkts erhalten und möchten nun ein Preisangebot für 20 Tonnen zehn Meter lange Kiefernbretter (*10-metre pine planks*), sowie Einzelheiten über Rabatte, Lieferzeiten und Zahlungsbedingungen. Schreiben Sie Herrn Enströms an. Denken Sie sich relevante Einzelheiten wie z. B. den Namen Ihres Unternehmens etc. selbst aus.

Business correspondence – Emails

6 An offer

This is Nina Bartlett's reply to Wolfgang Müller's email on page 156.

1 Look at the email and find the English for:

a Menge
b Beschreibung
c Gesamtbetrag
d Einführungsrabatt
e Skonto bei Barzahlung innerhalb von zehn Tagen
f Lieferung
g gültig
h Bezahlung in voller Höhe innerhalb von 30 Tagen nach Lieferung
i Warensendungen
j hochzufrieden

To: "Wolfgang Mueller" <w.mueller@maxwein.de>
From: "Nina Bartlett" <n.bartlett@goldenvalley.com>
CC:
Subject: Your quotation request
2 Attachments: Terms_and_conditions_of_business.docx; Maxwein_quotation.pdf

Dear Mr Mueller:

I also enjoyed our meeting at the trade fair. Thank you for your interest in our excellent wines and your request for a quotation. I am pleased to send you the attached offer.

These prices are DEQ Hamburg. I will be very pleased to offer you an introductory discount of 10% on this order and a further generous 5% cash discount for payment within 10 days of delivery. This offer is valid for three months.

Our terms are payment in full within 30 days of delivery.

You can normally expect to receive consignments from us around three weeks after we receive your order. I have attached our standard Terms & Conditions.

I am certain that you will be delighted with our products and I look forward to receiving your order in the near future. Please do not hesitate to get in touch with us immediately if you have any questions.

Sincerely yours

Nina Bartlett

Golden Valley Vineyards Inc.
2545 Las Amigas Road
Napa, CA 94559-2130
n.dasilva@goldenvalley.com
www.goldenvalley.com

> Denken Sie daran, bei Tausendern ein Komma als Trennungssymbol zu verwenden (z. B. 3,421). Im Englischen wird der Punkt nur bei Zahlen verwendet, die kleiner als eins sind (z. B. 2.50).

Quantity	Description	€ Price/case	Total
15	12 bottle case Chardonnay 2011	99.50	1,492.50
10	12 bottle case Cab. Sauvignon 2010	125.00	1,250.00
20	12 bottle case Merlot 2010	99.00	1,980.00
10	12 bottle case Zinfandel Res. 2009	476.00	4,760.00
GRAND TOTAL			9,482.50

Now you ...

2 Use these phrases and Nina's email to write the letter below.

Thank you for your request for a quotation of 29 August/August 29.					
We are pleased to		send you	the following: ...		
		quote you	as follows: ...		
We have pleasure in sending you			the following quotation: ...		
These prices		are	DDP your works/store/offices in ...		
All prices			EXW.		
The above prices			DAT Liverpool.		
We are pleased	to offer	you	a	trade	discount of ...%.
We are willing	to give			bulk/volume	
				cash	
			an	introductory	
Our terms of payment		are	payment in advance.		
			COD (*cash on delivery*).		
			payment within 30 days (of delivery).		
			by letter of credit.		
We will	dispatch	the	goods	immediately on receipt of your order.	
	deliver		consignment	within ... days of receipt of your order.	
	send		order		
You can normally expect to receive your goods/consignment ...					
... within three weeks / five days / around a week after we receive your order.					
This	offer	is valid	for ... months/weeks.		
	quotation		until ... (date).		
We look forward to			receiving your order soon.		
			doing business with you in the future.		

Email
Sie arbeiten für ein Unternehmen, das Schokoladenkekse herstellt. Ihr Chef hat eine Anfrage aus den USA erhalten und bittet Sie, das Antwortschreiben zu verfassen. Schreiben Sie diesen Brief unter Verwendung der Notizen Ihres Chefs.

Herr Peterson von Peterson's World Foods, 17 Quincy Market, Boston, MA 02122 schrieb uns am 4. Nov. bezüglich eines Angebots für 50 Kisten Chocolate Heaven Kekse, versandt per Luftfracht CIF New York. Bitte informieren Sie ihn:
- *Gesamtbetrag $2.100*
- *Zahlungsbedingungen: innerhalb von 30 Tagen*
- *(2% Skonto, wenn er innerhalb von 15 Tagen bezahlt)*
- *Lieferzeit: ca. 3 Wochen*

■ Writing tip
Die folgenden drei Sätze enthalten jeweils einen Fehler. Können Sie die Fehler finden und korrigieren?
- Our adress is 14 Richmond Street, London.
- Thank you for your letter from 3 March.
- I look forward to hear from you soon.

Business correspondence – Emails

7 An invitation

Public relations (PR) are an important part of business. Rebecca Perry is the HR manager with a logistics company in the east of England. In the first email below she receives an invitation to dinner from a recruitment agency that she often works with.

❶ Look at the two emails. Why is the Five Star Recruitment Agency organizing the dinner? Does Rebecca accept or refuse the invitation?

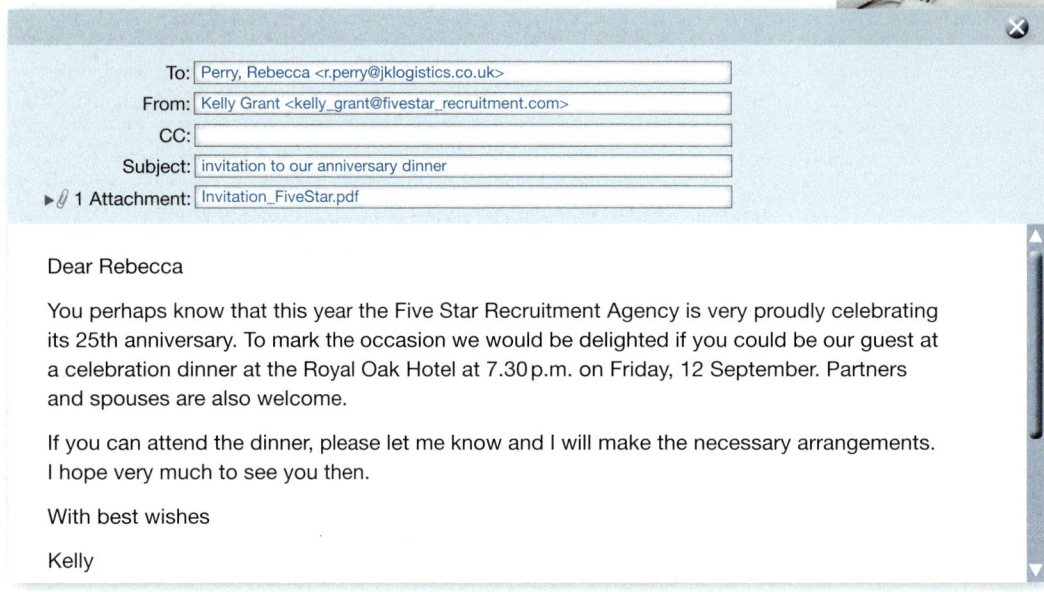

To: Perry, Rebecca <r.perry@jklogistics.co.uk>
From: Kelly Grant <kelly_grant@fivestar_recruitment.com>
CC:
Subject: invitation to our anniversary dinner
1 Attachment: Invitation_FiveStar.pdf

Dear Rebecca

You perhaps know that this year the Five Star Recruitment Agency is very proudly celebrating its 25th anniversary. To mark the occasion we would be delighted if you could be our guest at a celebration dinner at the Royal Oak Hotel at 7.30 p.m. on Friday, 12 September. Partners and spouses are also welcome.

If you can attend the dinner, please let me know and I will make the necessary arrangements. I hope very much to see you then.

With best wishes

Kelly

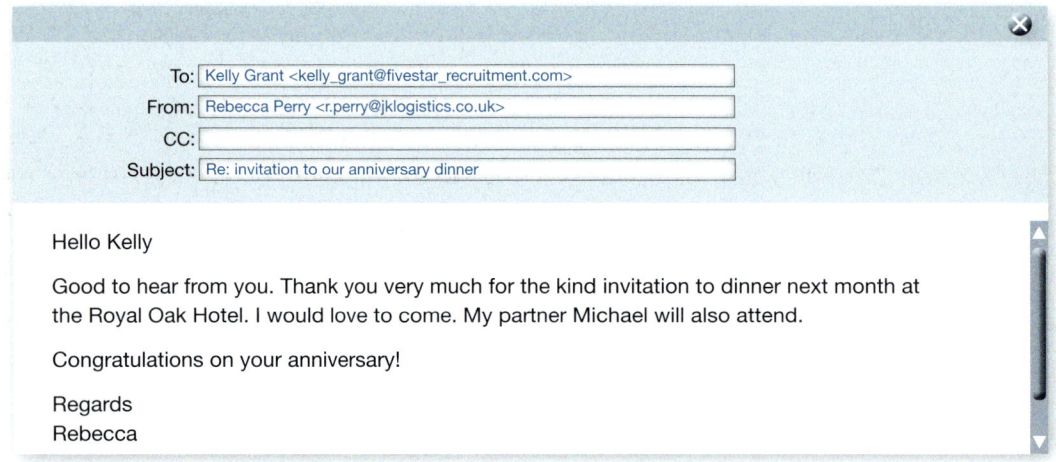

To: Kelly Grant <kelly_grant@fivestar_recruitment.com>
From: Rebecca Perry <r.perry@jklogistics.co.uk>
CC:
Subject: Re: invitation to our anniversary dinner

Hello Kelly

Good to hear from you. Thank you very much for the kind invitation to dinner next month at the Royal Oak Hotel. I would love to come. My partner Michael will also attend.

Congratulations on your anniversary!

Regards
Rebecca

Now you ...

2 Use these phrases and the emails on the previous page to write the emails below.

Sending an invitation		
This year we are celebrating our ... anniversary.		
We are currently organizing	a farewell dinner for Mrs Harrison.	
	a Christmas dinner for our most valued customers.	
The meeting/dinner/event will take place	at	the British Chamber of Commerce ...
		our offices ...
	on	Saturday, 29 April at 7.30 p.m. ...
We would be delighted if you could	attend the meeting.	
	be a guest at the dinner.	
Spouses and partners are welcome.		
Unfortunately, we cannot invite spouses and partners.		
Please	let me know as soon as possible if you can attend.	
	ring me on (01206) 449300.	
I look forward very much to seeing you then / at the dinner / at the meeting.		

Replying to an invitation		
(Friendly/informal)		
Thank you very much for your kind invitation to dinner on ... at ...		
I would	very much like	to attend.
	love	to come.
I'm very sorry but	I can't/won't be able to come	then / that day / that evening.
I'm afraid	I'll be away on business	
	I have another commitment	
(Formal)		
I have (great) pleasure in accepting	your invitation to dinner on ... at ...	
I regret that	I will be unable to accept your kind invitation.	
Unfortunately,	I have a prior commitment / will be away on business.	
I wish you a pleasant evening.		

Email 1
Sie haben eine Einladung von der örtlichen Handelskammer zu einem Abendessen bekommen, das von ortsansässigen Firmen organisiert wird, die Handelsverbindungen in die USA haben. Schreiben Sie eine E-Mail um die Einladung anzunehmen oder abzulehnen.

Email 2
Schreiben Sie eine Einladung an eine Kontaktperson in einem britischen Unternehmen, mit der Sie geschäftliche Beziehungen pflegen. Laden Sie die Person zu ihrem alljährlichen Firmenweihnachtsessen ein.

■ **Writing tip**
Wie bei jeder Art der geschäftlichen Kommunikation sollten Sie beim Verfassen von E-Mails sorgfältig abschätzen, welchen Eindruck Sie auf Ihren Geschäftspartner machen (könnten). Schreiben Sie also lieber förmlich (verwenden Sie Mr/Ms usw.), bis die Umstände eine andere Verhaltensweise nahelegen.

Business correspondence – Emails

8 A job application

Peter Scheibl works in Vienna as a translator for an online Austrian newspaper. He sees the advertisement below on an online media website and writes an email applying for the job.

❶ Look at the ad. What (and where) is the job? What qualifications and experience are necessary for it?

❷ Look at Peter's email. How does he present details of his CV? Do you think that he is a good candidate for the job? Why (not)?

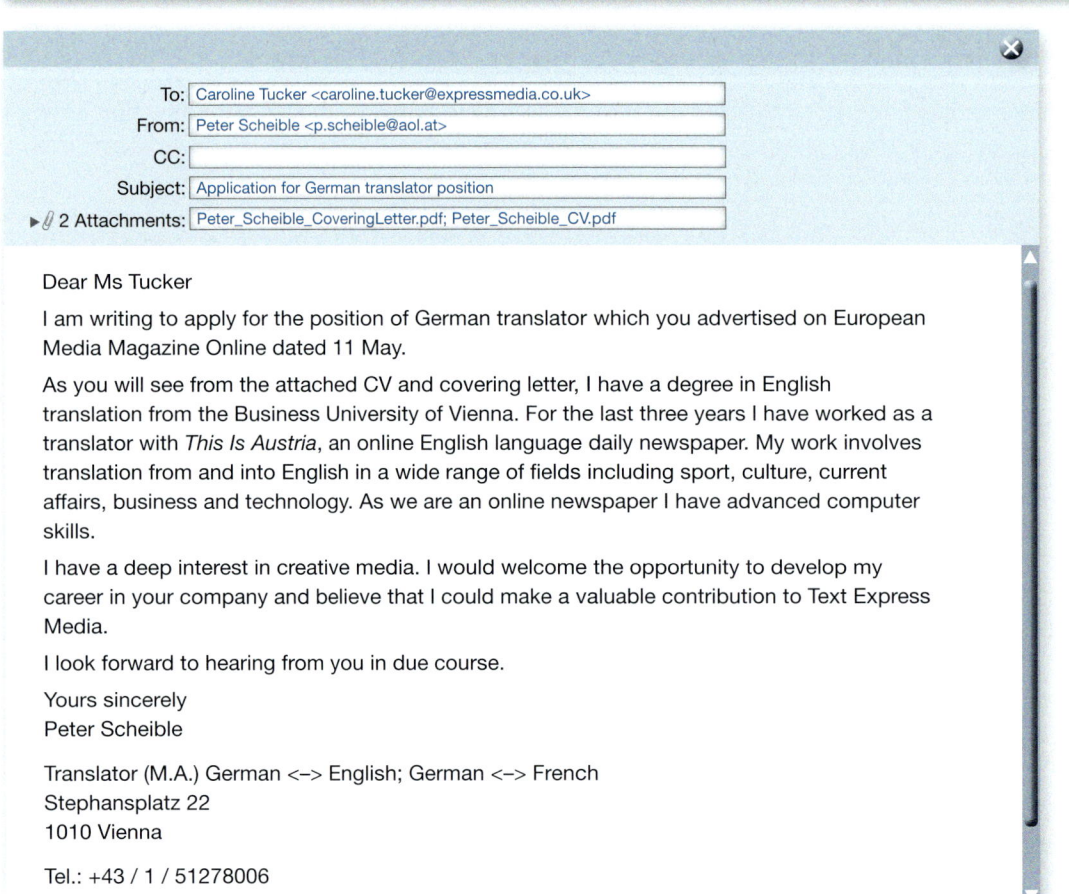

Dear Ms Tucker

I am writing to apply for the position of German translator which you advertised on European Media Magazine Online dated 11 May.

As you will see from the attached CV and covering letter, I have a degree in English translation from the Business University of Vienna. For the last three years I have worked as a translator with *This Is Austria*, an online English language daily newspaper. My work involves translation from and into English in a wide range of fields including sport, culture, current affairs, business and technology. As we are an online newspaper I have advanced computer skills.

I have a deep interest in creative media. I would welcome the opportunity to develop my career in your company and believe that I could make a valuable contribution to Text Express Media.

I look forward to hearing from you in due course.

Yours sincerely
Peter Scheible

Translator (M.A.) German <–> English; German <–> French
Stephansplatz 22
1010 Vienna

Tel.: +43 / 1 / 51278006

Now you …

3 Use these phrases and Peter's email to write an email applying for one of the job advertisements below.

I am writing I would like	to apply for the position of …,	which you advertised in the … of …
I am writing	in response to	your advertisement in the … of …
Please find my	covering letter and CV cover letter and résumé (US)	attached.
As you will see from	my CV/résumé, … the attached CV/résumé (and covering/cover letter) …	

I am a qualified accountant/engineer/…
I have a qualification/degree in business from (school/university) in …
I have three years' experience in production/manufacturing/advertising/sales/customer service.
I have worked for three years in the banking/automotive industry …

| In my present/current job, | I am responsible for …
my duties/responsibilities include … |

My current/present job involves …
I have (also) worked in / been responsible for / been involved in …

| I would welcome the opportunity | to work for your company.
to develop my career with your company. |
| I believe that I could | make a valuable contribution to your company. |

I feel that with my background and experience I could be a valuable asset.

I would be available for an interview at any time.
Please contact me at the above address if you require any further information.

| I look forward to hearing from you | in the near future.
in due course. |

CONFERENCE MANAGER

We are an international conference centre and are looking for a CONFERENCE MANAGER. The successful candidate will be responsible for an enthusiastic team of five people. You will have excellent communication skills, and at least five years' experience in the conference industry. Knowledge of English and some technical expertise is essential. If you are interested, please email your CV to:

caroline.goldie@centralconference.co.uk

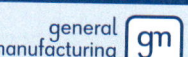

MARKETING ASSISTANT

We are a leading international manufacturing company based in the USA. We are looking for marketing assistants for our offices in Austria, Germany and Switzerland. You will have an excellent knowledge of English and be a good team player. We offer full training in marketing.

If you would like to apply, please email your résumé to:
david.wozynski@general-manufacturing.com
www.general-manufacturing.com

■ **Writing tip**

Denken Sie daran, dass sich E-Mails mit einem eindeutigen Betreff später leichter wiederfinden lassen. Der Betreff *Application* ist im Bezug auf den Inhalt der E-Mail eher vage. Besser wäre hier *Application as* mit Angabe der konkreten Stelle.

9 A confirmation

Paul Zydel works in the purchasing department of Online Media Marketing Inc. He has phoned a training provider to book Jamie Earle, a member of the company's sales department, on a training course. He then sends the fax below to confirm the arrangements.

1 Look at the fax. How long is Jamie staying in Washington? Is he going alone? Will he pay the invoice himself when he leaves?

05/19/20.. Th 08:15   FAX OMM INC.

Online Media Marketing Inc.
456 Broadway
New York, NY 10012
Fax: (212) 941-7482
Telephone: (212) 941-7400

FAX

To:	Sales Guru – training for sales professionals
Fax number:	202-555-78560
Date:	05/19/20..
Subject:	Confirmation of telephone booking
No. of pages including this one:	1
From:	Paul Zydel, Purchasing Dept (Tel: 212-941-7422)

This is to confirm the reservation made today by telephone for Mr. James Earle for the following training course:

Course title: Close more deals with Power Selling™
Dates: June 15-17
Cost: $1,700

Note that Online Media Marketing Inc. will pay the above invoice directly upon confirmation that the training has taken place. Please send an invoice to us at the above address after the course has been delivered.

Paul Zydel

A fax (message)

1. Die Angaben am Anfang eines Faxes sind unterschiedlich. Die hier aufgeführten (*To, Fax number; Date, Subject,* usw.) werden am häufigsten verwendeten. Ebenfalls üblich ist *For the attention of* (*Name*) oder einfach *Attention/Attn.* (*Name*).
2. Normalerweise wird auf einem Fax die Anzahl der Seiten angegeben, wobei diese Information oft als Standardaussage erscheint: *Number of pages including this one,* oder: *Number of pages including cover page/ sheet* (die erste Seite des Faxes).
3. Da viele unterschiedliche Arten von Dokumenten (Bestellungen, Rechnungen, technische Angaben und selbst Geschäftsbriefe) gefaxt werden, gibt es kaum Regeln oder Vorgaben. Wenn die Nachricht unkompliziert ist (wie im Beispiel hier), halten Sie Ihr Fax kurz und einfach. Eine förmliche Anrede und Schlussformel sind nicht unbedingt notwendig.
4. Faxe werden oft mit einer handschriftlichen Unterschrift versehen, um das Dokument rechtskräftig werden zu lassen.

Now you ...

2 Use these phrases and the fax on page 164 to write the faxes below.

This is I am writing	to confirm the booking/order made earlier today by telephone.
Please reserve	the following training course ... for (name). a single room for one/two/three nights
Our company	will pay the bill in full. will be responsible for payment (excluding food and drinks).
Please send an invoice	to us after the training has been delivered. to my attention on (name's) departure. as soon as you send the shipment.
(Name) will	pay the invoice personally on departure. settle the bill by credit card on departure. pay the invoice upon receipt of the order delivery note.

Faxes

Hier sind zwei für Sie bestimmte Notizen mit der Bitte, per Fax eine Buchung und eine Bestellung vorzunehmen.

Hiermit möchte ich einen Platz im Kurs „Moderne Verhandlungstechniken" vom 13.08. bis 17.08. in London reservieren.

Die Rechnung werde ich per Firmenkreditkarte vor Ort bezahlen werde.

Vielen Dank.

Tina Matthei

Wir brauchen mehr Büromöbel für unsere neuen Kollegen. Könntest Du deshalb bitte folgende Bestellung an unseren Lieferanten in Frankreich weitergeben:

4 Stühle, 4 Schreibtische und 3 künstliche Pflanzen.

Sie sollen die Rechnung mit der Lieferung bitte direkt an mich schicken.

Vielen Dank,

Dieter

Business correspondence – Text messages

10 Communicating with mobile devices

When communicating using mobile devices such as smartphones, the standard 'rules' of language regarding punctuation, spelling and grammar are often given a lower priority, both to save time and because there is often a limitation on the number of characters allowed.

Susanne Wölk and Peter Davenport are going on a business trip together and have arranged to meet at the airport. Peter is running late and is communicating with Susanne from the taxi.

1 Read the text messages and find the expressions/abbreviations which mean the following:

a at
b as far as I know
c see you
d you are / are you
e queue
f sorry
g today
h going to be
i before

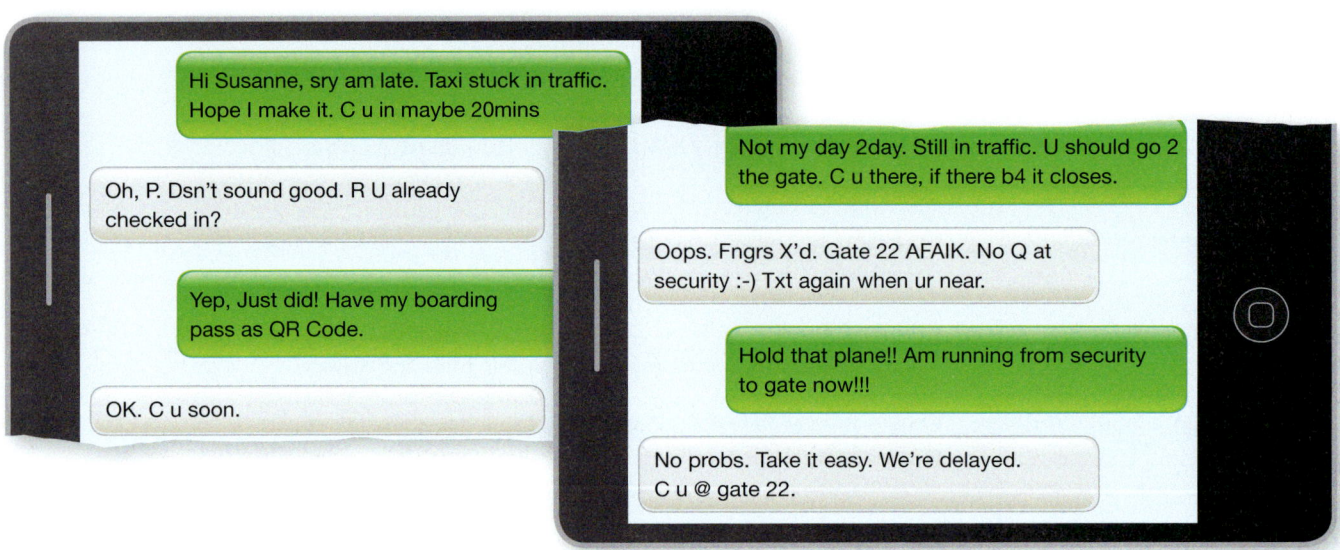

Now you …

2 Use these phrases and the text messages above to write the messages below.

Need to wrk late 2nite		I need to work late tonight	
Gonna c him 2mrw		I'm going to see him tomorrow	
Sry I'm l8		Sorry I'm late	
C U	soon / 2mrw in 20mins / @7	See you	soon/tomorrow in 20 minutes / at seven
R U hngry		Are you hungry?	

Text messages

Sie versuchen ein kurzes Treffen mit einer Kollegin/einem Kollegen zu organisieren. Sie schreiben ihr/ihm eine SMS. Schlagen Sie einen Treffpunkt und eine Zeit vor und informieren Sie Ihre Kollegin/Ihren Kollegen über den Anlass des Treffens. Wenn Sie mit der SMS fertig sind, entwerfen Sie bitte eine SMS, die Sie als Antwort auf Ihre erwarten würden. Das Zeichenlimit pro Nachricht sind 140 Zeichen.

Sie kommen zu spät zu einem Abendessen mit Kollegen. Schicken Sie ihnen eine SMS und erklären Sie, dass Sie sich verspäten, den Grund für Ihre Verspätung und wann Sie ungefähr ankommen werden. Wenn Sie mit der ersten SMS fertig sind, entwerfen Sie bitte eine SMS, die Sie als Antwort auf Ihre erwarten würden. Das Zeichenlimit pro Nachricht sind 140 Zeichen.

Extra practice – Answer key

Unit 1 pages 19–21

1
2 is/'s making; Do you like
3 start; am/'m starting; is/'s; am/'m doing
4 have; are/'re having
5 is/'s … doing; think; is/'s; is/'s making
6 are buying

2
1 e   3 f   5 c
2 b   4 d   6 a

3
2 Why do so many people like the iPhone?
3 How often does she update the files?
4 Where is your company based?
5 Are your company's products sold abroad?
6 When do you usually have a break?

4
1 is/'s divided
2 is/'s … based
3 Is … made
4 are manufactured, (are) exported
5 is/'s … used

5
1 c   3 a   5 d
2 b   4 e   6 f

6
1 division   4 staff
2 colleague   5 range
3 boss   6 culture

7
1 department   5 making
2 doing   6 boss
3 to   7 staff
4 supervisor   8 doing

8
1 Tzscheetzsch   4 0177 888 9433
2 Theodore   5 t_cheetz@online.co.uk
3 0044 20 7836 6652   6 www.xtratimes.com

9
Suggested answers:
1 He works for Toyota.
2 What's Anna doing now? She's making a phone call.
3 I usually drink/have coffee but today I'm drinking/having tea.
4 She sometimes meets up with her colleagues after work.
5 These products are usually bought by parents.
6 I'm afraid I can't help at the moment.
7 I work for a German company. I'm an engineer.
8 We are currently selling a lot of environmentally friendly products.

Unit 2 pages 31–33

1
1 went   6 lived
2 studied   7 didn't have
3 graduated   8 took
4 got   9 moved
5 worked   10 didn't like

used to
1 I used to go to school there.
5 I used to work in the marketing department.
6 I used to live in Nuremberg at that time.
8 I used to take the train to work.
10 I didn't use to like PTC at first.

2
1 Where did she go to university?
   She went to university in Munich/at the TU in Munich.
2 When did she graduate?
   She graduated in 2004.
3 Where was her first job?
   Her first job was at/with Tangelo/in Erlangen.
4 How did she get to work back then?
   She took/used to take the train.
5 When did she move to PTC?
   She moved there/to PTC in 2009.

3
1 was   6 weren't you
2 Were you able to   7 couldn't
3 didn't have   8 had
4 began   9 couldn't
5 was/were able to

167

Extra practice – Answer key

4
1. used to be done; is also done
2. could be seen; can also be seen
3. can be placed; were usually placed
4. used to be produced; are made

5
1. ordering process
2. job opportunity
3. product developer
4. team member
5. purchasing department
6. performance review
7. engineering industry

6
| 1 e | 3 b | 5 a | 7 h |
| 2 d | 4 c | 6 g | 8 f |

7
| 1 e | 3 a | 5 c |
| 2 d | 4 b | |

8
Suggested answer:
1. Franka
2. Paul Baker
3. Paul has the 15 netbooks from the GE3000 series that you ordered. He is upgrading the software at the moment. Everything should be ready next week.

9
Suggested answers:
1. Where were you born?
2. I got my first job in 1997 as a team assistant and then became a project manager in 2002.
3. We didn't always meet our deadlines.
4. I used to drive to work but now I take the bus.
5. She placed the order two months ago.
6. He can't answer the phone now because he's in a meeting.
7. I'm sorry that I can't do more/anything else to help you.
8. I'll give her the message when she returns/gets back.

Unit 3   pages 43–45

1
1. badly
2. careful
3. currently
4. easily
5. fast
6. well
7. lucky
8. possibly
9. thoroughly
10. usually

2
1. quickly
2. good; hard; right
3. urgently
4. lucky
5. badly; happy
6. immediately; important

3
1. were working
2. announced
3. were losing
4. launched
5. was introducing
6. expanded

4
2	b	Then it	is delivered
3	a	Next	is cut
4	f	During	is attached
5	d	After this	is done; is put
6	e	Finally	are checked; are shipped

5
1. must be worn
2. mustn't use
3. must be able to speak
4. needn't/don't have to start work
5. mustn't smoke
6. needn't/don't have to be shown

6
1. You must be
2. Nice to meet you.
3. Can I take your coat?
4. How was your flight?
5. Is this your first visit to London?

7

●··	·●·	·●··	··●·
compliment	appointment	competitor	information
document	arrangement	sabbatical	invitation

8

1. You can *make* an appointment, an arrangement or a compliment.
2. You can *take* a sabbatical.
3. You can *give somebody* an appointment, a compliment, a document, information or an invitation.
4. You can *attach* information, an invitation or a document to an email.
5. You want to be better than your competitor.

9

Suggested answers:
1. The translation of the safety instructions looks good.
2. We often have visitors on the premises.
3. Our CEO visited Mexico last year.
4. Visitors don't have to / needn't register at reception.
5. I'm afraid of fire.
6. We offer visitors a two-hour tour of the factory/plant.
7. I had an important appointment with the new factory/plant manager yesterday.

Unit 4   pages 55–57

1

2. He ~~are~~ going to look for new clients. *is/'s*
3. ~~Do will~~ it be more expensive? *Will*
4. The goods ~~will to arrive~~ tomorrow. *will arrive*
5. They're not ~~going make~~ a profit this year. *going to make*
6. The meeting ~~will be not~~ on Saturday. *won't be / will not be*
7. Who will be ~~ask~~ to attend the meeting. *asked*
8. We will ~~given~~ more information tomorrow. *be given*

2

1. won't be
2. will arrive ('will be' also possible)
3. will … collect
4. will come
5. will/'ll be
6. will … email
7. 'll do

3

1. going to be
2. will/'ll meet
3. going to learn
4. is/'s not going to be / won't be
5. will/'ll be able to
6. are going to go
7. is/'s going to be / will/'ll be
8. will/'ll send

4

2. Will … be given
3. will be presented
4. will be completed
5. won't be told
6. will … be sent
7. will be served

5

1. average consumer
2. product range
3. sales forecasts
4. Luxury products; high-end consumers
5. market pressure

6

1. from the graph
2. peaked
3. fell sharply
4. decreased steadily
5. rise
6. forecasts; an increase
7. drop slightly

7

Caller: Sabine Morel
Company: Digi-Shop
Order: Camera bags
1. 200, order number JG287XCB
2. 300, order number EP11YJD

8

Suggested answers:
1. I'm looking forward to testing the new product.
2. In 2010 there was a 10% decrease in sales.
3. I have some important information for you.
4. My opinion is that we could also work at the weekend. / In my opinion, we could …
5. What exactly do mean by 'weekend shifts'?
6. The installation will be finished by the end of January.
7. Marketing wants to postpone the meeting.
8. Don't worry. I'll call the project leader tomorrow.

Extra practice – Answer key

Unit 5   pages 67–69

1
2 If we hurry, we might be able to finish by 5 pm.
3 If you give me a discount, I'll increase the order.
4 If the quality is good, I'll order more.
5 If the delivery is late, we may have a problem.

2
1 e   3 a   5 b
2 c   4 d   6 f

3
1 When   3 when/if
2 if   4 if

4
3 ✔
4 easiest
5 more important
6 ✔
7 most famous
8 smaller
9 harder
10 ✔

5
1 oldest   5 faster
2 interesting   6 easier
3 most important   7 the worst
4 biggest   8 more useful

6
1 more   4 the most
2 the fewest   5 fewer
3 less

7
1 repeat   3 discount
2 free   4 to place a

8
1 e   3 a   5 d
2 c   4 f   6 b

9
1 Re   3 e.g.   5 FAQ   7 RSVP
2 IMO   4 BTW   6 asap   8 am

10
Suggested answers:
1 If the supplier offers a discount, we will/'ll place an order.
2 We may take two additional vending machines if the equipment is/'s good.
3 Call me when you arrive – I'll pick you up / collect you.
4 Most employees like taking part in Skype meetings.
5 A bad negotiation is much worse than no negotiation!
6 There are more stress-management seminars nowadays/today than 15 years ago.
7 The work processes/procedures here are not as complicated as in my former company.
8 I often use my mobile (phone) to arrange/make appointments with colleagues.

Unit 6   pages 79–81

1
2 Have you ever used SAP software?
3 Have you ever been late for an important meeting?
4 Have you ever applied for a visa?
5 Have you ever done business with the Chinese?
6 Have you ever given a presentation in English?

1 b   3 f   5 c
2 d   4 e   6 a

2
1 Has Mary ever worked
2 have/'ve never been
3 haven't tested
4 Have we been able to
5 has/'s had to
6 haven't attended
7 has/'s just uploaded

3
1 have/'ve travelled   6 had
2 have/'ve been   7 didn't try
3 have/'ve worked   8 spoke
4 worked   9 was
5 learned/learnt   10 have/'ve never forgotten

4
1 b yet   4 b yet
2 a already   5 a already
3 b yet   6 b yet

5
2 leaves   5 does your plane get
3 are you staying   6 am/'m not doing
4 am/'m seeing

170

6
1. Just a quick note
2. I really appreciated
3. I'm afraid
4. Otherwise
5. get back to me

7
Correct information:
1. Shufford
2. chairs
3. Charlie
4. shin

8
1. impressive track record
2. rewarding career
3. extensive knowledge
4. pioneering company

9
Suggested answers:
1. I had to work hard to become plant manager.
2. I have/'ve just been to an international conference.
3. My colleague is/'s taking part in a stand-up meeting this evening.
4. I was wondering if you could reschedule the flight?
5. Have you found the cable for the data projector yet?
6. I have noted down several appointments.
7. Could/Can you please confirm the appointment by 11 am tomorrow?
8. I'll pick up the brochures at nine o'clock tomorrow (morning).

Unit 7   page 91–93

1
1. were; haven't been
2. have risen
3. I gave; attended
4. were introduced
5. was
6. have already been launched; have been
7. had; went

2
1. for ten years
2. three months ago
3. for two weeks
4. since 1996
5. five minutes ago
6. since last May
7. for six years
8. since January last year

3
1. some; something
2. any; some
3. any; anywhere
4. some; anyone
5. any; someone
6. anything
7. any; someone/anyone

4
1. e
2. b
3. f
4. a
5. c
6. d

5
1. Is there anyone sitting here?
2. Can I get you anything to drink?
3. Could I have a glass of wine, please?
4. I'll bring them straight away.
5. Do you have any vegetarian dishes?
6. I'll have that.

6
1. There are three main things I'd like to show you in the next hour.
2. My presentation will take around 20 minutes.
3. By the end of this presentation, you'll have a better understanding of our new consumer products.
4. If you've got any questions, just ask.
5. I'd like to draw your attention to last year's results.
6. That brings me to the end of my presentation.
7. I have an extra slide here which will help answer your question.

7
1. revenue
2. interest rates; loans
3. mortgages
4. Turnover has; loans
5. borrow; lend

8
Suggested answers:
1. I need the new agenda for the kick-off meeting.
2. We are interested in a seminar on mortgage loans.
3. Our branch has offered this new service for two weeks.
4. Three months ago the turnover increased by 13%.
5. My colleague will give you an overview of our new loans.
6. The service was terrible! We didn't get anything / We got nothing to eat.
7. May I borrow your car this weekend?
8. Can we put some extra chairs at the back of the conference room?

Extra practice – Answer key

Unit 8   pages 103–105

1

2 His English was easy to understand.
3 This detergent is safe to use.
4 These goods have been difficult to transport.
5 The meeting is going to be complicated to organize.
6 His queries were hard to answer.

2

1 reasonably priced
2 technologically advanced
3 completely/perfectly safe to use
4 perfectly/beautifully designed
5 beautifully made

3

1 As a result
2 Although
3 For example
4 however
5 Nonetheless

4

2 had/'d seen
3 had/'d already phoned
4 had/'d tried
5 had you written
6 hadn't his boss been

5

1 cleared
2 had left / left
3 had
4 joined
5 walked
6 started
7 had left
8 didn't feel
9 got

6

1 I   Btw
2 F   appreciate
3 I   touch base
4 I   asap
5 F   Speaking of which
6 I   Hope

7

1 success
2 preparation
3 performance
4 completion
5 offer
6 responses
7 complaint
8 failure

8

1 e   3 a   5 f
2 c   4 b   6 d

9

Suggested answers:
1 The goods on the invoice are not the ones we received.
2 The visitors at the trade fair / The trade fair visitors were very price-conscious.
3 Our new product range offers good value for money.
4 We should translate the brochure into English.
5 The sales figures of the new KX model look good!
6 My colleague had left the brochures at the stand.

Unit 9   pages 115–117

1

1 have/'ve been producing/selling
2 has/'s been waiting
3 have been working
4 have been feeling
5 haven't been living
6 have you been selling

2

1 Have you been writing
2 have you written
3 Have you seen
4 has Bernd been attending
5 Have you ever thought

3

1 are … searching
2 adapt
3 have/'ve been making
4 international
5 range
6 mission
7 revolutionize

4

1 get across
2 get used to
3 get started
4 got to know
5 is/'s getting

5

1 me to translate
2 them to arrive
3 you to hurry
4 him not to come
5 her to wait
6 us not to smoke

6

1 It's a sort of
2 delicious
3 local speciality
4 Speaking of
5 I'd like to
6 Anyway

7

Model answer:
Customer: Jane Kaminsky
Order no.: XT4927DE
Reason for call: Order placed four weeks ago, still hasn't arrived.
Action plan: Check to see why order hasn't been processed yet. Find out when order can be delivered and whether we can offer compensation (discount?). Call back asap.

8

Suggested answers:
1 Meeting foreign visitors is a lot of fun. / It's a lot of fun to meet foreign visitors.
2 How long have you been business partners?
3 Last year our subsidiary in Poland was taken over by a Canadian company.
4 Could you please bring me the menu?
5 Do you want me to look for a new training provider?
6 You should adapt your style to the local culture.
7 We have been working on the complaints all day.

Unit 10   pages 127–129

1
1 had; could open
2 would happen; didn't deliver
3 would you do; was/were
4 knew; could help
5 would your company; wanted
6 didn't spend; would/'d get

2
1 e   3 a   5 c   7 d
2 g   4 b   6 f

3
1 in case   4 in case
2 Unless   5 Unless
3 unless   6 in case

4
1 He would buy a new laptop if he ~~would have~~ more money. *had*
2 We won't be competitive in Europe unless we ~~don't open~~ a new logistics centre. *opened*
3 In case we want to ~~opened~~ more factories, we need to increase the budget. *open*
4 Unless we finish now, we ~~wouldn't~~ finish in time for lunch. *won't*
5 If the delivery date ~~will be~~ OK, we'll sign the contract. *is*
6 Let's exchange phone numbers ~~if~~ we have to call each other later. *in case*
7 If he ~~would go~~ to the meeting, he could discuss the ideas in the report. *went*

5
1 tablet PCs   4 Tier-one suppliers
2 end users   5 e-book readers
3 business model   6 peripheral devices

6
1 market share   4 Fixed assets
2 copycat producers   5 depreciate
3 company reputation

7
1 depreciation   3 increase the
2 budget   4 products

8
1 the reason   5 market share
2 great opportunity   6 operating budget
3 financing   7 competitive
4 budget increase

9

Suggested answers:
1 Our plant/factory is owned by a Spanish company.
2 A good supplier should always have enough/sufficient spare parts in stock.
3 Besides projectors, we also supply tablet PCs.
4 She has specialized in project management.
5 If we increased the budget, we would reduce the risk.
6 We will lose customers unless we react quickly.
7 I need more data for the report.
8 At the end of the training course we took photos of everybody.

Transcripts

Unit 1

🔊 1.2 Part A, Exercise 4

Roger: Excuse me. It's Karin, isn't it? I'm Roger. I hope I'm not disturbing you.

Karin: Uhm, yes, I'm Karin Schröder. You're doing some research or something, aren't you?

Roger: Yes, that's right. Nice to meet you in person, Karin.

Karin: Nice to meet you too, uhm … Roger. Please, sit down. Would you like some coffee or something?

Roger: No, I'm fine, thanks. Right. Uhm, is now a good time for you, by the way?

Karin: Yes, no problem. So, what exactly do you want to know?

Roger: Well, as I mentioned in the email, I'm writing an article for the intranet. I'm profiling people in different departments here. I want to say something about their typical daily routines, that sort of thing, so that we can all get to know each other after the merger. By the way, I'm glad we can speak English; my German isn't very good yet.

Karin: No problem.

Roger: So, can I begin by asking about your role here?

Karin: Well, I'm Ms Balcke's personal assistant. I'm mainly responsible for diary management and general administration like …

Roger: Diary management? … Sorry, you first.

Karin: No, go ahead.

Roger: Diary management. What does that involve?

Karin: OK, I make a lot of appointments for my boss and I often arrange meetings for her too … that sort of thing. She has about ten meetings a day because of all the changes after the merger.

Roger: Yes, I can imagine there are lots of changes. But back to your job. General administration? Does that include payroll?

Karin: Employee reimbursement? No, I rarely deal with that. That's Sandra Beck's job. I usually do training schedules and I sometimes update HR documentation.

Roger: Are you working on anything special this week?

Karin: Well, a colleague of mine is off sick, so I'm doing some work for her too.

Roger: Does she work in this department?

Karin: No, she's a junior buyer in purchasing. As you probably know, we're doing more and more business with Asia at the moment, and Gina's boss – Jürgen Löwe – is visiting suppliers in Indonesia this week. I'm currently coordinating his travel arrangements.

Roger: I see. Another question, Karin. What do you like best about your job?

Karin: The flexitime! It's true – I have a young child. But I love the atmosphere here in the office too. We all have a great time here. I hope that won't change, you know, with the merger and all. Uhm, Roger, before we go on, can I ask you a question?

Roger: Sure, go ahead.

Karin: Why aren't you taking notes? You must have a great memory.

Roger: Oh, sorry, I forgot to mention it. Actually I'm recording everything on this little device here. Do you mind?

Karin: No, not at all.

🔊 1.3 Part A, Exercise 7

I'm in the retail, or rather the e-tailing, industry. We sell all kinds of products, from fashion to furniture, but we don't have a regular store: we sell everything online or through mail order.

I work in the human resources department of Logan Germany as a personal assistant. My immediate boss is Gabriele Balcke. She's head of HR and reports directly to our CEO. Within this department, I work closely with Sandra Beck. She's responsible for employee reimbursement, and her supervisor is Uwe Schmidt. Uwe also reports directly to Ms Balcke.

Outside of our department, I often give Gina Rossi some support. She's a colleague of mine in the purchasing department. Gina's a junior buyer and a member of a small team of seven people. Jürgen Löwe heads up the team. In fact, he's head of the purchasing department.

I have lots of nice colleagues in several other departments, too, like Anna Tafel from customer care. I sometimes meet up with her in the coffee break on a purely social basis.

🔊 1.4 Part B, Exercise 4

Hi, nice to meet you all. My name is Petra Weber and I work as a lab technician for Fresh Look, an innovative company in Düsseldorf. We are a British company and our head office is in Sheffield.

Fresh Look is a trusted brand name. We specialize in hair-care products but we're currently developing a new product range of body-care products for children, you know, soaps, shampoos, bubble bath.

The structure of our company is quite flat and divided according to product. Our products are made in factories in Germany and the UK and are exported to thirteen different countries, but our main customer base is in America and the UK. Obviously, a lot of our business is done in English so we require most of our employees to have a good level of English, and courses in business English are taught regularly throughout the organization.

1.5
My name is Johan Svensen. Pleased to meet you all. I'm Norwegian and I work for Lasco Energy, a utility company based near Oslo. I'm a safety engineer and am responsible for making sure that the plant meets national and international safety standards.

Our company structure is straightforward. Basically, it's like a pyramid. At the top we have the board of directors and at the bottom we have the workforce. In between we have a lot of senior managers, junior managers and that sort of thing. I work very closely with colleagues from all departments but especially the ones in the training department. Safe work habits are taught in different courses to managers and workers on a regular basis.

As to the plant itself, all our energy is generated through hydroelectric power. Lasco is a growing company, and we are currently constructing a new hydroelectric power station in Turkey.

Business file, Exercise 1
1.6
You have reached the voice mail of Elizabeth Parker of Vintage Rentals. I am not available to take your call at the moment. Please leave your full name and phone number and I will return your call as soon as possible.

1.7
Good morning, Ms Parker. This is Margaret Hughes, that's H-U-G-H-E-S, of Yarra Wines. I'm currently on a business trip here in the UK. The number I can be reached at here is 0744 5261333. I am calling to ask about car rentals. I'd love a brochure or something. I will be available today, Thursday, between one and 3.45. Again my number is 0744 5261333. Otherwise you can reach me by email at m_hughes@yarra-finewines.com. I look forward to hearing from you.

1.8
Good morning, Liz. This is Mohan Gupta. Remember, we met in Delhi last year. I am in the UK for a week and would love to catch up. I am staying at the Regent Hotel in London. The address is 115 Bayswater Road, and the telephone number is 020 for London, then 7836 7994. Please give me a call back and maybe we can arrange something. Goodbye.

1.9 Business file, Exercise 3

My name is Elizabeth Parker, but everyone calls me Liz. I work as a sales assistant for a unique sort of company called Vintage Rentals. We are the number one vintage vehicle hire company in Europe with the biggest range of vehicles. We hire out all kinds of vehicles from vintage limousines to old-fashioned farm tractors. Most of our customers are vintage car fans and hire our vehicles for weekend trips or as a special treat for the day. But we also do business with film companies that need our cars for movies or television commercials. This is the fun part of the job, of course, and – believe it or not – I sometimes even get to meet Hollywood film stars.

1.10
Hi, my name's Margaret Hughes and I run Yarra Wines, a winery in the Yarra Valley, near Melbourne, Australia. My parents founded the company, and I've worked there since I was a little girl. We export most of our production of Chardonnay wine to America and Europe. Our customers are very loyal and love our high-quality products and speedy service. So, what makes us so special? Well, for one thing, our wines are delicious. But we are also the only winery with our own small art museum.

1.11
Hello, my name is Mohan Gupta and I'm in banking. Our bank is in Delhi, India and it is a special kind of community bank. Most of our clients are very poor women. They live in villages near Delhi and they all need money to start up their own small businesses in the area. But what is so unique about our bank is that all of our customers have to send their children to school, otherwise we don't lend them any money. I sometimes talk at international conferences, and people are inspired by our results. I can see that we are really making a difference in the area and that's why I love my job so much.

1.12 Extra practice, Exercise 8
My surname is Tzscheetzsch. That's T-Z-S-C-H, double E, T-Z-S-C-H.
My first name is Theodore. That's T-H-E-O-D-O-R-E.
My telephone number is 00 44 (that's the country code for the UK) 20 (for London) 7836 6652.
You can also reach me by mobile phone on 0177 888 9433.
My email address is t_cheetz (that's C-H, double E, T-Z) @online.co.uk
Please visit my website at www.xtratimes.com. I'll spell that, W-W-W dot X-T-R-A-T-I-M-E-S, all one word, dot com.

Unit 2

1.14 Part A, Exercise 5
Well, my first job was at a company on the outskirts of the city. At that time, I lived in the city centre, so I used to get up very early every day so I could be one of the first in the office. It was my first job so I wanted to make a good impression! There was public transport, but I used to drive to work every day. It wasn't very economical – or environmentally friendly – but I didn't want to waste any time. Luckily, the company I work at now is located on the train line that goes by my flat, so I always take

Transcripts

the train. And these days I don't worry about being in first anymore.

I now have my own office, but I didn't use to. In my job at the start-up, for example, we all worked in an open-plan office. It used to get very noisy and hectic at times, which sometimes made it difficult to work. I was happy when, at ZMM, I could move to a smaller office with fewer people, and then later to my own office.

Another thing that is different now is the type of contract I have. I used to be on a temporary contract when I started with ZMM, but now I'm a permanent employee. It's nice to have that job security.

1.15 Part B, Exercise 1

Eleanor: Hi, Julia. Please come in and sit down.
Julia: Thanks, Eleanor.
Eleanor: So, I want to talk to you about an opportunity you might be interested in.
Julia: OK.
Eleanor: Well, you started here … uhm …
Julia: Two years ago.
Eleanor: Yes, two years ago, as a buyer in the purchasing department.
Julia: That's right.
Eleanor: And I can see from last month's performance review that things are going well. You dealt with a lot of large orders last year and you optimized the ordering process for the whole department. Very good. And the year before, you were able to integrate into your new team easily. It says here that 'your expertise helped you to quickly become a valuable member of the team'. Nice. It looks like you are able to deal with everything that comes your way, really.
Julia: Well, yes, I needed to learn quickly because we were understaffed at the time, and there was so much to do and so few people to do it. I could handle my main tasks easily after a couple of months …
Eleanor: OK.
Julia: … and I feel that I am ready for more challenge. I can definitely take on more responsibility.
Eleanor: OK. Good! Well, as you know, we're looking for a new team leader in the purchasing department, and I think you're the right person for the job.
Julia: Yes, I feel ready for it and know I can do it.
Eleanor: You understand that, as a team leader, you need to be able to delegate tasks and lead a team successfully. And manage budgets and deadlines, of course.
Julia: Well, yes, that's no problem. I was able to manage the team deadlines when I worked in the office supplies department. And I used to help with the budgets there.
Eleanor: OK, good. Here we expect you to coordinate your budget with the sales department too. And you're responsible for sourcing components from a range of suppliers, and for getting the best deals.
Julia: In my job now, I communicate regularly with our sales teams and suppliers, so that's no problem. I was able to create good working relationships with them from the beginning. I know I can use these business contacts now.
Eleanor: Another thing, in your current job your working hours are fixed. The working hours are flexible for team leaders, but you will probably need to work more hours than now. Will that be a problem?
Julia: Uh well, I guess not.
Eleanor: Good. Well, we still have to talk to the works council before we can officially offer you the job. But we can continue this discussion after lunch …

1.16 Business file, Exercise 1

Anne: Purchasing. Anne Bowen speaking.
Karsten: Hi Anne, it's Karsten Meier here from product development. Is Rachel there?
Anne: I'm sorry, the line's pretty bad. Could you repeat that, please?
Karsten: Yes, it's Karsten Meier here. I'd like to speak to Rachel Pennant.
Anne: Oh, that's better. Hi, Karsten. I'm sorry, she's not here at the moment. I think she's in a meeting. Could you call back later, say, in two hours?
Karsten: Well, I have to be in a meeting then myself. I need some information from her. Can you take a message?
Anne: Sure, go ahead.
Karsten: I placed an order with her purchasing team last week. Can she tell me when I can get the DC77 components I need for development.
Anne: OK, I'll give her the message when she returns.
Karsten: Great, thanks a lot. Bye, Anne.
Anne: Bye, Karsten.

1.17 Business file, Exercise 2

Karsten: Hello, Karsten Meier speaking.
Rachel: Hi Karsten, it's Rachel from purchasing. You called me earlier?
Karsten: Oh, hi Rachel. Thanks for calling me back. So, can you tell me the status of my order?
Rachel: Yes, sure. That's for the DC77 components, right? I checked, and we placed the order the same day you ordered from us. Our supplier has to source the components from the

	manufacturer, but they can get them to us by the 20th. Is that OK for you?
Karsten:	Hmm. Well, to be honest, I expected them sooner. I really need them asap.
Rachel:	I understand. I'm sorry, Karsten, but I'm afraid I can't do more to help you.
Karsten:	That's OK, Rachel. It's good to know about it, so I can plan accordingly. Thanks for the info.
Rachel:	OK, no problem. Talk to you soon, Karsten.
Karsten:	Yes, have a good week. Bye.
Rachel:	Goodbye.

1.18 Extra practice, Exercise 8

Hi, Marko. This is Paul. Paul Baker. I tried to call Franka but she's not in and for some reason I couldn't leave a message. Her phone just rang and rang. Strange. Anyway, could you give her a message for me?

She placed an order for some new hardware last week. It was for fifteen netbooks – that's netbooks, not notebooks, right? – for the GE3000 series. That's G for golf and E for echo, three thousand. OK? So, can you tell her that they are available, so that's no problem. We just have to upgrade the software and everything should be ready next week.

OK, thanks a lot. I have a meeting now till around four but she can try to call me then if she has any questions. I'm not sure if she has my mobile number, so it's 0176 654 3312. OK, thanks a lot, Marko. Bye.

Unit 3

1.19 Part A, Exercise 4

Julie:	Oh, you must be Petra! I'm Julie Chin. The driver called ahead and told me you were arriving. Welcome to Hong Kong. And welcome to Cantona's production site.
Petra:	Hello, Julie. It's nice to finally meet you in person after all the emails.
Julie:	Yes, it's nice to meet you too, Petra. And how was your flight? Did everything go smoothly?
Petra:	Fine. No problems there. Everything went according to plan.
Julie:	Good. So, what's your first impression of Hong Kong then?
Petra:	Well, it looks amazing from the air! But the driver got here so fast that I didn't have a chance to see much of the city itself. I can't wait to see more.
Julie:	Yes, well, we'll certainly make sure of that. We can go to a typical Hong Kong restaurant, if you like. Do you like Chinese food?
Petra:	Yes, I do. That sounds good. I always like to try new things when I'm in another country.
Julie:	Yes, me too. Uhm, would you like a cup of coffee or something while we're waiting for Li Wen? We can go to my office and you can leave your coat and your suitcase there too.
Petra:	Li Wen?
Julie:	He's the factory …
Wen:	Hi, Julie – excuse me, uhm …
Julie:	Oh, hi Wen. We were just talking about you! Petra, this is Li Wen, the factory supervisor. Wen, this is Petra Schöder.
Petra:	Nice to meet you, Mr Li.
Wen:	Please call me Wen.
Petra:	And I'm Petra.
Wen:	It's nice to meet you too, Petra.
Julie:	Petra's from Germany. Wen used to work in Germany, Petra.
Wen:	Well, not exactly in Germany. In Austria actually.
Petra:	Oh, really! Whereabouts in Austria, if you don't mind me asking?
Julie:	Oh, sorry, would you excuse me for a minute? I need to take this. Wen, can you look after Petra, please, and maybe go ahead and start the tour without me?
Wen:	No, problem, Julie. Petra, can I take your coat?

1.20 Part B, Exercise 3

Petra:	What's that over there? The canteen?
Wen:	Yes, we can go there for lunch after the tour if you like. Or would you like something to eat now?
Petra:	I'm fine, thanks.
Wen:	Ah, here is Julie.
Julie:	Hello. The call didn't take as long as expected.
Wen:	Good. So, Petra, shall we get started with the tour then. Ah, you have a question?
Petra:	Yes, it says something in the guide about earplugs. Are they really necessary?
Wen:	No, no, you needn't wear the earplugs today. It isn't really that noisy in the factory.
Petra:	OK, thanks.
Wen:	Uhm, before we start, I just wanted to give you a brief overview …
Julie:	Oh, sorry, Wen. Petra, I asked my assistant to check your shoe size. We want to give you a pair of SmartCommuter Pro's after the tour.
Petra:	Great, my own SCPs. That's really nice, thanks. Uhm … I take a size 38.
Assistant:	Size 38. Thank you.
Julie:	Thank you, Flora. Wen, you were saying …?
Wen:	Ah, yes, I was saying that I want to give Petra a brief overview of the shoemaking process before we start the tour. Uhm, well, you know that we use both leather and synthetic materials, right, especially for a product like the SCP. All the material is delivered to the unloading bay behind the factory and then is taken over to the cutting area, which is over there. The shapes have to be cut out by hand. A

Transcripts

	number of processes in shoe production have to be done manually, you know.
Petra:	Really? Why is that?
Wen:	Shoemaking is a very skilled profession – machines can't do everything. We need skilled workers who can understand design patterns and operate hand tools and machinery.
Petra:	I see.
Wen:	Anyway, where were we? Ah, yes. After the cutting, the upper parts of the shoe are sewn together, and then these upper parts are attached to the bottom part of the shoe, the sole. It's quite a tricky process.
Petra:	What happens exactly during that stage?
Wen:	Well, that's a good question. It's actually a bit complicated to explain without seeing it done, so I'd like to show you the process later, if that's OK with you?
Petra:	Yes, that's fine.
Wen:	So, let's move on.
Petra:	OK.
Wen:	Next, the shoes are given an attractive finish and then they are inspected for defects by quality control.
Petra:	Right.
Julie:	And finally – to wrap things up, so to speak – the shoes are packed in boxes and taken to the loading bay ready for shipment.
Wen:	Exactly. So, shall we start the tour now?
Petra:	Yes, indeed.
Wen:	OK, follow me. Here is a helmet for you. Please put it on and, remember, be careful. Do not touch any moving parts.
Petra:	Got it. So where are we going first?
Wen:	Let's start with the cutting area. It's just over there …

Business file, Exercise 2

1.21 1

Peter:	Excuse me, are you Miro Bernatsky from Alpeo, by any chance?
Miro:	Yes, that's me.
Peter:	Good morning and welcome to Manchester. I'm Peter Armitage.
Miro:	Hi, Peter. Nice to finally meet you in person.
Peter:	Well, I'm delighted to meet you too, Miro. Is this your first visit to Manchester?
Miro:	Yes, it is. I go to London quite frequently but this is my first time here. I'm looking forward to seeing this part of England.
Peter:	Right, I'd love to see more of Switzerland too. I just love Berne. I was there last summer with my girlfriend. We had a fabulous time.
Miro:	Yes, Berne is a very nice city – I know it well.
Peter:	Is that where you're from originally?
Miro:	No, I'm originally from the Czech Republic, but my family moved to Switzerland when I was a teenager. And I live just outside of Zurich now.
Peter:	Zurich? Is Zurich … oh, sorry, do let me take that.
Miro:	Oh, don't worry. It's on wheels.
Peter:	Oh, OK. Well, anyway, I'm parked just outside. Follow me. So, Zurich …

1.22 2

Peter:	Miro, may I introduce you to Fiona Smith. She's our Location Sourcing Manager. Fiona, this is Miro Bernatsky from Alpeo.
Fiona:	Oh, hello Miro. I'm thrilled to meet you. I know we can find some great locations for your stores.
Miro:	I'm happy to meet you too, Fiona. I'm looking forward to working with you.
Fiona:	Me too. Uhm, Miro, would you like some tea or coffee?
Miro:	Coffee, please.
Fiona:	Coffee? Good choice! Milk, sugar?
Miro:	Black is fine for me, thanks.
Fiona:	And please help yourself to the refreshments. These here are Kendall Mint Cakes. They're a speciality from the Lake District.
Miro:	Really? What are they exactly? I've never heard of them.
Fiona:	Please help yourself. They're a kind of energy bar. They're nice and minty.
Miro:	Mmm, it tastes good. You said something about the … Lake District? Is that somewhere near here?
Fiona:	The Lake District, yes. It's not far, only about 50 miles away. It's a beautiful area – well worth a visit. I could organize a trip there for you, if you like.
Miro:	Well, yes, if we have time, that would be nice.

1.23 3

Miro:	The Lake District is beautiful. The landscape here is quite impressive.
Fiona:	So, do you spend a lot of time outdoors then, Miro?
Miro:	Well, I live in Switzerland, so of course I do a lot of hiking. And skiing in winter.
Fiona:	Well, you can't do much skiing here. But there are a lot of nice treks to go on if you have the time.
Miro:	Yes, unfortunately my time is limited on this trip. But thanks for bringing me here today. It reminds me a bit of some parts of Switzerland. Especially the area around Zurich. Do you know that part of the world?

1.24 4

Peter: Is there anything particular you'd like to try? I can recommend this starter, but it's quite spicy.
Miro: I like spicy food. But I feel in the mood for something else this evening. I think I'll just have the chicken and noodle soup. So, Peter, do you come here often?
Peter: Yes, my girlfriend and I love Thai food.
Miro: Have you ever tried Swiss food?
Peter: Uhm, well, no. At least I don't think so. Is there anything you can especially recommend?
Miro: Well, there are so many different dishes. If you ever visit Zurich, please give me a call. I can take you to the Kunststuben.
Peter: Sorry, I don't speak German. What's that?
Miro: It's a traditional restaurant in an old art gallery close to Lake Zurich.

Unit 4

1.26 Part A, Exercise 1

The next story in our business segment is the strike by German dairy farmers and how the market is reacting to it. One of the firms most affected by the strike is Premier Dairies, with its headquarters in Regensburg, Germany. Premier Dairies is also an important supplier to the British market.

First a bit of background: this past summer Premier Dairies reduced the prices of its dairy products due to market pressure. To compensate for lost revenue, Premier Dairies then forced the farmers to accept lower prices for their milk. Other firms did the same and this caused the strike.

Premier Dairies CEO Wolfgang Meier says the company is going to keep its prices low for the general consumer market. But, they are also going to bring out a new luxury product line at the same time. This new brand will target those consumers who are willing to pay more for high-end products.

Unlike the average consumer, who is usually more interested in lower prices than what's fair for farmers, there is a growing number of consumers who can and will pay more for higher quality and image.

The strike will probably push milk prices up again, so Premier Dairies will most likely balance the revenue from both standard and luxury products so that they don't make an overall loss.

We are told that the new brand is going to be better than anything now on the market. Is this just marketing talk or are we really in for a treat? Whatever happens, it looks like it'll be an interesting time for Premier Dairies.

1.27 Part A, Exercise 7

Anja: OK, it looks like we're all here, or at least all except Hillary. We don't have much time so I'd like to get started straight away, if that's all right with everybody. Good. So, let's get started. First item on the agenda is the review. Martin, can I hand over to you?
Martin: Right! OK, ehhh, let me just turn the projector on. OK. Well, as you can see from the graph, sales in the yogurt segment rose steadily during the first two quarters of the year. We started the year with sales of approximately €7m. First quarter sales were around 7.5m and in the second quarter sales continued to rise, and peaked at €8.5m in June. This was because of the reduction in retail price. But the third quarter wasn't so good. Following the farmers' strike, we had to reduce production. This caused sales to fall sharply to €6m.
Anja: OK, thanks Martin. Well, it's clear that we need to increase sales in our yogurt segment and that's why we're planning to introduce the new product range, a luxury brand called Luxus. Hillary was going to tell us about the concept, but unfortunately she had to leave the office unexpectedly, so Paolo is going to take over. Paolo, over to you.
Paolo: Thanks, Anja. Well, we are going to introduce the new brand on the 10th of December, in time for Christmas. It will have a premium price, and target consumers who want higher quality and are willing to pay more. The yogurt will have a higher percentage of the key ingredient, such as fruit or high-quality cocoa. Early forecasts show that there will be an initial rise in sales in the first quarter of next year when the brand is new and the marketing campaign is fully in place. Sales will probably drop slightly before the second quarter, and then continue to rise again. We expect a steady increase from then on and into the third quarter.
Susan: Sorry to interrupt, Paolo. What will you do if the farmers strike again, and how will this affect your forecast?
Paolo: Good question, Susan. Well, we closed a negotiation last week with the farmers' union. We agreed to pay them 7% more and they're not going to strike for at least another 12 months. I have a summary of the agreement in my office. I'll send it over to you later today. If they break the deal, well, eh … we also have Plan B. Plan B means sourcing the milk from a farmers' cooperative in another country.
Susan: OK, sounds good. Could you send us a list of all potential countries for Plan B?

Paolo: Will do, no problem.
Susan: Thanks.
Anja: OK, good. Thanks, Paolo. Well, we need to move the discussion in the direction of item three on the agenda. Let's continue with questions later and start thinking about other Luxus products we want to add to the brand first.

1.28 Part B, Exercise 1

Well, as you know, it's only February and the Luxus brand is so successful that we need to have a new production line just for this brand. On this chart you can see an overview of the project schedule. The first step is to install the new production line. The installation, which will take two months, will be completed by the end of May, and we can begin then with testing to see how the new line works.

So, testing will take around six months and will be carried out on an ongoing basis in four to five-week trials. During this testing phase, regular optimization changes have to be made, of course. These will happen every four to five weeks. It won't take more than two to three days each time to get the machines fitted for the next trial.

In the first week of October, we'll start training the machine operators. Training will also take place on an ongoing basis and continue into the new year. Testing and optimization have to be finished by the end of November. That's our most important deadline as we need to start producing on the new line at the beginning of December.

Stage six is, of course, production on the current line. This will continue as normal until the middle of December when we stop producing on the current machinery and switch over to the new production line.

1.29 Part B, Exercise 5

Susan: So, that's the schedule then.
Martin: Sorry, those projections are unrealistic. With respect, Susan, I can't agree to that schedule. A two-week changeover period in December isn't going to be long enough to move active production from the current line to the new one.
Susan: What do you suggest then?
Martin: I think we need to bring the whole schedule forward and start with installation in March. That'll give us a whole extra month at the other end.
Susan: I understand your concern, Martin, but aren't you forgetting that we will produce less in December anyway?
Paolo: Susan's right. Any issues that arise will be dealt with during Christmas and the New Year. We can run night shifts and weekends if necessary so …
Martin: Wait a minute. Are you saying that we have to work nights and weekends over the holidays? I don't think my team will be happy with that at all.
Anja: OK, let's calm down a moment. That's not what we're saying. It's only a back-up plan. I'm sure we'll be able to stay on schedule.
Susan: Yes. I agree. We'll be fine.
Anja: Yes, Paolo?
Paolo: I think Susan's right. I think her schedule will work. There is enough time in the schedule for testing and optimization. By December the new line should be running perfectly so that we can make the transition from one day to the next. And we'll keep the current line running on standby just in case.
Martin: OK. I agree with you up to a point. I'd still be happier if we could bring the whole project forward.
Anja: Susan, is that possible?
Susan: It should work. I'll check the figures again and get back to you by the end of the week.

1.30 Part B, Exercise 6

1. Do you wanna postpone the meeting?
2. Lemme help you with the projector.
3. Waddaya gonna do after the meeting?
4. Wadja put on the agenda?
5. Gimme a call next week.
6. Can I getcha something to drink?

1.31 Business file, Exercise 2

Recording: Welcome to GIVE-IT, Corporate Gifts. Please press one for English. Press two for Dutch.
Karl: OK, *eins*.
Recording: Thank you. To place an order, press one. If you have a query about an existing order, press two. If you want to order a catalogue, press three. To hear this menu again, press four. For all other queries, please stay on the line.
Karl: OK, *nochmal eins*.
Nancy: Good morning. This is Nancy speaking. How may I help you today?
Karl: Hello, this is Karl Hempel from Premier Dairies in Regensburg, Germany. I have your catalogue from a business partner, but I have a couple of questions before I place an order.
Nancy: Sure. What would you like to know?
Karl: OK. You can print my company logo on your range of products, is that right?
Nancy: That's right.
Karl: So how do I send you the logo?
Nancy: Well, you can send it to us by email …
Karl: As a jpg file, for example?

Nancy:	Yes, that would be fine. Or if you prefer, you can just send us a page of your company notepaper or whatever, something that has your logo on it.
Karl:	And you can take the logo from that?
Nancy:	That's correct. It's all very simple.
Karl:	So, do the prices in the catalogue include printing the logo or is that extra?
Nancy:	No, the prices include the printing costs. But when you place your first order, there's a one-time charge for producing your logo or slogan. We call it a one-time logo development charge.
Karl:	How much is that?
Nancy:	Thirty euros.
Karl:	But I only pay that the first time, right?
Nancy:	Right. After your first order, we keep your logo here and we just use it again when you order more goods from us.
Karl:	OK. And what are your terms of payment?
Nancy:	Thirty days after you receive the items and you're satisfied with them.
Karl:	And shipping and handling costs?
Nancy:	Twenty euros if your order is under 500 euros. If you place an order for 500 euros or more, then shipping and handling is free.
Karl:	OK, well, that sounds good. I'd like to place an order with you, then.
Nancy:	OK, could you please repeat your name and the name of your company?
Karl:	That's Karl Hempel – H-E-M-P-E-L. And the company is Premier Dairies GmbH, that's capital G, small M for Mike, small B for Bravo, capital H. You should have the contact details. We placed an order … er … about a year ago.
Nancy:	One moment. Premier Dairies. OK, yes, Mr Hempel, here you are. Let me just put your name in here. Great. So, I'm ready for your order.
Karl:	First, men's T-shirts: I'd like to order 100. Women's T-shirts: 150.
Nancy:	Oh, I'm sorry, Mr Hempel. The minimum order on the T-shirts is 200.
Karl:	Well, 100 men's and 150 women's T-shirts makes 250. Do you see what I mean?
Nancy:	Oh, right. Well, they are two different products with different product codes. But, OK, as this is your first order, I think we can make an exception. So, which colours and sizes would you like?
Karl:	All light blue and medium.
Nancy:	OK.
Karl:	Next, 500 light blue spoons.
Nancy:	OK, 500 spoons, light blue.
Karl:	And then 175 of the travel bags, black.
Nancy:	Oh, yes. They're quite popular. Is there anything else you'd like to order?
Karl:	No, that's it.
Nancy:	I'll just read that back to you: 100 men's T-shirts, light blue, medium; 150 women's T-shirts, light blue, medium; 500 light blue spoons and 175 black travel bags. And should we use the company logo on file?
Karl:	Oh, no. All these items should have the product logo on them, not the company logo. The product line is called Luxus, OK? L-U-X-U-S.
Nancy:	Yes, that's important. L-U-X-U-S. OK, I've got it.
Karl:	I can send you the logo now.
Nancy:	Great.
Karl:	Oh wait, one more thing. When can I expect delivery?
Nancy:	Well, there'll be a lead time of about four weeks on this order.
Karl:	I'm sorry, what's a lead time?
Nancy:	Oh, that's the time we need from when you place your order until the order is ready to be shipped.
Karl:	Right! OK, That's fine. Thank you.
Nancy:	You're welcome, Mr Hempel. Thanks very much for calling and doing business with us. Have a nice day.
Karl:	Thanks, you too. Goodbye.

1.32 Extra practice, Exercise 7

Peter:	Foto-for-You, good morning. This is Peter speaking.
Sabine:	Hi, this is Sabine Morel from Digi-Shop in Lyon. I'd like to place a large order.
Peter:	OK, that sounds great. Could you please repeat your name and the name of your company?
Sabine:	It's Sabine Morel – M-O-R-E for Echo -L. And the company is Digi-shop. That's D for Delta, I for India, G for Golf, and I for India, hyphen, shop, S-H-O-P. My name should be in your computer. I ordered from you last year.
Peter:	One moment. OK, Ms Morel, yes, here you are. Digi-Shop. Right. OK, I'm ready for your order.
Sabine:	So, I'd like to order two types of camera bags. First of all, I'd like 200 bags with order number JG287XCB and 300 bags, order number EP11YJD.
Peter:	OK, I'll just read that back to you. Two hundred bags, order number JG287XCB and 300 bags, order number IB11JYD.
Sabine:	No, no. Wait a minute. That's EP, E for Echo, P for Papa, one, one, Y for Yankee, J for Juliet and D for Delta.
Peter:	Yes, thanks. That's 300 of EP11YJD. I've got it now.

Sabine: Great.
Peter: It looks like we'll be able to ship in about 10 days, so you should have the order in about two weeks. Is that OK?
Sabine: Excellent! OK, That's fine. Thanks.
Peter: You're welcome, Ms Morel. Have a nice day.
Sabine: Thanks, you too. Goodbye.

Unit 5

1.33 Part A, Exercise 1

Bob: And they agree that the new company gym will help motivate the staff to think more about a healthy work-life balance.
Sigrid: Good.
Bob: So, it looks like we're ready to place the order, then.
Sigrid: Well, wait a minute. We know which equipment we want to buy, but that doesn't mean that we should order directly from the catalogue. I mean, look at the prices!
Bob: Well, we could always order used equipment.
Sigrid: No, we can't do that. We want our employees to be motivated and to see the investment in the new gym as a sign of our commitment to them and their well-being. I know the new equipment is more expensive, but it'll look like we're only half trying if we buy used equipment. There might also be safety and insurance issues if the equipment isn't new.
Bob: I see what you mean.
Sigrid: And we need to think about discounts. For example, if we order 14 fitness machines in total, we'll most likely be able to get a bulk discount.
Bob: Good point. And we won't use up our entire budget if we manage to get a discount. Maybe we'll then have enough left in the budget to get the drinks machine we were looking at.
Sigrid: Yes, good idea. OK. How about this? We tell the supplier that we want 12 different pieces of equipment and see if we can get a bulk discount. Then if he agrees, we can 'spontaneously' order another weights machine and another cross-trainer. This will bring the total number up to 14.
Bob: That's a good strategy. I think it's a good way to go.
Sigrid: Good. Can you complete the order form and send it off on Monday to – eh, what was his name?
Bob: Manfred Schmidt.
Sigrid: Yeah, right – so he'll have it before our meeting on Thursday?
Bob: OK, sure.

Sigrid: Right, we also need to talk about the delivery terms. Normally they charge extra for delivery so let's try to get free delivery.
Bob: OK, maybe after we order the two additional pieces of equipment, we can also put in a last-minute order for a drinks machine. Then he might agree to free delivery to the top floor, so we won't have to move the equipment later.
Sigrid: Yes, nice idea. OK. Let's see how it goes.

1.34 Part A, Exercise 5

Bob: Well, thanks for coming, Mr Schmidt. Did the completed order form arrive OK? We sent it over on Monday.
Manfred: Yes, I got the order, thanks, but I'm a bit confused. The total order is only for 12 pieces of equipment: six weights machines, four bikes, one cross-trainer and one stepper.
Bob: Yes, that's right.
Manfred: Oh, OK. That's it?
Bob: Well, yes. Your prices are rather high, and our budget is quite tight. We might be able to order more if you can give us a discount.
Manfred: Well, I'm sorry, that's just not feasible. The prices are the way they are because you're ordering top quality. Our equipment is better than the competition's, and on an order of this size I'm afraid we can't offer a discount.
Sigrid: Well, don't you think that a discount could be possible because we're a new customer?
Manfred: I might be able to agree to that. Hmm. I'll tell you what: if you can increase your order by another two fitness machines, I'll give you a 5 % discount on the complete order. How does that sound?
Sigrid: OK, now that's getting interesting. How about if we increase our order by another two fitness machines and a drinks machine? Will you give us an 8 % discount and free delivery?
Manfred: You drive a hard bargain, Ms Petík. I'm sorry, I can't increase the discount though. However, if you increase your order that much, I can throw in mats and hand weights for free, as well as free delivery.
Sigrid: With a 5 % discount?
Manfred: Yes, that's right. How does that sound?
Sigrid: OK, that sounds fair. I can agree to that. It's a deal!
Manfred: Great! So when can I expect to receive the new purchase order?
Bob: I'll call the purchasing department later today and take care of re-issuing the order form. Meanwhile we can …

Part A, Exercise 8

1.35 1
A: I'm sorry, but that's the lowest I can go.
B: But that's still much too high for me.
A: I'm sorry. It looks like we can't reach an agreement

1.36 2
A: How about if I reduce the price by 10%?
B: Yes, I think I can agree to that.
A: Great, so it's a deal.

1.37 3
A: We need to make a decision now. Time is running out.
B: Well, I'm sorry. We can't both get on the flight.
A: Yes, I know. It looks like we have a win-lose situation here!

1.38 Part B, Exercise 1

Dirk: Hey, Sue. What can I get you?
Sue: Oh, I'll have a coffee please, Dirk. White, no sugar.
Dirk: OK, this one's for you.
Sue: Thanks.
Dirk: So, how's it going?
Sue: Ah, pretty good, thanks. I just got back from visiting the Dublin subsidiary.
Dirk: Ah, how'd that go?
Sue: Yeah, good. Everything went fine. You know, they've got the highest workload of all our European offices these days, but they still have the best results. They get everything done.
Dirk: That's great.
Sue: They're really into this whole work-life balance thing in Ireland at the moment.
Dirk: (groans)
Sue: I think it's a good idea. I think it's becoming more and more important.
Dirk: You can't be serious! Some people are just lazier than others and look for reasons to work less.
Sue: Maybe, but not the Dublin group. Look at their performance. It's about being more responsible for having a life outside of work. People who only work all the time, like some people I won't mention, will burn out eventually. That's just counterproductive. You need to balance your work with something like sport or something to help you switch off.
Dirk: Switch off?
Sue: Yeah, you know, relax, take your mind off work, think of other things. There are things in life other than work, you know. You'll get more satisfaction from work and also have better results with a healthy work-life balance. I really think you should …

1.39 Part B, Exercise 2

Dirk: OK, I see what you mean. Sometimes I do feel that I just live for work. It would be nice to be more active outside of work.
Sue: Well, how about coming jogging with me? It's one of the easiest sports to start. I go running along the river twice a week at around 7 pm. I started about two months ago.
Dirk: Mmm.
Sue: No, it's great. The air, well, it's fresher than in the office, that's for sure. And jogging's definitely more convenient than going to a gym; you can start directly from the door of the office. Why don't you come with me on Thursday?
Dirk: Oh, I don't know. I'm not as fit as I used to be.
Sue: Oh, come on! We'll take it easy. I know you'll find it more enjoyable than staying here in the office so late.
Dirk: OK, fine. I'll give it a go. Let's meet at the front door around ten to seven. That will give me time to …

1.40 Business File, Exercise 1

Brian: You've got a great selection of food and drinks here, Andrea. Some nice healthy choices, too, I see.
Andrea: Oh, thank you, Brian. Most of my customers are companies, and there's more and more demand for that kind of thing.
Brian: So, how did you like the vending machine I sent you? Were you happy with it?
Andrea: Yes, I liked it very much. The functionality and the quality are both very good.
Brian: So, do you think you'd like to place an order with us, then?
Andrea: I have some questions first.
Brian: Oh, fine. Go ahead.
Andrea: About the prices on your price list: Are they ex works or do they include delivery?
Brian: They're the basic, ex works prices. The delivery costs depend on the size of your order. Just a minute. Yes, here we are. This is the breakdown of the delivery charges showing insurance, fees, etcetera, etcetera.
Andrea: Breakdown?
Brian: *Aufschlüsselung*.
Andrea: You speak German!
Brian: No, not really. Just some words, you know: *Haus, Wasser, Bier* …
Andrea: The important words! Yes, that's clear. Yes, that's OK, quite normal, I think. And that includes insurance, does it?
Brian: This line here, yes. Everything. That's the total cost of the vending machines to your door.
Andrea: Yes, OK. About payment: What are your terms?

Brian:	We normally say 30 days. If it's a first order and if it's very big, we sometimes ask for payment in advance or COD but, for you, payment in full within thirty days will be fine.
Andrea:	Good, thanks. And how should I pay?
Brian:	Well, our preferred method of payment is a bank transfer. It's quicker and easier. Our IBAN, the International Bank Account Number and BIC, Bank Identification Code, will be on the invoice. You'll need those for the transfer.
Andrea:	OK, fine. And what do I do if there's a … err … a problem with the vending machines?
Brian:	Well, obviously that depends on the problem. If it's a question of you just, well if you change your mind when you see the vending machines, …
Andrea:	I don't understand.
Brian:	OK. For example, if you order the double size, then decide that you really wanted just the single size …
Andrea:	OK.
Brian:	Then you have to pay to send the double-sized vending machines back.
Andrea:	Of course.
Brian:	But if it's the quality of the machines, basically if it's our fault, then we'll refund – give back – your money immediately and pay the transport costs.
Andrea:	Yes, that's clear. Fine. Now, what discounts can you offer me?
Brian:	We have a very clear company policy about that, Andrea. We never give discounts on a first order.
Andrea:	But if I order more vending machines, if I place more orders later …?
Brian:	Well, of course we can talk about discounts then. What I can say is that with our good customers we normally give a rebate after six months. So, six months after your first order, if you place more orders with us, we can give you a discount that goes back to the beginning on all your orders.
Andrea:	How much?
Brian:	Four, maybe five per cent.
Andrea:	Can we agree that now? Say, a five per cent rebate after six months?
Brian:	OK, agreed.
Andrea:	Can you let me have that in writing?
Brian:	Of course. Fine. So, Andrea. Would you like to place an order today?
Andrea:	Yes, I would. But let's go and have a cup of coffee first …
Brian:	And I'll get the order form ready.

Unit 6

2.2 Part A, Exercise 2

Welcome back to The Edge – the podcast that highlights creative companies and innovative people.

Have you ever worked with diamonds? I've only ever worn them myself! But today I'm looking forward to talking to Ms Aysun Greenfield, who is the new Head of Research and Development at DPN, a company that processes diamonds for industrial use in drills, knives, blades and machines. DPN, a pioneering German company in the field of diamond processing, was founded in Dortmund back in 1999 by current CEO Patrick Heilbronner.

Ms Aysun Greenfield, whose mother is Turkish and whose father is British, grew up in Ankara, Turkey. She is very adaptable and has worked as an engineer and in management positions in a number of diamond processing companies in Europe, Australia, Africa and the United States. She even has her own YouTube channel called 'Breaking the Glass Ceiling'. She has made several videos for the channel, profiling successful female professionals, like herself, who have had to work very hard, and who now have very rewarding careers in different industrial and business fields.

Ms Greenfield and her husband of twenty years have travelled widely – Turkey, Tanzania, Chile, China: you name it! She has learned four languages fluently: English and Turkish, of course, Spanish and French – she even knows a little Swahili, and this is something we're going to talk about later. So, let's welcome our next guest, Aysun Greenfield. Aysun, it's good to have you on …

2.3 Part B, Exercise 2

David:	Hi, there. I just wanted to touch base. What are you two doing this week?
Wiebke:	Don't ask. Things have been so busy around here. We're doing a lot of demos this month so there's a lot to prepare.
Anton:	And Wiebke and I are flying to Berlin this afternoon. We're giving a presentation to some potential clients there.
David:	Oh, that's right – I forgot about that. Good luck with the pitch! I hope it won't be too tough to convince them.
Anton:	Thanks.
David:	When are you coming back?
Wiebke:	Tomorrow evening.
David:	Well, I'll keep my fingers crossed for both of you!
Anton:	It's a shame you're not coming, David. Maybe next time.
David:	I hope so! Anyway, Wiebke, are you taking Wednesday off after all? Did that work out?
Wiebke:	Well, yes and no. I talked to Aysun and unfortunately I can only take the morning off.

	You see, we're running tests on the new prototype in the afternoon.
David:	What about Thursday, Wiebke? Another busy day?
Wiebke:	Not really. Why?
David:	I was just wondering whether you have any time this week for a chat? I … uhm … need some help with the paperwork for the Braun project.
Wiebke:	Let me see. Thursday, I'm seeing … uhm … I have an appointment in the morning. And in the afternoon I'm meeting with Aysun. Sorry.
David:	Don't worry, it can't be helped. But how about Friday afternoon perhaps? After the workshop? It will only take five minutes and I'll buy you a drink afterwards.
Anton:	But on Friday you're flying to South Africa with Aysun, aren't you, Wiebke? To meet with the suppliers?
Wiebke:	No, that flight's been postponed. We're not leaving until Sunday now. I think the flight leaves at 5 pm and we get to Cape Town about fifteen hours later. Something like that. Anyway, I'll be able to go to the workshop after all.
David:	Great, so that's drinks after the workshop then.
Wiebke:	Fine … uhm, Anton, would you like to join us?
Anton:	Sure, I'd love to!

2.4 Part B, Exercise 5

Aysun:	So, Bettina, I've just noticed that it's almost five o'clock. I have to leave for my German course in a minute so I'm afraid I don't have much time, but can we just check the diary for this week before I go?
Bettina:	Sure. I … uhm … have already rescheduled your flight to Cape Town. You and Wiebke are leaving on Sunday at five o'clock.
Aysun:	Great, and have you ordered a taxi to the airport?
Bettina:	No, not yet. But I'll see to it straight away.
Aysun:	Oh, and did you remember to call Philip?
Bettina:	You mean, about chairing the meeting?
Aysun:	Sharing the meeting?
Bettina:	Yes, whether he's chairing the meeting or not.
Aysun:	Oh, chairing the meeting, being the chair. Right. Have you called him?
Bettina:	I've left him several messages but he hasn't called back yet. I think he's still off sick.
Aysun:	Mmm, well, I suppose that can't be helped. I'll try to get in touch with him this weekend. What else? Oh, yes, the projector. Have you picked up the new projector yet? I'll need it for the trip.
Bettina:	Yes, I have. I picked it up yesterday. But …
Aysun:	Yes?
Bettina:	Well, I think you wanted an extra cable. I'm afraid I haven't been able to find one yet.
Aysun:	Mmm … Maybe Anton has one I can use. Can you ask him, please? That would be great. OK, then …

Part B, Exercise 6
2.5 Part 1

chip, ship   shoes, choose   cheese, she's
chew, shoe   shop, chop

2.6 Part 2

My name is Charlie Shen. I own the Chester Silicon Chip Company. My partner and I live at 165 Shutter Court in Chelsea, England.

My name's Shirley Chelton and my husband's name is Shane. We live on Chattleford Drive in Shelltown, Maryland, and we sell ships.

Business file, Exercise 1
2.7 1

Tom:	Hello.
Malcolm:	Hi, Tom. This is Malcolm.
Tom:	Oh, g'day Malcolm. How are things?
Malcolm:	Fine, thanks. Tom, look, I'm sorry, but I have a problem with our breakfast meeting on Thursday morning. I can't make it.
Tom:	Ah, that's OK. We can find another time.
Malcolm:	Well, I was thinking … . I can see from my diary that we have another meeting next week anyway, on Tuesday morning. Can't we just cancel this one and deal with everything next week? I don't think there's anything particularly urgent to discuss anyway.
Tom:	No problem. Let's just forget Thursday, and meet next week then.
Malcolm:	Great, Tom. I appreciate that. I look forward to seeing you next Tuesday then.
Tom:	Right you are! Bye now. See you.
Malcolm:	See you.

2.8 2

Jean:	Jean Yates speaking.
Malcolm:	Good morning, Jean. This is Malcolm from Mercury Insurance.
Jean:	Good morning, Malcolm. What can I do for you?
Malcolm:	It's about our meeting on Thursday.
Jean:	Yes, is there a problem?
Malcolm:	Yes, I'm afraid so. Unfortunately, something unexpected has come up, and I'm afraid I won't be able to make our appointment.
Jean:	Oh, I see. Well, never mind. It can't be helped, I suppose.

Transcripts

Malcolm:	I'm really sorry for the inconvenience, Jean, but I would still like to see you if possible.
Jean:	Of course. When do you think you could manage?
Malcolm:	Well, I'm busy all day on Wednesday, but at the moment I'm free tomorrow at the same time as on Thursday.
Jean:	Let me just check my diary. Tomorrow looks good, Malcolm. It looks like I'm free, although I will have to check that with my assistant. She isn't in yet.
Malcolm:	Well, shall we pencil it in and you can confirm it later?
Jean:	OK, let's assume it will work. So, that's tomorrow at 9.30 then … unless you hear from me.
Malcolm:	Thank you very much for being so flexible, Jean.
Jean:	No problem. Bye.

2.9 3

Woman:	Paul Berry's Office.
Malcolm:	Good morning. Could I speak to Paul, please? It's Malcolm from Mercury Insurance.
Woman:	One moment, please.
Paul:	Hi, Malcolm. How are you this morning?
Malcolm:	Morning, Paul. I'm doing fine, thanks. It's a glorious morning. First day back at work too.
Paul:	Ah, right. Did you enjoy Bondi Beach?
Malcolm:	Yeah, the surfing was great. And how are you doing?
Paul:	Things are OK – lots of work though. Anyway, Malcolm, as a matter of fact, I wanted to phone you this morning too. Look, I'm really sorry but I can't make our appointment on Thursday.
Malcolm:	Don't worry about it. In fact, that's why I was phoning you. I can't make it either.
Paul:	Oh, well, that's OK then. Shall we try and find another time?
Malcolm:	Yeah, let's. This week is a bit hectic – I've got a big workshop planned for Wednesday. But I have some time on Friday morning. Would that suit you?
Paul:	Hold on a sec. Yes, Friday morning would be fine. How about at around ten o'clock again?
Malcolm:	Great, and can you still make lunch afterwards?
Paul:	Yes, that should work out too. OK, Malcolm, see you then.
Malcolm:	See you. Bye now.
Paul:	See you, bye.

2.10 4

Pamela:	Hello.
Malcolm:	Good morning, it's Malcolm Minsky here from Mercury Insurance. Is that Pamela?
Pamela:	Yes, it is.
Malcolm:	Great. I got your voicemail message this morning.
Pamela:	Oh, right. I do hope you can fit me in today.
Malcolm:	Yes, I was wondering if you could make it later this morning. Would that work for you?
Pamela:	That would be wonderful. Thanks for fitting me in.
Malcolm:	No worries. How about ten o'clock? Or is that too soon for you?
Pamela:	No, ten o'clock is great.
Malcolm:	Could you just spell your surname for me, please? I didn't quite catch it on the voicemail.
Pamela:	Yeung – that's Y–E–U–N for November–G.
Malcolm:	OK, Pamela, thank you. I've got that. See you soon then.
Pamela:	Yes, at ten o'clock. Bye.
Malcolm:	Bye.

2.11 Extra practice, Exercise 7

A: Hello.
B: Hello, can I speak to Mr Shufford, please?
A: Mr Shufford or Mr Chufford?
B: Shufford, Peter Shufford.
A: Sorry, Mr Shufford isn't in today. Can I take a message?
B: Yes, can you ask him to check the chairs before our next meeting? There weren't enough available for everyone last time.
A: Certainly, I've noted that down. Is there anything else, madam?
B: Oh, yes, tell him that Charlie can't make it to the meeting. I'm afraid she hurt her shin while she was playing volleyball last weekend.
A: Charlie's hurt her shin and can't attend the meeting. Got it. Was that all?
B: Yes, thank you very much.

Unit 7

2.12 Part A, Exercise 1

I work in Munich for the Credmasse Group, a holding company that is active in the financial sector. The group's head office is in Milan, but the main market in the Central European region is Germany, so we have three main business units operating out of Munich: Consumer Banking (that's where I work), Corporate Banking and SAOR Financing. SAOR Financing is a new division that has recently been taken over by Credmasse.

I'm a product manager for loans and mortgages, and I've worked in the Group's Consumer Banking Unit for 13 years now. We specialize in loans and mortgages for consumers in the 18–30 age range, and have branches all over Germany. As I said, I normally work in Munich but I'm in Milan for two days to attend a meeting at head office. In fact, I've just arrived at the airport and am waiting for Max Baker, a colleague of mine. Well, he's not really a colleague; he works in SAOR Financing, the new subsidiary specializing in loans.

After SAOR Financing was acquired, Max and I were asked to work together to find a way to improve the types of loans we offer and, at the same time, help the company increase its turnover. We first met about six weeks ago, and had the idea to create a new range of loans with special interest rates for consumers. We've spent a lot of time since our first meeting working out the details and are here in Milan today to present our ideas and get approval.

Max and I haven't seen each other for about ten days – he's been on a business trip to the UK. As soon as his plane lands, we'll go to the business lounge over there and put the finishing touches to our presentation. Fingers crossed it all goes well.

2.13 Part A, Exercise 7

Maria: Well, thanks again for coming and telling us about your new ideas. We've enjoyed listening to them and think that you are on the right track. Let me get your coats.
Max: Thanks, Maria. We're happy you think so. Eh, mine's the black one.
Maria: OK, and so this one must be yours then, Stefan?
Stefan: Yes, that's it.
Maria: Is this your first time in Milan?
Stefan: No, I've been here once before, on holidays. It's a nice city. I especially like the area around La Scala.
Max: La Scala?
Maria: That's the famous opera house here.
Max: Oh, yes, of course. I've heard about it but, as I'm sure you can guess, I haven't been here before. This is my first time. Luckily, we're not flying back till tomorrow morning. That will give us some time this evening to look around.
Maria: Again, I'm sorry I can't join you tonight. I'm afraid I can't change my appointment.
Max: That's OK. Maybe it will work out next time.
Maria: That sounds good. So, when is next time? When are you coming back?
Stefan: In around three months. Isabella said she needed to check something before agreeing a date. Her assistant's going to send out an invitation, right, Max?
Max: Yes, that's what she said.
Maria: OK, as soon as we know the exact dates, I'll make sure I'm free.
Max: Great.
Stefan: Sounds good.
Maria: Oh, and sorry, again, that Roberto couldn't stop by to say hi today.
Stefan: That's OK. He told me he had to go to London on business but I wasn't sure when. Hopefully, we'll see him next time. Please say hello to him for me, though.
Maria: Of course I will. So, would you like me to call you a taxi?
Max: No, that's not necessary, thanks. It's a nice evening and I think we'll walk back to the hotel. We've been indoors all day and some fresh air will be nice.
Maria: OK. Well, have a good trip home and keep in touch.
Stefan: We will, Maria. Thanks a lot.

Part B, Exercise 1

2.14 1

Receptionist: Reception.
Max: Oh, hello. This is Max Baker in room 304. I'm afraid there aren't any towels in my room. Could you please send some up?
Receptionist: Yes, of course, Mr Baker. I'm very sorry about that. I'll send some up straight away. Is everything else OK?
Max: Yes, everything else is fine. Oh, yes, uhm, could you tell me what time breakfast is in the morning?
Receptionist: Breakfast is served from 6 until 10 am, sir. Would you like a wake-up call?
Max: Yes, please, that would be great. Let's see, my plane leaves at 8.45, so could you give me a call at six o'clock, and could you also order me a taxi for seven, please … to the airport?
Receptionist: Of course. I'll do it straight away.
Max: Great, thank you. Goodbye.

2.15 2

Max: Oh, there you are. Hi.
Stefan: Hi, Max. I hope you got some towels in the end.
Max: Yes, they brought me some, no problem. The service is great. I don't think I've ever stayed in a friendlier hotel.
Stefan: Can I get you something to drink?
Max: Yeah, sure. I'll have a beer and some peanuts, if they have any.
Stefan: Eh, excuse me. Could I have another beer and some peanuts, please?
Barman: I'm sorry. We don't have any peanuts left. Would you like some crisps instead?

Transcripts

Stefan: Yeah, sure. That's fine. Oh, can you recommend somewhere good to eat in the area?
Barman: Well, the hotel restaurant is quite nice and it's just on the other side of the reception area.
Stefan: OK, that sounds good. What do you think? Should we try that?
Max: Sure. Uhm … do you know what time it closes?
Barman: Don't worry, sir. We're in Italy. It'll be open for at least a couple more hours.

2.16 3
Max: Hello. Is there anyone sitting at this table?
Waiter: No, sir. They've just left. Let me clear it for you. One moment, please.
Max: OK, thank you. Let's take this table, Stefan.
Stefan: Sure, that's fine. But … oh, there's something on my chair.
Max: Why don't you sit here then?
Stefan: OK, great. That's better. Right. Now let's have a look at the menu. Though I'm actually not that hungry, to tell you the truth …
Max: … and I think he was in Rome then. Ah, here comes the waiter.
Waiter: Excuse me. Are you ready to order?
Max: Yes, I am, at least. I'd like some crostini to start and the ossobuco for my main course.
Waiter: Yes, sir. The crostini followed by the ossobuco.
Stefan: Uhm, I don't eat meat or fish. Do you have any vegetarian dishes?
Waiter: Yes, sir. They're on the third page and marked with a leaf.
Stefan: Ah, OK. … Well, then I'll have the vegetable soup for my starter and … let's see … the asparagus risotto for my main course.
Waiter: Certainly, sir.

Part B, Exercise 4
2.17 1
Waitress: Here you go, sir. A bottle of Chianti and a large bottle of still water.
Man: Oh, no. I'm afraid that's not what we ordered. We ordered a bottle of Rioja and sparkling water.
Waitress: I'm very sorry, sir. I'll bring the right drinks straight away.
Man: Great. Thanks a lot.

2.18 2
Woman: Eh, excuse me, … sorry…
Waitress: Yes, madam?
Woman: I've just dropped my knife and fork. Sorry. Could you please bring me a new set of cutlery?
Waitress: Yes, of course. One moment … here you go.

Woman: Thanks. And, … ehm, would it be possible to move tables? There's a draught coming from the back of the restaurant and the people at the next table are smoking. Their smoke is blowing in our direction.
Waitress: No problem. How about a table near the front of the restaurant? There's one over there by the window.
Woman: Yes, that'll be fine. Thank you. We'll move over now.

2.19 3
Woman: Ehh, excuse me. Excuse me …
Waiter: Yes, madam. Is everything OK?
Woman: Well, actually no. Unfortunately, no, everything's not OK. I'm sorry to say that we had to wait a very long time for our main courses. We finally have them, but I'm afraid that my meal is overcooked and my colleague's is cold.
Woman 2: Yes, it really is!
Waiter: Oh, I'm very sorry about that. Let me take them back and sort it out. You ordered your steak medium rare, right?
Woman: Yes, I did. And look at it. It's so tough, it's like a piece of leather. I'd like to eat my steak, not make some shoes and a handbag from it.
Waiter: I'm sorry, madam. I'll be back with them both in just a few minutes.
Woman: Well, I suppose it could be worse, Susan. At least I didn't order the sushi. It might have come out hot.

2.20 Business file, Exercise 3
Speaker: Good morning, everyone. Thanks for coming. I'd like to tell you about our new virtual meeting software. It's easy to use, will reduce travel expenses and allows for faster communication between the whole team. It's like having a teleconference, but with a few differences: you use a headset to listen and speak, we can see each other via webcam, and you can share your screen with others and vice versa. All of these elements will make it easier to work in remote teams than by using standard teleconferences.

OK, so in the next hour, there are three main things I'd like to show you. First, the platform itself, then I'll show you some of the basic functions. By the end of the presentation, you'll have a better understanding of this software. This next slide gives you an overview of the presentation. Oh, and if you've got any questions, just ask. So, if you're ready we can look at the platform itself. …

Speaker: OK, so that was the platform and how it looks. I'd now like to move on and look at the basic functions. The first one is the webcam function. Uhm … I need a volunteer. John, how about you? Can you come up here and be our test person?
John: Huh, me? Uh, OK.
Speaker: Thanks. OK, John, take a seat there. Great. OK, everyone. So, as you can see, John and I can see each other on our computers. The most obvious advantage of this is that we can now read each other's body language and build more rapport than we could just on the phone. Furthermore, it's also quite useful … Right, let's now move on to the last feature, which is screen sharing. Why is it useful to share your screen? Well, with screen sharing, everybody at the virtual meeting can see the same version of a file. When you, the person whose screen everybody is looking at, make changes, for example, to a set of figures or the title of a report, then everybody can see exactly what you change as you change it. I'm currently sharing my screen with John, so if I do this, John can simultaneously see it on his screen. It's as easy as that. Another advantage of the virtual meeting software. And here it's just the two of us in our virtual meeting, but you can just add more people to the invitation list depending on how many need to attend. Right. Thanks, John. So, that brings me to the end of the presentation. Are there any further questions?
John: Well, yes, I have one actually. What if I need to …?

Unit 8

2.21 Part A, Exercise 3
Uli: Good morning, can I help you?
Mary: Yes, I was just looking at your range of detergents.
Uli: Are you interested in it for professional use or for yourself?
Mary: Well, for professional use actually. My name is Mary Burton. I'm a buyer for Value It. We're an eco-supermarket chain in the UK.
Uli: Oh, yes. I've heard of you, of course. I'm Uli Rietz, HTR's sales manager for Western Europe.
Mary: Nice to meet you.
Uli: Nice to meet you too. So, Ms Burton, if you have a couple of minutes now, I can give you a few more details.
Mary: Yes, that would be nice.
Uli: Good. Shall we sit over there? It's a bit quieter. … OK, I assume that you're looking for an environmentally sustainable detergent.
Mary: Yes, that's right.
Uli: What kind of quantities did you have in mind?
Mary: Well, that depends on the price, of course. But we have 158 outlets in the UK.
Uli: I see. Well, we have a great product called Ecoclean. Customers bring their own reusable containers to your outlets and buy it in bulk. Do you stock any products like that at the moment?
Mary: We do. But not Ecoclean.
Uli: Why is that?
Mary: Well, several reasons but, at the end of the day, I suppose it's basically just a question of price.
Uli: I see. Uhm, may I ask you some more questions?

2.22 Part A, Exercise 4
Uli: I see. Uhm, may I ask you some more questions?
Mary: Go ahead.
Uli: Are any of your current detergents produced in an environmentally sustainable way?
Mary: Some, but not all. But our customers are becoming more and more interested in this sort of product. That's why we are interested in offering even more.
Uli: OK, and my second question is: Are you happy with what you're getting from your current suppliers?
Mary: Yes, we are, for the most part. Our wholesalers offer good products at a reasonable price. Certainly a lot lower than yours. And I don't really see any differences in quality.
Uli: Well, although Ecoclean seems expensive at first glance, it is better value for money than you may think. It is simply more effective than any other green detergent on the market. I can show you some statistics for both our pre-packaged and bulk options.
Mary: Mmm, but your prices per kilogram are, well, around 10% above what I'm paying at the moment. That's a big difference.
Uli: Well, it isn't always easy to immediately see the difference in quality between an ordinary organic detergent and a really high-quality eco-detergent like ours, because they both look very similar. But Ecoclean sets the standard for laundry detergents and thus I'm sure you'll see your sales improving over a longer period of time.
Mary: So, what are these differences exactly?

Uli: Well, for one, Ecoclean in bulk is the most environmentally friendly detergent around due to the fact that there is no packaging and over 60% of the ingredients come from renewable resources.

Mary: Well, I can see that your detergent is environmentally friendly, but will UK customers pay extra for it?

Uli: Of course they will. We'll help you promote the product. We'll provide you with giveaways for the launch, and when customers start using Ecoclean, they will see how much cleaner their clothes look and how much fresher they smell. They'll never go back to other detergents because Ecoclean really is …

Part B, Exercise 1
2.23 Message 1
Hello, Tracy. This is Pauline Dubois from La Reine in Metz. I've got a couple of queries about your last invoice. I've just sent you an email with my comments. Do you think we can touch base as soon as possible? I'm on holiday from Thursday onwards, so am only here today and tomorrow, and I don't think my new assistant is up to handling this. Thanks.

2.24 Message 2
Hello, this is Mary Burton from Value It speaking. I'm trying to reach Mr Rietz but he isn't answering his mobile, so I am trying this number instead. The reason I'm calling is that the display stands he sent me are the wrong size. I wanted stand-alone displays and I have received small counter displays instead. I'd appreciate it if you could send me an email to confirm you have received this message. My email address is mary dot burton at valueit (that's all one word) dot co dot UK.

2.25 Message 3
Tracy, hi! Giovanni here. How's things? I need some more company brochures, the Italian versions obviously. Could you send me two thousand? I've just opened the last box of a hundred and as you know I'm attending the Milan fair with Uli the week after next, so please send them subito? Thanks. Ciao.

2.26 Message 4
Hi. My name is Svenja Karlsson and I run a small chain of organic supermarkets in Northern Sweden. We're currently expanding our range, and I've just seen your products on the Internet. I'd like to talk to someone about the Ecoclean range. Do you have a representative in Sweden, and if so, how might I be able to contact him or her? My phone number is 0046 23861253.

Unit 9

2.28 Part A, Exercise 7
Sorry, it's real noisy here … Amy, I'm stuck in Heathrow. I've been waiting for three hours for my flight to Munich. … flight's been delayed … won't be in Munich until late afternoon European time. At least I hope so … Do me a favour and write Mr Müller an email … offer him the following alternatives. I could meet up with him this evening for dinner, you know, a get-to-know-you session. Then we could set up an appointment for later this week. Or I can call him tomorrow … and arrange to meet him – either in his office or in our seminar centre in Munich. And please confirm that we offer on-site seminars in the Munich office. Tell him we've been doing so for quite a few years. And don't forget …

2.29 Part B, Exercise 1
Tony: Well, Kurt. Here's to a long and happy partnership! Cheers! Or should I say Prost actually?

Kurt: Prost, it is! So, Tony, what do you think of the wheat beer?

Tony: I love it. It's always one of the highlights when I come to Germany.

Kurt: So, you can't get this type of beer in Cleveland then?

Tony: Well, you can if you try, but it's hard to find.

Kurt: It's hard to find a good cross-cultural training provider, too.

Tony: Yes, but you've come to the right company.

Kurt: I hope so. We need you to get started with the training as soon as possible.

Tony: No problem.

Kurt: So, you think our staff will learn to adapt to the new way of doing business?

Tony: If they're willing to learn, yes, of course.

Kurt: Yes, they are. It's just that they're a bit nervous at the moment because they don't know what the new management expects them to do. They've been worried ever since they heard the rumours of the takeover. They know things are going to change.

Tony: Change. That's the heart of the matter, isn't it? Nobody likes dramatic changes. We'll take things slowly. We'll make sure that everybody gets to know each other early on. We'll have a 'getting to know each other' meeting in September before the real work starts, so to speak. And, you know what? I'd like them all to subscribe to our newsletter before they start the programme, so they can get a feeling for the way other countries do business. It's easy reading; we try to get the ideas across in a light and humorous way.

Kurt: Yes, that sounds like a good idea. We really need the atmosphere to change soon.

Tony: Talking of atmosphere, it's very nice here, isn't it? Someone from our Cleveland office recommended it. It's more modern than I thought it would be, though. It's not what you would call a typical German restaurant, is it?

Kurt: Well, it's hard to say what 'typical German' means really. I come from Northern Germany and the restaurants can be very different, especially in terms of the food. They seem to have lots of regional specialities here, but you're right, the restaurant is quite modern looking.

Tony: Well, it's certainly a lot different from the places you find in Cleveland. A lot more elegant for one. We have a lot of all-you-can-eat buffet style places with servers everywhere filling up your coffee cups and water glasses.

Kurt: Yes, I remember a place called Talk of the Town from my last visit to the States. There were more servers there than customers. They certainly make sure the coffee cups never get empty.

Tony: I wish they'd do the same with the beer over here. Mmm … that tastes so good. I always eat and drink a lot more than I should when I'm in Munich. I love German food, especially all the local delicacies here like liverwurst and Weisswurst. Speaking of which, I'm getting hungry. Do you know what you'd like to order yet, Kurt?

Kurt: No, I need to study the menu a bit. I've only been living here for a few months so I'm still getting used to Bavarian cuisine. By the way, do you want me to help you translate anything?

Tony: Yes, please, if you wouldn't mind.

Kurt: Well, I'll try my best …

2.30 Part B, Exercise 3

1 heart 3 peas 5 simple 7 built
2 cab   4 life 6 spice   8 save

2.31 Business file, Exercise 1

Megan: Sunrise Electronics, Megan Taylor speaking. How may I help you?

Customer: Good morning. I'm calling about some goods we ordered. I'm afraid we haven't received them yet.

Megan: Oh dear, I'm sorry to hear that. When exactly did you order the goods?

Customer: Three weeks ago. My name is Andrew Clarke. That's Clarke with an 'e'.

Megan: Yes, Mr Clarke, I appreciate your call. I'll sort this out for you immediately. Uhm, do you have an order number for me, please?

Customer: Yes, it's 023-SX-8743-2015.

Megan: Ah, I've got it. A consignment of platinum microchips.

Customer: Yes, that's right. It's very annoying because we were expecting them to arrive last week. We have an important order to fill.

Megan: Oh dear, I'm really sorry about this. Let me just check the order status. Yes, I'm afraid there's been a bit of a delay here, Mr Clarke. The Sunrise Platinum microchips are a new brand, and there's been an enormous demand for this product. I'm afraid your order hasn't been processed yet. I'll get in touch with our shipping department immediately. Should I ask them to send the goods by express – at no extra charge to you, of course?

Customer: Yes, that would be great. When can I expect delivery?

Megan: They'll be with you tomorrow afternoon. Does that sound OK?

Customer: Yes, that sounds good.

Megan: Thank you so much for calling, Mr Clarke. I apologize again for the delay.

Customer: Well, thanks for sorting everything out. Bye now.

Megan: Goodbye, Mr Clarke, and have a nice day.

2.32 Extra Practice, Exercise 7

Agent: Customer care. Bill Sawyer speaking. How can I help you?

Customer: Hello. My name is Jane Kaminsky. I'm calling to find out what's happened to my order. I placed it four weeks ago and it still hasn't arrived.

Agent: Oh dear. I'm sorry to hear that. Do you have an order number for me, Mrs Kaminsky?

Customer: Yes, it's XT4927DE.

Agent: XT4927, D for Delta, E.

Customer: That's right.

Agent: One moment. Let me just check. Ah, I see. I'm afraid the order hasn't been processed yet.

Customer: What? How did that happen?

Agent: I'm not sure, but I'll look into it immediately and call you back. Would that be OK?

Customer: Yes, I guess so. But I hope you can offer me some sort of compensation. Perhaps a discount? I've been waiting for weeks.

Agent: I'll see what I can do. Let me talk to my colleagues and find out what's happened. I'll call you right back.

Customer: Thank you. Bye.

Agent: Good-bye.

Transcripts

Unit 10

2.33 Part A, Exercise 3

Welcome to our logistics centre. As you can see in our brochure, we offer our customers personalized products, and the most efficient way for us to produce them is using a JIT – or just-in-time – production strategy. So, for instance, if a customer wanted two or even 20 different personalized products, we'd only begin production when we received the order.

OK, of course we have most of the components already here in our inventory, and it's a matter of assembling them and adding the personalization elements. However, our goal is to keep our inventory low as we need to be efficient with the space we have. This is why we operate a Kanban system for our standard components. It's a system of planning which tells us what to produce, when to produce it and how much of it to produce. With the Kanban system we can operate a JIT strategy and not really have to wait until the last minute to produce the orders.

The software we use to manage all of this is ERP from SAP. ERP stands for Enterprise Resource Management. It can manage all of the communication both internally and between us, our suppliers and our suppliers' suppliers. We keep a small inventory here, but our tier one and tier two suppliers are constantly aware of the current situation through a connection to our ERP system. A benefit for us is that they can keep their inventory where they are, but deliver components to us quickly as our standard stock runs low.

We also run a similar supply chain for the production of personalized features, but this needs to move much faster. These days a growing number of our customers here in Ireland, but also in mainland Europe, want to personalize the products they buy. This is a very important part of our business. If we didn't have the flexibility to deal with personalized orders quickly, we would go out of business – it's as simple as that.

Our logistics centre uses RFID chips – that's chips with radio frequency identification – on all our packaging so that we can identify the packages as they move through the centre and into the lorries before shipping throughout Europe. We're currently looking at options for faster delivery to mainland Europe, which includes the possibility of setting up another logistics centre. In fact, I've asked two of my analysts to prepare a report, so we'll see what they recommend.

Oh, and finally, we also have QR codes on our packages not only for us to identify products, but also for our customers. Those are quick response codes. They're similar to barcodes, but our customers can scan them with the cameras on their smartphones and see 3D designs, or get linked to more information about our products on the Internet.

2.34 Part B, Exercise 2

Declan: OK, thanks for coming today, Ilke, Henry. I've read your report and understand the situation. So, where do we go from here?

Henry: Thanks, Declan. Well as you know, our location in Ireland is negatively affecting our delivery times to mainland Europe. Unless we can speed up our delivery times, we're going to lose customers. The best and most-efficient long-term way to achieve this is to open another production site in mainland Europe. If we opened another production site, we could aim to increase our market share.

Declan: OK, I understand, but we're already operating under a tight budget after last years' cutbacks and we're having difficulty staying within it.

Henry: Yes, but we need to protect our brand in case our competitors launch another attack like they tried two years ago. And if you want long-term sustainability of the brand and company, you need to increase the annual budget of the company, and also the supply chain budget in the short term.

Declan: What do you mean by 'in the short term'?

Henry: Ilke, you can probably answer this best.

Ilke: Sure. Well, if we want to increase market share, and not just maintain it, we'll need to increase the budget by 30% for the next two years.

Declan: Thirty per cent! For two years! That's just not possible. I can't approve such a high budget increase.

Ilke: Yes, I know it sounds very high and might seem to be an almost unreasonable request. But we need to aim high in case we have delays in implementing our new ideas. We can't afford for this not to work or to take too long. Besides, unless we do this, we'll see a slow and steady decrease in revenue and market share. You should also look at the long-term benefits of this budget increase and change in strategy. Sales and market share will both rise, and transport costs will be reduced.

Declan: Yes, I see your point. And you think this is really necessary, do you?

Ilke: Well, you've seen the report and the findings. It doesn't look good for Rosco's future if we do nothing.

Declan: Right. If I approve this, we'll also need to have a back-up plan to minimize our risk, just in case.

Henry: Exactly. That's why we recommend purchasing the new site in Germany rather than in another country, and purchasing rather than leasing. Germany is our fastest growing market and so being nearer to those customers will be better. Germany is also economically stable, so the

	value on the property should rise. We should see it as an investment.
Declan:	Hmmm. OK, well you're my analysts, so I should trust you. You can have your budget increase, but first could you prepare a full proposal including a SWOT analysis and a timeline?
Henry:	We already prepared one in case you asked that question. Here's a full proposal with all of the strengths, weaknesses, opportunities and threats in detail.
Declan:	Very nice, thanks. If I agreed to this, how quickly would you need approval without delaying the process too much?
Ilke:	How about the end of the month?
Declan:	OK. That'll give me time to look through everything in detail and get back to you if I have any questions.
Henry:	Yes, of course, if you have any questions, just give one of us a call.

2.35 Part B, Exercise 9

I used to drive to work, so obviously I couldn't really use my phone while driving. But I could listen to my coursebook CDs on my car stereo, so I did that a lot. After that I started commuting using public transport and my commute took around 25–30 minutes. I just had a standard mobile phone with a standard camera and no video or Internet access. With that, I could take pictures of interesting things to talk about during my lessons. It was also possible to get books as text messages, so I got to read a little bit of a story every day.

Ever since I got my smartphone, it's given me many more possibilities for language learning in my free time and also in my lessons. In fact, in our lesson last week, our teacher made a QR-code treasure hunt. We had to use our phones to read the codes, which contained clues – all in German of course – for the next step. I'm also currently reading a very interesting book using the e-book reader function.

I'm going to visit Germany soon and am of course bringing my smartphone with me. I've just downloaded a translator app to help me with reading signs and menus. And I've started subscribing to a few German podcasts. It's really helping me get used to hearing lots of different accents and how German is spoken outside the classroom, which …

Business file, Exercise 1
2.36 Pitch 1

Well, the reason I want to talk to you today is because we have an issue with the budget for the Alpha project. We're making really good progress, but we're only halfway through and we're getting very close to the budget limit. We'd like to ask for a 30 % increase in the budget. I know that's high, but we would definitely double the return on our investment with this increase. In that sense we should look at the long-term benefits rather than the immediate cost of the budget increase. Unless we increase the budget, we won't be able to finish the project. It will fail. It's really as simple as that. So, what do you think?

2.37 Pitch 2

Well, the reason I want to talk to you today is because we've identified a great opportunity to reduce costs in the department by 30 %. We're calling it the Bravo project! I'm sure you'll agree that it's a great opportunity, but it does need some financing. We need to increase the department's operating budget by just 15 % for this year. We need this budget increase to implement a couple of changes and communicate these to the whole team. If we do this properly, then we'll achieve the savings we're aiming for. If we don't, well, then the costs will remain the same next year. Actually, they'll probably need to rise by about 5 % to deal with rising costs and salaries. So, what do you think?

2.38 Pitch 3

Well, the reason I want to talk to you today is because we're having problems with the Charlie project. It's going well, but our hardware is just too old and too slow. We didn't calculate this into our original budget for the project and now it's costing us time. The computing speed is unreliable and we've recently lost some data. That's why we need to buy more computers and a data input terminal. If we do this, we'll be able to stay on schedule and finish the project on time. Productivity and efficiency will both rise and the problems we've been having will disappear. However, it's not looking good if we do nothing. Unfortunately, if we don't update, we might lose more data and it's difficult to say how delayed the project will become, but it'll definitely be late. I have a full analysis in my proposal here for you to read through. So, what do you think?

2.39 Business file, Exercise 3

Thanks to all of you for your ideas and also for bringing me up to date on the situations in your departments. You have all presented very good cost-saving ideas, but as you know our financial situation is not what it used to be, and we have to limit how much we increase our budgets. For that reason, we've decided to give the budget increase to the Alpha project. It's been quite successful so far and we want to build on that success. Increasing the budget there will mean that project can continue the success it's been having so far. We are also aware that doing nothing for the Charlie project will have consequences, but we are currently prepared to take that risk. Any extra budget that's left over will be used for project Bravo in case the costs and salaries do in fact rise, as was suggested. I hope you understand.

Irregular verb list

Infinitive	Simple past	Past participle	
be	was/were	been	*sein*
become	became	become	*werden*
begin	began	begun	*beginnen, anfangen*
break	broke	broken	*brechen, kaputtmachen*
bring	brought	brought	*bringen*
build	built	built	*bauen*
buy	bought	bought	*kaufen*
catch	caught	caught	*fangen*
choose	chose	chosen	*(aus)wählen, aussuchen*
come	came	come	*kommen*
cost	cost	cost	*kosten*
cut	cut	cut	*schneiden*
deal	dealt	dealt	*handeln, sich beschäftigen (mit)*
do	did	done	*tun, machen*
draw	drew	drawn	*zeichnen*
drink	drank	drunk	*trinken*
drive	drove	driven	*(Auto)fahren*
eat	ate	eaten	*essen*
fall	fell	fallen	*fallen*
feel	felt	felt	*(sich) fühlen*
find	found	found	*finden*
fly	flew	flown	*fliegen*
forget	forgot	forgotten	*vergessen*
get	got	got (US: gotten)	*bekommen, gelangen*
give	gave	given	*geben, schenken*
go	went	gone	*gehen, fahren*
grow	grew	grown	*wachsen*
have	had	had	*haben*
hear	heard	heard	*hören*
hide	hid	hidden	*(sich) verstecken*
hit	hit	hit	*schlagen*
hold	held	held	*halten*
hurt	hurt	hurt	*schaden*
keep	kept	kept	*behalten*
know	knew	known	*wissen, kennen*
lead	led	led	*führen, leiten*
learn	learnt/learned	learnt/learned	*lernen*
leave	left	left	*(weg)gehen, (ver)lassen*
lend	lent	lent	*(aus)leihen, borgen*
let	let	let	*(zu)lassen, erlauben*
lose	lost	lost	*verlieren*
make	made	made	*machen, tun*
mean	meant	meant	*bedeuten*
meet	met	met	*(sich) treffen*
pay	paid	paid	*(be)zahlen*
put	put	put	*legen, stellen, setzen*

Infinitive	Simple past	Past participle	
read [riːd]	read [red]	read [red]	*lesen*
ride	rode	ridden	*(mit)fahren, reiten*
rise	rose	risen	*steigen, sich erheben*
ring	rang	rung	*klingeln, anrufen*
run	ran	run	*laufen, verwalten*
say	said	said	*sagen*
see	saw	seen	*sehen*
sell	sold	sold	*verkaufen*
send	sent	sent	*senden, schicken*
set	set	set	*setzen, stellen, legen*
shake	shook	shaken	*schütteln*
show	showed	shown/showed	*zeigen*
sing	sang	sung	*singen*
sit	sat	sat	*sitzen*
sleep	slept	slept	*schlafen*
speak	spoke	spoken	*sprechen*
spell	spelt/spelled	spelt/spelled	*buchstabieren, schreiben*
spend	spent	spent	*ausgeben, verbringen*
stand	stood	stood	*stehen*
swim	swam	swum	*schwimmen*
take	took	taken	*nehmen*
teach	taught	taught	*unterrichten*
tell	told	told	*erzählen, sagen*
think	thought	thought	*denken, meinen*
throw	threw	thrown	*werfen*
understand	understood	understood	*verstehen*
wear	wore	worn	*tragen, anhaben*
win	won	won	*gewinnen*
write	wrote	written	*schreiben*

Notes

Notes

Copyright

Fotos

Titel: © Mauritius Images, Pixtal; – **S. 6** © alamy, Andres Rodriguez | Somos Images | Denkou Images, © Shutterstock, Yuri Arcurs, © Fotolia, RTimages, © alamy, Paul Bradbury, © iStockphoto, bortonia; – **S. 8** © iStockphoto, Kai Chang, © Shutterstock, StockLite, © iStockphoto, AIMSTOCK, © Fotolia, WavebreakMediaMicro, © iStockphoto, nyul; – **S. 8-9** © Shutterstock, Mario Tarello; – **S. 9** © iStockphoto, gilaxia, © Shutterstock, Dean Mitchell | Yuri Arcurs, © alamy, GlowImages, © Shutterstock, Noam Armonn; – **S. 10** © iStockphoto, Dean Turner, © Shutterstock, StockLite, © alamy, Juice Images; – **S. 11** © Shutterstock, StockLite; – **S. 12** © iStockphoto, Leontura; – **S. 13** © Fotolia, Eray, © iStockphoto, Yang Yin | Greg Brookes; – **S. 14** © Fotofinder, Caro Fotoagentur – Rupert Oberhäuser, © Shutterstock, Yuri Arcurs | StockLite; – **S. 15** © iStockphoto, Eric Foltz, © Shutterstock, Kitch Bain, © Fotolia, Eric Isselée, © iStockphoto, Aleksandra Smirnova, © Shutterstock, vnlit, © Fotolia, Michael Flippo; – **S. 16** © iStockphoto, DSGpro, © Shutterstock, Elena Elisseeva | Noam Armonn, © istockphoto, Pgiam; – **S. 17** © iStockphoto, Alex Slobodkin; – **S. 22** © Shutterstock, Andresr; – **S. 24** © Shutterstock, Andresr, © iStockphoto, lacreme; – **S. 25** © iStockphoto, Phillip Jones; – **S. 27** © iStockphoto, Yunus Arakon; – **S. 28** © Fotolia, WavebreakMediaMicro, © iStockphoto, Yulia Popkova; – **S. 29** © iStockphoto, Leontura | wsfurlan | DSGpro; – **S. 35** © alamy, Glowimages, © Shutterstock, leungchopan; © iStockphoto, Leontura; – **S. 36** © alamy, Mar Photographics; – **S. 40** © alamy, Directphoto.org, © Fotolia, Pavel Losevsky, © iStockphoto, amriphoto, © alamy, Alex Segre | Michael Willis; – **S. 41** © iStockphoto, Leontura | Andresr; – **S. 46** © Shutterstock, RTimages; – **S. 48** © Fotolia, WavebreakMediaMicro; – **S. 49** © Shutterstock, wavebreakmedia ltd; – **S. 50** © Fotolia, WavebreakMediaMicro (2); – **S. 52** © iStockphoto, Jani Bryson | Evgeniy Ivanov | Hans-Joachim Schneider | Skip O'Donnell | Danny Hooks | JackJelly | ODV | Evgeny Karandaev | Floortje | Oliver Blondeau; – **S. 53** © alamy, Westend61 GmbH; – **S. 58** © iStockphoto, Izvorinka Jankovic | Sandra O'Claire; – **S. 59** © iStockphoto, Izvorinka Jankovic | Leontura; – **S. 60** © iStockphoto, Artur Figurski; – **S. 61** © iStockphoto, Radoslaw Korga; – **S. 62** © iStockphoto, nicole waring, © alamy, Catchlight Visual Services, © iStockphoto, Joshua Hodge Photography; – **S. 63** © iStockphoto, paul kline | Lisa Gagne; – **S. 64** © Sielaff GmbH & Co. KG, © Shutterstock, Dean Mitchell; – **S. 65** © Shutterstock, Alja Lehtonen; – **S. 70** © iStockphoto, franckreporter | nyul; – **S. 71** © iStockphoto, nyul; – **S. 72** © iStockphoto, Chris Pecoraro, © alamy, Jorge Fernandez, © Shutterstock, Kitch Bain, © iStockphoto, leluconcepts, © Shutterstock, Monkey Business Images, © iStockphoto, blackred; – **S. 73** © iStockphoto, Catherine Yeulet; – **S. 74** © iStockphoto, nyul; – **S. 76** © iStockphoto, claudiobaba; – **S. 77** © iStockphoto, wavebreakmedia; – **S. 82** © Shutterstock, Yuri Arcurs; – **S. 84** © Shutterstock, Stephen Coburn; – **S. 87** © Shutterstock, Goodluz; – **S. 88** © Shutterstock, Monkey Business Images | Peter Hansen; – **S. 94** © CEBIT, Hannover; © ITB, Messe Berlin GmbH; – **S. 95** © iStockphoto, gilaxia; Natexpo, Paris; – **S. 97** © iStockphoto, Pali Rao; – **S. 98** © iStockphoto, Pali Rao; – **S. 100** © SFM GmbH (Sachs Bikes); – **S. 106** © iStockphoto, Alex Slobodkin | Nicole S. Young | Marcy Smith, © Shutterstock, Kenneth Sponsler; – **S. 108** © iStockphoto, AIMSTOCK | kristian sekulic / AIMSTOCK; – **S. 109** © Fotolia, Alta C., © iStockphoto AIMSTOCK; – **S. 112** © Shutterstock, LVector, © iStockphoto, Sascha Deforth; – **S. 113** © iStockphoto, digitalskillet | nicolas hansen; – **S. 118** © iStockphoto, Fotowizje studio@bartektomczyk.pl | Dan Driedger, © Fotolia, Ramona Heim; – **S. 119** © iStockphoto, Kai Chiang; – **S. 121** © iStockphoto, Kai Chiang; – **S. 122** © iStockphoto, Leontura; – **S. 123** © iStockphoto, Kai Chiang; – **S. 124** © Fotolia, WavebreakMediaMicro (3); – **S. 130** © HARIBO GmbH & Co KG; © Beiersdorf AG; – **S. 136** © iStockphoto, Leontura; © Birkenstock Orthopädie GmbH & Co. KG, © PLAYMOBIL | geobra Brandstätter GmbH & Co.KG; – **S. 146** © Shutterstock, Kolesov Sergei (2); – **S. 147** © iStockphoto, webphotographeer; – **S. 152** © Messe Düsseldorf | Tillmann; – **S. 154** © iStockphoto, nyul; – **S. 155** © iStockphoto, Jeff Salvant; – **S. 156** © iStockphoto, TEMISTOCLE LUCARELLI; – **S. 158** © iStockphoto, sean boggs; – **S. 160** © iStockphoto, Ye Liew; – **S. 164** © iStockphoto, Darren Mower; – **Umschlagseite 4:** © Ed Benn | runrabbitrun.eu

Wir danken für die freundliche Abdruckgenehmigung:
S. 64 Sielaff GmbH & Co KG, Automatenbau, Herrieden; – **S. 94** CEBIT, Hannover | ITB, Messe Berlin GmbH, Berlin; – **S. 100** SFM GmbH – Sachs Bikes, Nürnberg; – **S. 130** HARIBO GmbH & Co. KG, Bonn; Beiersdorf AG, Hamburg; – **S. 136** Birkenstock Orthopädie GmbH & Co. KG, Vettelschoß; PLAYMOBIL | geobra Brandstätter GmbH & Co. KG; – **S. 152** Messe Düsseldorf GmbH

Audio CDs – Track list

CD 1

#				Time
1		Copyright		00:50
Unit 1				
2	A	ex. 4		03:07
3		ex. 7		01:29
4	B	ex. 4	1	01:12
5			2	01:07
6	BF	ex. 1	1	00:30
7			2	00:58
8			3	00:40
9		ex. 3	1	00:58
10			2	00:45
11			3	00:55
12	EP	ex. 8		01:47
Unit 2				
13	A	ex. 1		00:59
14		ex. 5		01:30
15	B	ex. 1		02:51
16	BF	ex. 1		01:01
17		ex. 2		01:06
18	EP	ex. 8		01:17
Unit 3				
19	A	ex. 4		02:18
20	B	ex. 3		03:21
21	BF	ex. 2	1	01:28
22			2	01:21
23			3	00:48
24			4	01:00
25	EP	ex. 7		00:39
Unit 4				
26	A	ex. 1		02:08
27		ex. 7		03:31
28	B	ex. 1		01:28
29		ex. 5		01:46
30		ex. 6		00:50
31	BF	ex. 2		06:02
32	EP	ex. 7		02:33
Unit 5				
33	A	ex. 1		02:38
34		ex. 5		02:14
35		ex. 8	1	00:22
36			2	00:15
37			3	00:22
38	B	ex. 1		01:35
39		ex. 2		01:03
40	BF	ex. 1		04:01
Total running time				**64:54**

CD 2

#				Time
1		Copyright		00:50
Unit 6				
2	A	ex. 2		02:07
3	B	ex. 1		02:12
4		ex. 5		01:45
5		ex. 6	1	00:30
6			2	00:30
7	BF	ex. 1	1	01:10
8			2	01:32
9			3	01:32
10			4	01:09
11	EP	ex. 7		01:01
Unit 7				
12	A	ex. 1		02:03
13		ex. 7		02:15
14	B	ex. 1	1	01:11
15			2	01:12
16			3	01:26
17		ex. 4	1	00:36
18			2	00:50
19			3	01:03
20	BF	ex. 3		03:31
Unit 8				
21	A	ex. 3		01:40
22		ex. 4		02:19
23	B	ex. 1	1	00:40
24			2	00:57
25			3	00:35
26			4	00:40
27		ex. 5		01:22
Unit 9				
28	A	ex. 7		00:57
29	B	ex. 1		03:27
30		ex. 3		00:43
31	BF	ex. 1		01:57
32	EP	ex. 7		01:29
Unit 10				
33	A	ex. 3		03:05
34	B	ex. 2		03:39
35		ex. 9		01:39
36	BF	ex. 1	1	00:51
37			2	00:56
38			3	01:04
39		ex. 3		01:13
Total running time				**57:48**

Studio:
Clarity Studio Berlin

Aufnahmeleitung:
Christian Schmitz

Tontechnik:
Pascal Thinius
Christian Marx

Regie:
Christian Schmitz
Janan Barksdale
Anna Batrla

Sprecher/innen:
Noémi Besedes
Kieran Breen
Laura Cameron
Tania Carlin
Silvia Cavallari
Peter Cotton
Helena Ekre
Elisabetta Gaddoni
Daniel Godor
Andreas Goebel
Marianne Graffam
Merlene Griffin
Melissa Holroyd
Sylvie Krause-Grégoire
Pierpaolo de Luca
Nicola Devico Mamone
Kim Pfeiffer
Helena Prince
Christian Schmitz
Peter Scollin
Dharmander Singh
Darren Smith
Tomas Spencer
Ian Wood
Felix Würgler